1ˢᵗ September 2018.

# Fire Metaphors

GW00644862

Dear Chris & Mary

On the occasion of your 70ᵀᴴ and 80ᵀᴴ
birthdays (ages that one no longer needs to
conceal) I (and Clare) present you with
"Fire Metaphors".

You are two of only a few friends
who I think may actually open this book –
though if not please enjoy the cover.
Very Best Wishes

Jonathan & Clare.

**Also available from Bloomsbury**

*Contagious Metaphor*, Peta Mitchell
*Metaphor and Intercultural Communication*, edited by Andreas Musolff,
Fiona MacArthur and Giulio Pagani
*Political Metaphor Analysis*, Andreas Musolff
*Sex in Language*, Eliecer Crespo-Fernández

**Also by Jonathan Charteris-Black**

*Analysing Political Speeches: Rhetoric, Discourse and Metaphor*, (2014)
*Politicians and Rhetoric: The persuasive power of metaphor*, (2011, 2nd edition)
*Gender and the Language of Illness*, (2010)
*The Communication of Leadership: The Design of Leadership Style*, (2007)
*Corpus Approaches to Critical Metaphor Analysis*, (2004)

# Fire Metaphors

## Discourses of Awe and Authority

Jonathan Charteris-Black

BLOOMSBURY ACADEMIC

LONDON • NEW YORK • OXFORD • NEW DELHI • SYDNEY

BLOOMSBURY ACADEMIC
Bloomsbury Publishing Plc
50 Bedford Square, London, WC1B 3DP, UK

BLOOMSBURY, BLOOMSBURY ACADEMIC and the Diana logo are trademarks
of Bloomsbury Publishing Plc

First published in Great Britain 2017
Paperback edition first published 2018

Cover image: Artist: Blake, William / God Judging Adam, 1795 © Tate, London 2015

A catalogue record for this book is available from the British Library.

ISBN: HB: 978-1-4725-3254-1
PB: 978-1-3500-7009-7
ePDF: 978-1-4725-3258-9
ePub: 978-1-4725-2813-1

Library of Congress Cataloging-in-Publication Data
A catalog record for this book is available from the Library of Congress.

Typeset by Integra Software Services Pvt. Ltd.

To find out more about our authors and books visit
www.bloomsbury.com and sign up for our newsletters.

*For the two sparks of my life, my beautiful daughters Sara and Tanya:
may your flames always burn brightly!*

# Contents

# List of Figures

# Acknowledgements

I would especially like to thank Zoltán Kövecses for his insightful comments on a draft of the whole manuscript. In addition, I would like to thank Jenny Rose for her detailed comments on a draft of the chapter entitled 'Fire in Zoroastrianism'. I would also like to thank Clive Seale for his comments on a draft of Chapter 1, Lisa El Refaie for her comments on a draft of Chapter 10, Mark Davies for making accessible material in the Corpus of Contemporary American English (COCA) and the British National Corpus (BNC), the cartoonist Dave Brown for permission to use Figure 10.5 titled 'The boy stood on the burning deck' (©Dave Brown/The Independent 2007), the cartoonist Steve Bell for permission to use his cartoon in Figure 10.6 titled 'Liar, liar pants on fire' (©Steve Bell/The Guardian) and Zoltán Kövecses for permission to use the material in Figure 3.2 titled 'the CONTAINER structure for "anger" metaphors'.

Part One

# Fire in Culture, Language and Thought

# 1

# The Meaning of Fire

## Introduction: Fire and power

On the 17th of December 2010, a young street vendor, Tarek Bouazizi, set himself on fire as a personal protest against the confiscation of his wares and the humiliation he had experienced at the hands of the Tunisian authorities. This symbolic action, and his resulting death soon afterwards, sparked off the Tunisian revolution leading to the fall of President Zine Ben Ali, and ignited civil protest against the authorities in many parts of the Arab world in a series of related protests that spread rapidly and became known as 'the Arab Spring'. While the 'Arab Spring' is easily recognized as a metaphor, if only from being placed in inverted commas, the other metaphors in the previous sentence – 'sparked off', 'ignited' and 'spread' – are less readily recognized as metaphors for two reasons. The first is because when passions are 'inflamed', it seems natural to employ a 'fire' metaphor because of our embodied experience of a rise in temperature when emotionally aroused. The second is because the events that they describe actually involved the use of fire; angry people tend to burn cars and buildings and, more tragically, people set fire to themselves. Metaphors of fire derive from our experience of heat and fire, either within our bodies or in the external world, and they communicate powerful psychological and emotional responses. It is such fire metaphors that form the topic of this book.

While our scientific understanding of fire has grown in disciplines such as climatology and environmental management – accelerated by the burning of fossil fuels and the carbonization of the atmosphere – this has not yet been accompanied by an equivalent understanding of how fire works in the human mind. Our relationship with fire has influenced our understanding of a wide range of spiritual, psychological and social relationships. Fire has come to represent divine punishment, personal creativity, social protest and private emotion. It is little surprise that a very successful form of electronic reading device has been branded as the 'kindle' because fire metaphors are *inherently* persuasive and are therefore commonly used in the language of product 'branding' (itself originally a 'fire' metaphor). A study of metaphors derived from the fire lexicon in a range of religious and political discourses provides insight into how they contribute to a language of power that I will refer to as discourses of awe and of authority. As Sontag's study of 'war' metaphors in illness experience has illustrated, an in-depth exploration of an apparently narrow linguistic area can offer a much broader understanding of the mental constructs that underlie the role of language in constructing the social world.

There was nothing essentially novel about the act of self-immolation committed by the young Tunisian street hawker; what was novel was that acts of self-combustion are more commonly associated with Indian and Buddhist cultures rather than Islamic ones where suicide is strictly forbidden. The practice of Buddhist self-immolation became more widely known in the West after its use by Buddhist monks in Vietnam during the anti-colonial protests of the 1960s. In June 1963, a Buddhist monk named Thich Quang Duc set himself on fire while seated in a meditation position at a major crossroads in Saigon. The act of self-immolation came to symbolize Buddhist resistance to President Diem's suppression of Buddhism. Western media coverage of this symbolic action made the practice more widely known to audiences who had previously associated death by fire with the martyrdom of religious non-conformists. The original meaning of immolation was 'killing a sacrificial victim' and its etymology can be traced to the Latin 'immolare' to sprinkle with sacrificial meal (mola salsa).

While burning at the stake is not an exclusively European practice, it was one extensively employed by European powers during their sixteenth- and seventeenth-century wars of religion, and, to a lesser extent, in their overseas colonial conquests. Burning heretics was the most visible, final and theologically grounded means for eliminating ideological opponents. This practice was employed by the Jesuits of the Inquisition when enforcing religious conformity through the trial known as the *auto-de-fe* – a ritual re-enactment of the Last Judgement. The sight of heretics being publicly burnt at the stake was intended to remind the audience of the divine punishment that awaits all sinners in the form of eternal hell-fire. The public display of suffering was a highly persuasive means for enforcing conformity. Those who repented during the *auto-de-fe* would be strangled or garrotted prior to being burnt and so would be saved from the punishment that awaited the damned. As Foucault (1975: 58) reminds us: it was a 'policy of terror', whose aim was 'to make everyone aware, through the body of the criminal, of the unrestrained presence of the sovereign. The public execution did not reestablish justice; it reactivated power'.

As well as the almost unimaginable pain, what is most significant about self-inflicted death by fire is that it implies a spiritual motivation as the perpetrator could only bear such sacrifice as a result of psychological suffering, or with a view to making a spiritual point. When Joan of Arc was asked at her trial, 'Do you not, then think yourself bound to submit your words and deeds to the Church Militant, or to any other but God?', the heroic young militant replied:

> What I have always said in the Trial, and held, I wish still to say and maintain. If I were condemned, if I saw the fire lighted, the faggots prepared, and the executioner ready to kindle the fire, and if I myself were in the fire, I would not say otherwise, and would maintain to the death all I have said.[1]

In the margin of the original manuscript the Registrar Manchon wrote: 'Responsio Johanne superba'. The terror of such a fate eventually forced her to recant – albeit too late to satisfy the 'Church Militant'. But her testimony of courage and of resistance remains.

A Jesuit, Bocanegra, recorded a similar act of defiance by a heretic:

All along the way the confessors and the Catholic bystanders shouted at him to repent and the heretical ways answered with gestures that showed his rebelliousness … (Once they got to the brasero) they held a torch to his beard and face to see if the grief would make him sane and the pain would make him open his eyes. But with words and actions he consummated his last impenitence, and dragging the wood closer with his feet, he let himself burn alive, showing no signs of remorse. What is more, no longer being able to speak, one could see him shake his head and hands as if he were saying no to the common voice that was claiming his conversion, experiencing already in this life the prelude of the eternal flames.[2]

The voluntary embrace of the flames – whether by a sixteenth-century heretic, or by a 21st century protestor – is a symbolic action that rejects all forms of human authority. Self-immolation reclaims the divine motivation as the victim re-asserts control over his own body by complete acceptance of suffering; the immolated therefore ceases to be victim and becomes the agent of his own salvation: a martyr!

Isolated acts of self-immolation are relatively rare, and it is their imitation that enhances their significance as symbolic actions. Bouazizi's self-immolation in Tunisia sparked off many others in countries across the Middle East and Europe: in the six months after his death, at least 107 Tunisians sought to commit suicide in this way. Social psychologists refer to the contagious, or spreading, effect of self-immolation as the 'Werther effect'. A study of fire metaphors contributes to an understanding of how and why fire takes on this symbolic meaning. I hope to explain the dual and apparently contradictory role of fire in human conceptualization that may account for how an apparently nihilist act of self-destruction may be interpreted as meaningful. Since fire changes the state of the material world it has agency: it is transformational and this capacity to change the state of matter forms the basis of its symbolic meaning. An understanding of the symbolism of fire therefore contributes to an understanding of martyrdom: when an act of individual protest – through imitation and replication – itself becomes a form of communication.

Evidence is provided in the fire metaphors in the official English language publication of the Islamic State (also known as ISIL and ISIS and Dabiq); each edition of the publication has the following strapline on its contents page: 'the spark has been lit here in Iraq, and its heat will continue to intensify … until it burns the crusader armies in Dabiq',[3] here we have a deliberately ambiguous use of fire words that activate metaphoric and literal senses. The 'spark' is a metaphor that refers to their religious beliefs, but the burning of 'crusader armies' is quite literal: the 'heat' could refer to embodiment or to actual fire.

Although my primary concern is the insight into human conceptualization offered by such fire terms, I also believe that a detailed study of fire metaphors has implications for a more general understanding of the relationship between thought, language and social action. I propose that the fire lexicon contributes to discourses of awe – language that creates feelings of reverence and wonder – and that these are then integrated within discourses of authority: language that expresses and imposes power relationships. By identifying how a single semantic field creates social meanings, I hope to provide a general account of language and power relationships.

There are other related areas of human experience such as illness, contagion and the human body that are also exploited through metaphor to contribute to discourses of awe and discourses of authority that underlie legitimacy claims (see for example Sontag 1991; Mitchell 2012; Musolff 2010). Mitchell (2012) provides a historical overview of the contagion metaphor and traces ideas of moral panic and Dawkins's meme theory back to the root concept of contagion. While power theorists – political scientists and philosophers such as Hobbes, Machievelli and Nietzche – have accounted for discourses of authority, fire provides a historically earlier, more tangible and probably less well-understood model for establishing legitimacy claims. Perhaps it is for this reason that fire metaphors – although not the most frequent – are the most prototypical of all metaphors. Fire offers a complex and rich frame for understanding the interrelationships between the bodily experience and society. Although both disease and fire are entities that motivate by arousing fear, disease is instantly recognizable as something inherently threatening to human survival, conversely, fire is conceptually ambiguous because it brings both gains and losses – both warmth and destruction; such ambiguity demands an explanation.

## Fire, evolution and survival

Fire has contributed in significant ways to human survival and evolution. As well as providing protection, warmth, light and the means to cook, fire was also at the basis of scientific thinking by encouraging observation to understand causation, and gaining control over the environment through technology. Pyne (2001: 24) puts this eloquently:

> All humans manipulate fire, and only humans do so. We are truly a species touched by fire. Fire opened the night by providing light and heat. It protected caves and shelters. It rendered foods more edible, leached away toxins from cassava and tannic acid from acorns, and killed bacteria that caused salmonella, parasites that led to trichinosis, and waterborne microbes. It interacted with every conceivable technology from flint mining to ochre painting, Fire was a god, or at least theophany; fire was myth, fire was science, fire was power, We could call it forth as we could not call forth floods or hurricanes or earthquakes or droughts.

While he may be right in claiming that the manipulation of fire is the exclusive preserve of humans, recent research into chimpanzees (Warneken and Rosati 2015) indicates that they share with early hominins some of the cognitive capacities that are involved in cooking. These include having the motivation to cook and having the patience to collect ingredients rather than eat them straight away. Cooking also involves understanding causal relationships between behaviours, such as putting ingredients in a cooking device, and their outcomes. The chimpanzees in the study showed a preference for cooked over raw food and demonstrated self-control by sacrificing food in their possession. They could also save food in anticipation of future cooked food;

deferment of gratification to obtain the benefits of future consumption shows an orientation towards the future.

A fascinating implication of this research is that if chimpanzees and early hominins *do* share common cognitive capacities, then the ability to cook may have originated much *earlier* in human evolution than was previously thought. It suggests that early hominins may have been able to cook with *naturally occurring fire* some time before they had mastered the ability to use hearths and ovens. Such opportunistic use of fire would then have created the conditions for the development of more complex uses of fire to cook in an enclosed space. Irrespective of whether or not there is a cognitive link between the behaviour of chimpanzees in a twenty-first-century empirical experiment and early hominins, it is certain that the emergence of cooking-related behaviours contributed significantly to the development of human cognition.

Fire that occurs naturally will necessarily spread: control over fire is only fully established when it is contained in some way. A hearth provides warmth and when contained within an oven, fire can be used for cooking; when within a kiln, it can be used for technological transformations. Controlled fire is therefore a source of physical comfort and cognitive development – partly because it freed up time and energies that were otherwise spent hunting and gathering *and* because it provided the opportunities and incentives for technological experimentation. Not only did fire provide warmth and protection from animals, it assisted in human cognitive and physical development.

Searching for ingredients *and* firewood developed greater planning skills than collecting fruit and berries and encouraged a more erect posture. Understanding how to produce fire led to increasingly complex understanding of cause and effect relationships in combustion. This involved experimenting in how to generate sparks, and identifying sources of tinder and fuel; such accumulated knowledge then needed to be preserved, and transmitted. It also encouraged social organization, for example through the division of labour required in scavenging for firewood, searching for raw food and cooking itself. Social rules needed to develop to overcome divisions arising from the theft of firewood, of ingredients, of food or even of the fire itself.

The functional and technological application of fire opened up numerous opportunities for control over the environment through the development of tools; this reflects in terms such as 'The Iron Age' and 'The Bronze Age', which imply that periods of human evolution are strongly associated with technological development through the ability to smelt different materials. The 'Industrial Revolution' and 'The Nuclear Age' reflect increasing knowledge over the physical cause and effect relationships involved between heat generation and social power. By understanding more about *how* fire has been used by humans, from the earliest times onwards, we can also understand the evolutionary basis for fire metaphors in language and their contribution to human cognitive and social development.

Fire is the only element that is generative in the sense that, like living creatures, it reproduces itself when supplied with fuel and oxygen. The mystery of fire is partly because humans have not always been sure as to whether to think of it as something that is alive or dead: while fire is not alive in a biological sense because it is not an organism, it still has some of the common defining characteristics of living organisms. Living organisms require nutrition; move of their own accord; grow; feed; are able to reproduce themselves; to respire; and to be sensitive to their environment and excrete. Fire satisfies each of these criteria: it requires fuel; it appears to move of its own volition – although in reality it is external influences such as wind that govern this; it can grow when it has access to fuel and oxygen. Fire can appear to reproduce itself when sparks fly from a forest fire to reignite elsewhere; like organisms, it requires oxygen to survive and will only do so in favourable conditions; just as organisms produce excreta, so fire produces cinders and ashes. In this respect fire can be viewed as having a cycle of existence: of being born, growing and dying. Like humans, fire also has needs and Pyne develops the metaphor of fire as a living entity with social demands:

> Domestication itself most likely began with the tending of flame. Like a being, it had to be conceived, fed, protected, put to bed, awakened, trained, controlled, exercised, bred – in effect, socialized into human life. It required constant attention, it needed a protective shelter ... Someone had to gather the endless fuel, someone had to fuss over the flames and nurture the coals, and someone had to oversee its proper use. (Pyne 2001: 24)

We know that fire is highly responsive and, if ignored, a fire will often go out – however, a small re-arrangement of logs or coals can soon re-activate the flames. Fire has needs that can either be met or ignored – each of these courses of action will bring their own consequences. It can thrive and increase, or it can decline and fade. It proves to be most beneficial to humans when tended and when constraints are placed on it, and at its most destructive when it is ignored or given insufficient respect – then it can truly spread, like wildfire. The contrasting role of fire in human evolution provides the basis for its ambiguous nature and I will consider some literary evidence for this in the next section.

## The ambiguity of fire

The argument of this book is that fire metaphors feature extensively in the formation of 'discourses of awe' and 'discourses of authority' because fire itself offers *our earliest experience of contradiction and ambiguity*. Bachelard identifies the essentially ambiguous nature of fire when applied to the moral order:

> Among all phenomena, it is really the only one to which there can be so definitely attributed the opposing values of good and evil. It shines in Paradise. It burns in Hell. It is gentleness and torture. It is cookery and apocalypse. It is a pleasure for the good child sitting prudently by the hearth; yet it punishes any disobedience when the child wishes to play close to its flames. It is well-being and it is respect. It is a tutelary and a terrible divinity, both though good and bad. It can contradict itself thus is it one of the principles of universal explanation. (Bachelard 1964: 7)

By attributing ambiguous moral qualities to fire Bachelard views it as offering the fundamental metaphor for understanding good and evil. Notice also how it is attributed with agency and is construed as a force that can 'punish' disobedience. Awareness of the inherently ambiguous nature of fire is not a contemporary phenomenon: the same conceptual ambiguity has motivated fire metaphors in literature from its earliest forms – such as the creative language play in Anglo-Saxon riddles:

> A wonderful warrior exists on earth.
> Two dumb creatures make him grow bright between them.
> Enemies use him against one another.
> His strength is fierce but a woman can tame him.
> He will meekly serve both men and women
> If they know the trick of looking after him
> And feeding him properly.
> He makes people happy.
> He makes their lives better.
> But if they let him grow proud
> This ungrateful friend soon turns against them.

Here fire is used in both making love and making war; it is something both meek and controllable and something wild and uncontrolled. Ambiguity and metaphor constitute the style of the riddle: it is only by interpreting the metaphor that we can resolve the ambiguities. First we have to work out the figure of personification, so that the inanimate entity – fire – is described as if it were an actual person – a warrior. The warrior symbolizes a physical force with the potential for improving life, and emotions such as anger and love are also forces. When interpreting the riddle we draw on our knowledge of warriors, war and emotions. Fire is a force that, like our emotions, can either overwhelm or be overwhelmed. Ambiguity therefore draws on two primary tropes: metaphor and metonymy; we know that love and war can be *like* fire, but fire can also *be* strongly associated with destruction *and* with our experience of being embodied creatures.

Fire occurs in a wide range of discourses because it offers a model for understanding contrastive relationships and ambiguity that is rooted in experience. But because it is agentive in the sense that it *actually* burns and transforms the concrete, material or known world and its biomass into gases, it is the ultimate and prototypical transformative agent. It enacts in the material world what metaphor enacts in the world of language and thought: it changes one thing into another, and in the process transforms both itself and what it acts upon.

A metaphor is a word or phrase that undergoes a transformation of meaning so that a new sense comes into being alongside a literal sense. This new, more recent sense is typically less tangible, concrete or embodied than the earlier sense. Metaphor is therefore, metaphorically speaking, *fire in language*. Just as fire transforms the visible material world into something immaterial and less visible, so metaphor shifts the senses of words away from their visible, material senses towards invisible, immaterial senses. Fire is therefore the perfect model for how metaphor works because cognitively metaphor allows us to understand what is less known, with reference to what is tangible and better known. Fire metaphors are easily recognized because while fire is visible, fire metaphors usually refer to something that is not visible. Typically, they describe emotions and power-related aspects of social relationships and it is these that I will now illustrate in literature.

## Fire, desire and death in literature

In literature and poetry fire is a widely accepted metaphor for describing human passions – especially those related to love and sexual desire. The transformative power of fire as a force in the physical world forms the perfect analogy for describing the transforming effect on the individual who is in love. Fire is extensively used as an image in the poetry and fiction of DH Lawrence; his poem 'The Enkindled Spring' is based entirely around the trope of a regenerative life force as 'fire'; here and elsewhere in the book I have put 'fire metaphors' in bold:

> This spring as it comes **bursts up in bonfires green,**
> Wild puffing of emerald trees, and **flame-filled bushes,**
> Thorn-blossom **lifting in wreaths of smoke** between
> Where the **wood fumes up** and the watery, **flickering rushes.**
> I am amazed at this spring, **this conflagration**   5
> Of **green fires lit** on the soil of the earth, **this blaze**
> Of growing, and **sparks that puff in wild gyration,**
> Faces of people streaming across my gaze.
> And I, what **fountain of fire** am I among
> This **leaping combustion of spring?** My spirit is tossed   10
> About like a shadow buffeted in the throng
> **Of flames**, a shadow that's gone astray, and is lost.

The power of the emotions that are activated by witnessing recrudescent nature at the time of spring is so overwhelming that the author is unable to resist the force of fire. More commonly, Lawrence draws on the trope of fire to describe the overwhelming power of sexual love in his poem 'Wedlock'[4]:

> Come, my little one, closer up against me,
> Creep right up, with your round head pushed in my breast.
> How I love all of you! Do you feel me wrap you
> Up with myself and my warmth, **like a flame around the wick?**
> And how I am not at all, **except a flame that mounts off you.**
> Where I tough you, **I flame into being;** but is it me, or you?
> Your breasts, your knees and feet! I feel that we
> **Are a bonfire of oneness, my flame flung leaping round you,**
> You the core of the fire, crept into me.
> And oh, my little one, you whom I enfold,
> **How quaveringly I depend on you, to keep me alive,**
> **Like a flame on a wick!**

Here the fire is equated with survival through the power of love: the flame is the emotional and sexual force that sustains the author and blends desire with its object. Throughout Lawrence's work the image of fire has a close association with the force of sexual desire: it is irresistible and potentially dangerous. In his fiction, fire becomes a highly explicit metaphor for sexual desire; for example in Lady Chatterley's Lover (Lawrence 1928):

> And softly, with that marvellous swoon-like caress of his hand in pure soft desire, softly he stroked the silky slope of her loins, down, down between her soft warm buttocks, coming nearer and nearer to the very quick of her. **And she felt him like a flame of desire, yet tender, and she felt herself melting in the flame.** (Chapter 12)

Here fire is a symbol of the totality of union that takes place in the sexual act. The embodied experience of lovers is developed systematically throughout the novel:

> She was nearly at the wide riding when he came up and flung his naked arm round her soft, naked-wet middle. She gave a shriek and straightened herself and the heap of her soft, chill flesh came up against his body. He pressed it all up against him, madly, the heap of soft, chilled female flesh that **became quickly warm as flame,** in contact. (Chapter 15)

Later in the novel fire is also employed to describe a form of spiritual purification that can take place through the sexual act:

> Though a little frightened, she let him have his way, and the reckless, shameless sensuality shook her to her foundations, stripped her to the very last, and made a different woman of her. It was not really love. It was not voluptuousness. It was sensuality **sharp and searing as fire, burning the soul to tinder.**
>
> **Burning out the shames,** the deepest, oldest shames, in the most secret places. It cost her an effort to let him have his way and his will of her. She had to be a passive, consenting thing, like a slave, a physical slave. Yet **the passion licked round her, consuming, and when the sensual flame of it pressed through her bowels and breast,** she really thought she was dying: yet a poignant, marvellous death. (Chapter 16)

Here shame is 'burnt out', so that sexual passions of lovers are beyond moral judgement. Eventually, towards the end of the novel, the fire trope takes on a spiritual meaning that replaces the earlier embodied one:

> So I believe in **the little flame between us.** For me now, it's the only thing in the world. I've got no friends, not inward friends. Only you. And now **the little flame** is all I care about in my life. There's the baby, but that is a side issue. It's my Pentecost, **the forked flame** between me and you. The old Pentecost isn't quite right. Me and God is a bit uppish, somehow. But the **little forked flame between me and you:** there you are! (Chapter 19)

The image of Pentecost activates other more spiritually based associations for fire and the trope of fire integrates the emotional, the physical and the spiritual so that no borders remain between them. Ultimately, it is this transforming power of fire that makes it such a potent and widespread image in his work.

But fire is not only transforming in relation to the human passions: historically fire was used for the disposal of dead bodies following military conflicts. Not only did it offer the fastest means of sending dead warriors to the afterlife, it also removed the dangers of disease from rotting bodies and therefore contributed to the survival of the victors. The use of fire in cremation contributes to the association between fire and destruction so that although fire was not necessarily used to *cause* death, it was the means of disposal of the dead. Fire is the final stage in a cognitive script that originated in experience of military conflict; because we know that a series of warlike events leads to the death of many warriors and sometimes non-combatants too, we also know that the last act in these events is the burning of the dead; hence the fire is a metonymy for the destruction or conflict in which these lives were lost.

In much literature, fire has become a prime trope for death – both as an instrument of destruction in war and in disposing of dead heroes. In the Anglo-Saxon poem Beowolf, the hero, Beowolf, is involved in a life and death struggle with the monster Grendel; Grendel is frequently described in terms of fire and fire terms are in italics:

> In off the moors, down through the mist-bands    710
> God-cursed Grendel came greedily loping.
> The bane of the race of men roamed forth,
> Hunting for a prey in the high hall ….
> Pacing the length of the patterned floor
> With his loathsome tread, while a baleful light,
> *Flame more than light, flared from his eyes* …
> The story goes
> That as the pair struggled, mead benches were smashed
> And sprung off the floor, gold fittings and all.
> Before then, no Shielding elder would believe
> There was any power or person on earth
> Capable of wrecking their horn-rigged hall
> *Unless the burning embrace of fire*    780
> *Engulf it in flame.*

An association is established between the monster and the most destructive force of which the Anglo-Saxons had experience: fire. The monster Grendel becomes such a terrifying opponent precisely because of its power to wield destructive fire:

> The dragon began *to belch out flames*
> And *burn bright homesteads*; there was a *hot glow*
> That scared everyone, for the vile sky-winger
> Would leave nothing alive in his wake.
> Everywhere the havoc he wrought was in evidence.

Far and near, the Geat nation
Bore the brunt of his brutal assaults
And virulent hate. Then back to the hoard
He would dart before daybreak, to hide in his den.   2320
He had *swinged the land, swathed it in flame,*
In *fire and burning,* and now he felt secure
In the vaults of his burrow; but his trust was unavailing.

Eventually, it is the dragon's capacity to breathe fire that enables him to destroy Beowolf. It is noticeable how the expression 'belch out' implies a degree of force since it was the emission of fire that gave its owner power over opponents. Earlier in the poem (lines 1107–1125) the metonymic association between fire and death had already been established through burning the bodies of fallen warriors. This account of the cremation of well-born Danes is then echoed in the description of Beowolf's cremation at the end of the poem:

The Geat people built *a pyre* for Beowulf,
Stacked and decked it until it stood four-square,
Hung with helmets, heavy war-shields
And shining armor, just as he had ordered.    3140
Then his warriors laid him in the middle of it,
Mourning a lord far-famed and beloved.
On a height *they kindled the hugest of all*
*Funeral fires; fumes of wood smoke*
*Billowed darkly up, the blaze roared*
And drowned out their weeping, wind died down
And wrought havoc in *the hot bone-house,*
*Burning it to the core.* They were disconsolate
And wailed aloud for their lord's decease.

There is no doubt about the finality and absoluteness of death in the image of the 'hot bone-house'; so fire is both the primary supernatural attribute that empowers Grendel and the means of cremating the dead. This association of fire with power, pain, death and destruction provides a frame for social prohibition. By 'frame' (a term originating in the work of Charles Fillmore) I mean the 'characteristic features, attributes, and functions of a denotatum, and its characteristic interactions with things necessarily or typically associated with it' (Allan 2001: 251). Fire is typically associated with life, nature and human productive enterprise. But it is also associated with the imposition of authority:

> In reality the social prohibitions are the first … This, then, is the true basis for the respect shown to flame: if the child brings his hand close to the fire his father raps him over the knuckles with a ruler. Fire, then, can strike without having to burn … Thus fire is initially the object of a *general prohibition*; hence this conclusion: the social interdiction is our first *general knowledge* of fire. What we first learn

about fire is that we must not touch it. As the child grows up, the prohibitions become intellectual rather than physical; the blow of the ruler is replaced by the angry voice; the angry voice by the recital of the dangers of fire, by the legends concerning fire from heaven. (Bachelard 1964: 11)

He then goes on to discuss the problem of 'clever disobedience' when a child secretly steals matches to start a fire. I will argue that this contrary role as a force for enforcing or challenging conformity provides the basis for fire to be used metaphorically in discourses of authority and rebellion. It is because fire provides its owner with great power that it is a contested element. The suggestion that fire metaphors enforce social prohibition invites an exploration of how they are used by those with political and religious authority – inquisitors and judges – and by those who challenge such authority – the self-immolators and heretics. The language of fire forms the basis for a system of command and control because, as the prototypical force in nature, fire provides a metaphor for socially imposed power relationships. A study of fire metaphors therefore provides insight into how power and authority are imposed through language.

We find early literary evidence for fire as a form of social prohibition in literary texts that – like the paintings of Bosch – offer visual images of divine punishment. Consider the use of fire terms (in italics) in Milton's depiction of the place prepared for the punishment of Satan for his act of rebellion against God in Paradise Lost:

Him the Almighty Power
Hurld headlong flaming from th' Ethereal Skie
With hideous ruine and *combustion* down
To bottomless perdition, there to dwell
In Adamantine Chains and *penal Fire*,
Who durst defie th' Omnipotent to Arms ....
There the companions of his fall, o'rewhelm'd
With Floods and Whirlwinds *of tempestuous fire* ....
He soon discerns, and weltring by his side
He lights, if it were *Land that ever burn'd*
With solid, as the Lake with liquid fire;
He walkt with to support uneasie steps
Over the *burning Marle*, not like those steps
On Heavens Azure, and the torrid Clime
Smote on him sore besides, *vaulted with Fire*;
Nathless he so endur'd, till on the Beach
Of that *inflamed Sea,* he stood and call'd
His Legions, ...

Milton describes a fire that overwhelms other elements such as wind and water as lakes and even seas become 'liquid fire'. 'Fire' occurs sixty-seven times in Paradise Lost. Another biblical text evoked by Milton is the *Book of Revelations* where 'fire' occurs twenty-five times (in the New King James version)[5] and is the predominant trope of divine punishment:

The first angel sounded: and *hail and fire* followed, mingled with blood, and they were thrown to the earth. And a third of the trees were *burned up*, and all green grass was *burned up*. Then the second angel sounded: and something like a great mountain *burning with fire* was thrown into the sea, and a third of the sea became blood. And a third of the living creatures in the sea died, and a third of the ships were destroyed. Then the third angel sounded: and a great star fell from heaven, *burning like a torch*, and it fell on a third of the rivers and on the springs of water. (Revelations 8: 7–10)

Fire also occurs 163 times in the Qur'an,[6] as for example in the following:

And death and hell were *cast into the lake of fire*. This is the second death. And whosoever was not found written in the book of life was *cast into the lake of fire*. (Qur'an, 20)

One reason that fire has provided the ultimate symbol of divine punishment in literary and religious texts is because throughout history it has been the predominant weapon of war. From Sodom and Gommorah, through the conflagrations of the European religious wars in the seventeenth century, to the fire bombings of the Second World War as described in the works of Arthur Koestler, uncontrolled, human-initiated fire has been the primary means for imposing power through fear and destruction. At the time of writing, the most sophisticated ground attack missile of Britain's Royal Air Force is named the 'Brimstone'. It has a radar homing device to ensure accuracy and is designed to limit collateral damage. Its fire-related name is designed as a metaphor that inspires awe among friends and foe alike.

But there is always ambiguity: the match, the lighter and the candle are the tools of the cook, the terrorist and the lover, of the pleasure-taker and the pleasure-breaker. Just as the work of Sontag and others sought to cure society of unguarded language by the use of metaphors of war and combat in relation to illness – a linguistic detoxification – I hope to undertake the work of the bomb-disposal expert by taking apart the fire metaphors of politicians, theologians and prophets. Fire is at the very basis of human imagination, and once a process of thought has started, its natural tendency is to continue of its own volition – provided that the necessary 'spark' and the necessary 'fuel' in the form of ideas, thoughts and the time to pursue them have been provided.

## Myths about the origin and discovery of fire

Frazer (1930) argues that in narratives accounting for the discovery of fire there is an implicit distinction between three ages according to man's knowledge of how to make fire: the Fireless Age, the Age of Fire Used and the Age of Fire Kindled. In the Fireless Age, people were ignorant of the existence of fire and suffered considerable hardships such as coldness and the consumption of raw or sun-dried food alone. In the Age of Fire Used, people knew about fire and were able to use it for cooking and heating but lacked an understanding of how to *kindle* fire; they relied on natural fire that arises in one of two ways: when lightening kindles a fire by striking flammable material or when the wind causes two branches to rub together generating the friction and heat necessary to cause a fire. The Age of Kindled Fire was when man had knowledge of how to control ignition and combustion but also therefore had less need for mythic explanation of fire.

The Age of Fire Used accounts for the majority of the myths described by Fraser and their primary theme is to provide an explanation of the origins of fire. For example, many stories provide accounts of how fire was given to man by a bird or a beast: curiously, these imply that animals possessed fire *before* humans. A typical example of such a story is that of the aborigines of Victoria, Australia:

> It was a small bird, variously described as the fire-tail wren and the fire-tail finch, which first brought fire to men, either having fetched it from the sky or stolen it from the crows, which alone possessed it; but the bird has still a red patch on its back where the fire burned it. (Fraser 1930: 209)

Many animals – woodpeckers, robin red breasts, monkeys or coyotes – are the bearers of fire in these myths. As Fraser notes, these myths are also concerned with explaining the physical characteristics, or other attributes, of their animal protagonists, though I would not agree that this was their primary purpose. In Fraser's third age, the Age of Fire Kindled, the narrative concerns how fires were kindled by human rather than divine agency. The most frequent of these methods was by the fire drill – a method involving two pieces of wood: an upright drill and a horizontal board. The upright one was rapidly rotated in the hands into the horizontal board until it made a hole. The rotation continued and once the friction had generated sufficient heat, a spark could ignite the tinder placed in the vicinity of the drill hole for that purpose.

A gendered dimension is given to some myths about the origin of fire, for example the idea that fire originated from the female genitals. In such myths, the position and function of the two sticks symbolize the sexual act: the vertical, pointed stick has a male penetrative role and the horizontal recipient board takes on a passive female role. In this frame, the action of drilling is analogous to sexual intercourse. Because the fire is extracted from the horizontal board, some myths interpreted fire as originally *belonging to* women before it came into the possession of men.

There was a long period of time when the kindling of fire was both time-consuming and problematic and implied significant differences in power between groups – as Pyne (2001: 122) describes:

> Nor for early hominids, was fire easy to make. They had to hold on to it once they had it. If they lost it, they could get more only by begging, borrowing, or stealing from others. Yet it was rare for groups to give fire away, it was too precious. They shared only within a clan, from a common source, and shared with outsiders only during core ceremonies like marriage or treaty-signings, where the commingling of fires symbolized the merging of their interests. To lose fire would be disastrous the very symbol of catastrophe. So they stove to preserve fire, slow matches, banked

coals, embers insulated with banana leaves, or birch bark, perpetually maintained communal hearths – all kept fire constantly alive – with suitable kindling and coaxing, new fires could be ignited from this source.

There was a shift from myths of fire's origin to a new type of meaning that arose from awareness of fire's scarcity and hence its power to create a symbolic meaning that reinforced social identity:

> As a socio-cultural regime, the fire regime tended to strengthen group ties. It was by virtue of their membership of a group that people enjoyed the benefits of having a fire. The extent to which, from early on, a group may have been identified with its fire can be inferred from the custom, noted among gatherers and hunters in our own times, of referring to one's group affiliation by saying to 'which fire' one belonged. (Goudsblom 1994: 39)

The development of symbolic meaning of fire arising from its role in creating social identities marks the transition from a mythological to a religious form of understanding, though there was a long period of transition in which fire became used increasingly in ceremony:

> The efforts to preserve the fire or the Sacred Fire of the larger community had thus an immensely practical purpose, eventually coded in elaborate ceremony and symbolism. Many people moreover, carried their glowing fires with them when they travelled. It was first believed that Australians, Tasmanians, and Andaman Islanders, for example did not know how to start fire because for long decades they were never seen to kindle one. Instead they carried their firesticks with them. (Pyne 2001: 122)

So, it is probably an oversimplification on Fraser's part to divide myths for the origin of fire into three distinct phases; in reality there would have been overlap in all sorts of different ways. A group could have worked out how to kindle fire, but then lost that knowledge because they moved to another area lacking in adequate materials for tinder. It may be that the origin of fire in religious rituals depended on developing a caste of fire experts: fire priests whose social role was to retain the knowledge of how fire should be prepared, sustained and maintained; without such knowledge a group could relapse into a dark, cold, primitive period – a Fireless Age. It is in the context of a cultural shift to preserving fire so as to maintain a religious worldview that we need to understand a new 'fire' concept – that of Sacred Fire that I develop in the Introduction to Part Two (page 65).

## Outline of the book

The first part of the book – this chapter and the following two chapters – provides context for the study of fire in language. In the next chapter I illustrate how semantic analysis and concepts such as 'lexical field' can assist us in understanding the concept of 'fire'; I then show how a large corpus of language can be used to examine particular fire metaphors for evidence of their basis in thought. In Chapter 3, I outline cognitive linguistic views on fire metaphors in relation to emotions such as love, desire, lust and anger; a central idea will be that the concept of force integrates knowledge of fire with knowledge of the embodied effect of the emotions. I consider evidence for such universally embodied conceptualizations; I argue that the use of fire metaphors to describe human emotions originates in correspondences between fire as *a physical force in nature* and the human experience of *emotion*. Fire- and heat-related metaphors also originate in the rise in temperature that is associated with bodily experience of emotions.

In the second part of the book I examine the concept of fire in religious discourse. In Chapter 4, I describe and compare the use of fire metaphors in the Abrahamic religions – Judaism, the Bible and the Qur'an. In Chapters 5 and 6, I consider fire symbols and metaphors in the Indo-Iranian religions of Zoroastrianism and Hinduism. Drawing on the evidence of their sacred texts, I consider whether fire has a primarily metonymic role because it is used in symbolic ritual, for example in making sacrifices, or whether it is primarily metaphoric, by communicating spiritual understanding. I trace a gradual shift from the symbolic meaning of fire in ritual towards linguistically based fire metaphors.

In the third part of the book I explore fire metaphors in discourses of authority. The concept of fire as a contested element is introduced in Chapter 7, where I undertake a study of *Foxe's Book of Martyrs*. This is a sixteenth-century account of the courage of the English Protestants who were martyred – usually by fire – for rejecting the doctrines of the Roman Catholic Church and who refused the opportunity to recant their beliefs. In Chapters 8 and 9, I examine the use of fire metaphors in political speeches. I first examine such metaphors in 167 British political speeches, supplemented by searches of 7.6 million political speeches from Hansard and then in 123 American political speeches. I examine the relationship between metaphor and metonymy and the extent to which fire metaphors are triggered by situations in which 'fire' stands for some aspect of political and social reality – such as protests or demonstrations.

Because of the importance of satire in disrupting and undermining discourses of authority, in the last chapter I analyse fire metaphors in British political cartoons. I argue that the same fire metaphors that contributed to discourses of authority also contribute to subversion in the semiotics of the political cartoon. Drawing on the resources of the British Cartoon Archive, I present findings for fire terms in cartoon captions and in verbal descriptions of the entities depicted in the cartoon. I argue – drawing on evidence of the pervasiveness, salience and expressive force of fire metaphors across different genres – that our understanding of communication is at least partly modelled on our observation, experience and understanding of fire.

# 2

# Investigating Fire Metaphors

## Linguistic methods

Corpus linguistics can be used to 'detoxify' fire metaphors by demonstrating a strong link between words according to how they are actually used in the language. A corpus is simply a large 'body' of language stored on a computer that allows identification of the meaning of words by examining their distributional patterns and contexts: by examining the contexts of words we can know about their subtle shades of meaning. I will illustrate this with words relating to language, disease and authority and show how these three semantic fields are conceptually related because of their common association with 'fire'. A semantic field is a group of words that are conceptually related in the mind, so that the semantic field for 'fire' includes concepts or ideas related to the causes of a fire, its appearance, its properties such as heat and light, its motion and its action. These concepts will tend to be universal but how they are verbalized will vary in different languages.

'A semantic field' can be compared with a 'lexical field' which is the actual words used to describe concepts in a particular language; so, for example, in the English lexical field for fire 'spark' describes the cause of a fire; 'glow' refers to the appearance of a fire; 'spread' refers to the motion of a fire and 'burn' refers to the action of fire. All these words are included in the semantic and lexical fields for 'fire'. Semantic fields allow the comparison of concepts across different languages, whereas lexical fields are specific to particular languages. So most languages have a word that refers to the cause and action of fire, but in English these words are 'spark' and 'burn'. Thought and language are like parent and child: one is a precondition for the other and meaning arises from the interaction between them.

To illustrate how a large electronically stored database can assist in investigating 'fire' metaphors I will draw on the Corpus of Contemporary American English (COCA)[1]; this is a large database of spoken and written English. It can either be searched as a whole or by selecting one of its various sub-corpora such as 'newspapers'. We can search for particular words, either in their root form or with all their grammatical variations – plural and so on. We can also search for words that co-occur with other words: these are known as its collocates. In either case we can restrict our search to particular word classes such as nouns or verbs. For example, if we search for the grammatical variations of verbs that often occur directly before or after 'word' and 'words' (its 'collocates') in COCA, we get the results shown in Table 2.1.

**Table 2.1** Sample of verb collocates of 'Word' in COCA (>50)

|          | 'word' | 'words' | Total |
|----------|--------|---------|-------|
| spoken   | 102    | 180     | 282   |
| spread   | 233    | 0       | 233   |
| sent     | 211    | 0       | 211   |
| received | 207    | 0       | 207   |
| written  | 0      | 187     | 187   |
| echoed   | 20     | 103     | 123   |
| sounded  | 0      | 108     | 108   |
| leaked   | 64     | 0       | 64    |

As well as verbs associated with sound ('spoken', 'echoed' etc.) and writing ('written'), we find verbs related to transmission – 'spread' or 'send' and 'leaked'. There is also a difference between plural and singular, so the 'word' is 'spread', 'received' or 'leaked', whereas 'words' are 'written', 'spoken' or 'sounded'. We may ask ourselves what other type of things often 'spread' and what is the semantic effect of this? And to answer this question we would need to search the collocates of 'spread' because if two different entities are conceptualized as 'spreading', it is possible to establish a connection between them through this mutual association: importantly, it is one that may form the basis for a metaphor. For example, 'disease' also 'spreads' as seen from the list of verbal collocates directly before and after the word 'disease' (shown by 1,1, in brackets) (see Table 2.2).

Here there are verbs concerned with causation, naming, preventing and curing disease. But the only verb that occurs in both the 'word' and 'disease' lists of collocates is 'spread'. This supports Mitchell's view of metaphor itself as a form of contagion. If we search collocates of 'spread', we find that there are eighty corpus lines where 'fire' is followed by a verb form of 'spread'. Why is it that language, disease *and* fire are all commonly used as subjects of the same verb 'spread'? A possible explanation is that our understanding of the behaviour of language and disease arises from *our understanding of the behaviour of fire*: fire is after all more visible and concrete than language or disease.

**Table 2.2** Sample verb collocates of 'Disease' (1,1)

|          |     |
|----------|-----|
| cause    | 544 |
| prevent  | 231 |
| called   | 182 |
| spread   | 135 |
| cure     | 85  |
| treat    | 80  |
| progress | 56  |

**Table 2.3** Semantic grouping of collocates of 'Spread' (1,1)

| Semantic field | Collocates of 'Spread' |
| --- | --- |
| DISEASE [2] | cancer; virus; infection; disease; aids; flu; epidemic |
| LANGUAGE & COMMUNICATION | word; processing; fashion; rumor |
| AUTHORITY | prevent; halt; stopping |
| COOKING | pan; evenly; bread; pepper; spatula; sheet; smooth; dish; cheese |
| BODY | legs; smile; arms; fingers; wings; grin; wrinkles |
| FIRE | fire; flames; wildfire; conflagration; ashes |
| SPEED | quickly; rapid; slow; slowly; rapidly; gradually |
| EXTENT | wide; continues; widely |
| OTHER | began; helped; excel; stain; upward |

To develop this argument further, let's consider in more detail words that are commonly found in close proximity to 'spread'. Table 2.3 shows the most common collocates of 'spread' when they are organized into semantic fields.

Since we may 'know a word by the company it keeps',[3] these groups show us something about the meaning of 'spread'. Spread in its physical sense is related to ideas of physical motion and movement; but the movement of more abstract entities – such as disease and language – are also viewed as 'spreading'. A third group is related to authority and includes 'preventing' or 'stopping' things from spreading. Cooking is a fourth group since 'spreading' is often referred to in recipes. Another group is related to the body, as well as those in the table, 'blush', 'flush' and 'wrinkles' also 'spread' (unfortunately!). Other groups relate to the speed and range of spreading. Finally, an important group that forms the basis for the research in this book is 'fire'. Other fire-related collocates of 'spread' are 'wildfire', 'conflagration', 'warmth' and 'ashes'.

Once we have organized words that occur with 'spread' into semantic fields, we can then identify meaning-related patterns between these groups. For example, entities that 'spread' can be either concrete or abstract. By 'concrete' I mean tangible and material, whereas 'spread' refers to physical motion or an increase in physical surface; this is the case when words are from the semantic fields of cooking or the body, as in 'spreading jam' or 'spreading one's legs'. By 'abstract' I mean intangible and immaterial, where 'spread' refers to an increase in the extent of influence, effect or knowledge, as in 'spreading a virus' or 'spreading a rumour'; this is the case with words relating to disease, language or authority. When a rumour is 'spread' via twitter, it has an influence and this can be viewed as a metaphor because of the availability of a more concrete and physical meaning of 'spread'. The distinction between concrete and abstract senses differentiates between literal and metaphoric meanings because a metaphor can be defined as 'a word or phrase that is used with a sense that differs from another more common or more basic sense' (Charteris-Black 2011: 31). For example, when we speak

**Table 2.4** 'Spread' (1,1) – metaphoric uses

| Semantic field | Example | Frequency |
|---|---|---|
| DISEASE | The speed with which the *disease spread* surprised everyone, its transmission bolstered by the fact that the vaccination rate had dropped below what was necessary for herd immunity. In the context of changing patterns in international travel, immigration and global *disease spread,* understanding the socio-economic determinants of existing disease risks is prudent. | 116 |
| LANGUAGE & COMMUNICATION | At dawn, *word spread* that a lieutenant had raped a girl. Soldiers followed suit, testified Cesar Ibanez, the second Kaibil. By 6 am, a supervisor radioed his bosses, then relayed that residents would be 'vaccinated'. Last week, *word spread* among gay service personnel on the West Coast that investigations of gay soldiers have been initiated at Fort Lewis, Wash. | 322 |

of fire as 'spreading', we are using a literal sense of 'spread' because fire is tangible and visible, but when a rumour 'spreads like wildfire', this is metaphoric because we cannot actually see it happening and therefore this sense is less basic. Table 2.4 shows the frequency of some metaphoric uses of 'spread' – again searching in positions directly adjacent to 'spread' – and some examples of these.

Once we look at the contexts of 'spread', we find that entities that 'spread' are often negatively evaluated – since disease is inherently 'bad', it needs to be 'halted' or 'prevented'. Similarly, with authority – there is an effort to prevent the spread of dangerous entities. When we speak of preventing the spread of some social ill, it indicates that there is evidence of metaphoric thinking in relation to authority.

On examining contexts more fully, a group of social behaviours that typically 'spread' are forms of social unrest such as 'protests', 'demonstrations', 'discontent', 'rioting', 'insurgency', 'clashes' and 'unrest' itself. Our understanding of authority may therefore be metaphorically related to our understanding of disease and of language. Taking metaphor further, the negative meaning that can arise from these three concepts could have originated in our primary understanding of the destructive effects of fire. What seems to connect our understanding of disease, language and authority is the shared concept of force of transmission. Table 2.5 shows some examples of the force of transmission concept by collocates of all forms of 'spread' (i.e. spreads, spreading etc.) within the wider range of four words before and after each of the words in the second column (shown by 4,4):

Concepts relating to the transmission of ideas, illness and social protest are indirectly connected by their shared use of the verb 'spread' to describe something essential to their nature: their tendency to increase as a result of a force. A further concept related to authority concerns the response by authority to social protest that

**Table 2.5** 'Spread' and FORCE OF TRANSMISSION collocates (4,4)

| Semantic field | Word | Example | Frequency |
|---|---|---|---|
| TRANSMISSION OF IDEAS | word | After six years of slavery, he escaped and left the country. But after training in the church, he returned to *spread the word of* Christianity throughout Ireland. | 1770 |
| | message | For McCain, the town hall is more than just a chance for him to *spread his message* of staying the course in Iraq and cutting taxes and spending. | 312 |
| | gospel | In the near future, expect the option to watch a single game with multiple camera angles. Though MLB.com says that a big part of its mission is *spreading the gospel* of baseball. | 228 |
| | democracy | Yet it also showed that the least popular American policy is the US push to *spread democracy* in the Middle East. | 200 |
| CONTAGIOUS DISEASE | disease | … but in a gradual whimper of environmental collapse as soaring temperatures and rising seas submerge cities, parch farmlands, crash ecosystems and *spread disease* and chaos worldwide. | 1164 |
| | Aids | the headstrong opposition to the use of condoms in Africa to prevent the *spread of AIDS.* | 351 |
| | infection | but those treatments didn't halt the *spread of infection.* | 270 |
| SOCIAL PROTEST | protest | *Protests also spread* to the ancient city of Fez, in the northeast. | 77 |
| | demonstra-tion | *Demonstrations* quickly grew and *spread* to Yemen's main urban centers | 28 |
| | discontent | The *discontent* also could *spread* to other restive pockets and deepen insecurity over Indonesia's political future after the 72-year-old Suharto steps down from power, | 13 |
| | riot | Drawing inspiration from Tunisia, an unprecedented wave of protests and *rioting has spread* to Algeria, Libya, Jordan and Egypt. | 20 |
| | unrest | A protester in the Sinai desert shot dead as he ran. The *unrest* in Egypt has *spread* like wildfire. | 40 |
| | insurgency | Since frustrated farmers tipped the 2004 national elections and a rural Maoist *insurgency spread* across the heartland | 18 |
| | clashes | *Clashes spread* across Israel's northern border with Lebanon, and Hezbollah guerrillas there kidnapped three Israeli soldiers. | 8 |

is spreading: this is by a forceful action to stop or prevent the transmission of protest. This is illustrated in Table 2.6:

**Table 2.6** 'Spread' and STOPPING TRANSMISSION (4,4)

| Semantic field | Word | Example | Frequency |
|---|---|---|---|
| RESPONSE BY AUTHORITY | prevent | It had become accepted wisdom that the openness of the United States and its acceptance of minority faiths and communities had helped to *prevent the spread* of the kind of Islamic radicalism that has gripped Western Europe over the past decade. | 562 |
| | stop | To help *stop the spread* of Islamic terrorism, governments around the world should censor and block websites that encourage murder of the innocent. | 385 |
| | halt | Qariout, a rocky village of 2,600 people about 20 miles north of Jerusalem, illustrates why Palestinians are desperate to *halt the spread* of Jewish settlements. | 74 |

What I hope to have illustrated empirically by drawing on a large body of language is that we understand communication in a way that is similar to how we understand disease and authority and that *all three of these concepts originate in our understanding of the behaviour of fire.* Observing fire as a force in nature, and understanding the way that it moved across the land served as a model for understanding the force of ideas and their transmission through language and how illnesses moved between populations. Controlling the force of fire also became a model for controlling the force of social protest. Language, disease and authority are related because of their common conceptual grounding that originates in knowledge of the force and transmission of fire. In his study of crowds and power, Canetti (1960: 89) argues that crowds behaved in very much the same way as fire:

> If we consider the several attributes of fire together we get a surprising picture. Fire is the same wherever it breaks out: it spreads rapidly; it is contagious and insatiable; it can break out anywhere, and with great suddenness; it is multiple; it is destructive; it has an enemy; it dies; it acts as though it were alive, and is so treated. All this is true of the crowd...these likenesses between fire and the crowd have led to close assimilation of their images; they enter into each other and can stand for each other. Fire is one of the most important and malleable of the crowd symbols which have always played a part in the history of mankind.

The findings of the corpus study of 'spread' supports Canetti's view of fire as an important crowd symbol.

At this point I should explain that a frame is a gestalt-like structure; this means that a particular fire metaphor can trigger a whole frame structure. For example, reference to a rumour 'spreading like wildfire' activates a conceptual structure that might have other fire-related slots for speed of transmission and danger. Authority responds to social unrest when it is described as 'spreading like wildfire' because this frame also has ideas of disease. The nature of governance is in controlling the spread of what is viewed as harmful. The notion of 'spreading' is fundamental in discourses relating to awe and authority: power has a force tendency to spread or to control spreading. Power spreads those ideas that are favourable to its purposes but it resists those that are opposed to it. The social order emerges from a struggle of opposing forces that is modelled on the behaviour of fire and responses to it.

This discourse of governance and control takes its origin in the frames we have for fire: this is why acts of self-immolation can take on a symbolic meaning in social protest. The 'Arab Spring' was sparked off by an actual fire, one that then spread, and subsequent responses were either to extinguish this metaphoric 'fire' or to spread it further afield. It is also why the Islamic State predicts that 'the spark has been lit in Iraq, and its heat will continue to intensify ... until it burns the crusader armies in Dabiq'. Analysis of 'spread' – and its patterns of use in a large corpus of language – provides evidence that the behaviour of fire has provided a frame for how illness, language and social protest have worked as force systems of transmission and governance. Metaphors and similes provide evidence that our understanding of fire underlies this conceptualization. Further evidence of this claim is by identifying the type of entities that are described as 'spreading like wildfire'; these are summarized in Table 2.7.

Of course, fire can be made safe, contained within a hearth, or an altar – but the spreading of fire, by combustion with a release of heat, light and smoke, when used metaphorically allows us to draw on a complex range of experience. As long as there are flammable substances, a source of fire and oxygen, fire will necessarily have a tendency to 'spread', creating a living model for the force of transmission. The use of the expression 'spread like wildfire' was in relation to the concepts previously identified: transmission by language in words such as 'news', 'rumors' and 'stories'; transmission of illness ('bug'; 'flu'; 'cholera'; 'infection' etc.) and the transmission of social protest ('protests'; 'sit in'; 'strike' etc.). Mitchell (2012) explores how ideas of social and moral contagion emerged in late nineteenth-century France. Early studies of social psychology such as Le Bon (1895) saw analogies between contagion and the behaviour of crowds. However, there was also an extension of the frame of transmission that emphasized the *speed* and *force* of transmission especially in relation to the rapid spread of novel sports such as basketball and yoga:

**Table 2.7** Agents that 'Spread like wildfire'

| Semantic fields | Words |
| --- | --- |
| TRANSMISSION OF IDEAS | news; word; rumours; stories; idea; social media posts; belief; scandal; picture; information; music-sharing service; baseball; fashion; trend |
| CONTAGIOUS DISEASE | bug; flu; sarcoma; diseases; infection; cholera; virus; abuse; cancer; AIDS |
| SOCIAL PROTEST | protests; violence; unrest; sit in; revolution; mass suicide; secret lodges; strike |

The game arrived on Cuba's shores in 1869, when some university students brought bats and balls home from the mainland. El beisbol spread **like wildfire**, partly because it was viewed as a modern American activity, a refreshing break from the traditions of the dying Spanish colonial empire. Within decades, the game was catching on in every U.S.-embracing corner of the Caribbean.

The rapid spread of novel activities can be positive – for example in relation to ideas about education:

Adding a twist to the traditional nighttime curfew, Monrovia, Calif., a community of 39,000 in Los Angeles County, in 1994 became the first city in the nation to fight truancy by adopting a daytime curfew to keep kids in class during school hours. The idea has spread **like wildfire** to other California cities and even earned Monrovia a visit from President Clinton during the 1996 campaign.

Fire also creates a frame for understanding how new ideas and inventions are spread and the phrase 'spread like wildfire' is often used to describe the spread of new ideas through technological innovation:

State securities regulators emphasize that the problem of illicit and abusive on-line investment schemes is a new one that has the potential to spread **like wildfire** as the result of the increasing popularity of commercial bulletin board services and the Internet.

Here the emphasis is on rapid transmission, and this is negative when the entities that are transmitted are viewed as socially damaging – for example the spread of new ways of making drugs:

First introduced on the market in 1995, OxyContin abuse has been spreading **like wildfire**. Its active ingredient is a synthetic form of morphine called oxycodone.

What motivates metaphors such as 'spread like wildfire' is the experiential knowledge that the effects of the transmission of disease and of ideas may be accompanied by experiences similar to a salient attribute of fire: the force of its uncontrolled transmission. But what motivates the metaphoric use of 'wildfire' can be compared with situations where fire *actually* occurs since these experiences of real fire influence metaphoric senses. For example, we may describe protests and riots as 'spreading like wildfire' because they are literally accompanied by the lighting of fires and explosions, and the use of fire-making equipment such as bombs. Such uses lead us towards metonymy because when social protests occur, people burn things and this gives rise to *the actual presence of fire*. Conceptually, a metonymy is when one entity stands for another to which it is closely related in experience: in this case the fire stands for the beliefs, the feelings and the emotions of the protesters. So the fire started by the protesters becomes a metonymy, or verbal symbol for their protest.

## Discourses of fire

In the previous section I have tried to demonstrate how the metaphoric meaning of fire can be explored by identifying how 'spread' is used in a corpus. This shows it often has 'fire' as a subject. Then, I have explored other concepts that are conceptually related to fire because they also 'spread' and therefore share the concept of transmission; these include ideas, diseases and authority. Because 'spread' is used to refer to both tangible and to abstract entities, this creates the possibility for metaphor. The force of transmission of ideas, social protest movements and contagions can all be framed in terms of the behaviour of fire. These metaphoric uses form the discourses of awe and of authority that are the topic of this book; these are summarized in Figure 2.1.

My proposal is that analysis of the word 'spread' shows that our conceptualization of transmission is grounded in our understanding of fire because fire is a prototypical entity that spreads. Fire is thought of as if it were alive, as in expressions such as 'fire my imagination' or inventions and new ideas as 'spreading like wildfire'; these metaphors form discourses of 'awe' because the force of fire creates a symbolic connection between fire and being alive – as in the notion of 'life force'. Conversely, when fire metaphors are used to communicate prohibition, as in the prevention of disease, I

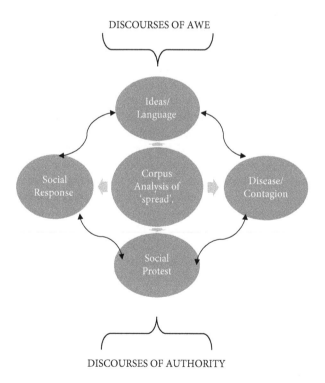

**Figure 2.1** Discourses of awe and authority

will be interpreting such concepts as instances of discourses of 'authority' – ideas that originate in the knowledge that controlling a force is necessary when that force is dangerous and therefore make a symbolic connection between control of fire and control of threatening forces.

To explore discourses of awe, I have tried to select texts that are representative of religious language: the Torah, the Bible, the Qur'an, the Avesta, the Rig Veda and the Upanishads. To explore discourses of authority I use *Foxe's Book of Martyrs* and large samples of British and American political speeches. To identify fire metaphors I first need to describe the semantic and lexical fields for 'fire', which I will do in the next section; I will refer to these words as 'the core fire lexicon' (words such as 'burn' and 'flame'). These words can then be used to investigate religious and political texts (either in their original forms or in translation). Exploring collocations in the fire lexicon allows me to identify metaphoric senses of fire.

Analysis of lexical patterns enables the identification of a theme, or concept, that underlies a number of different metaphors. For example, in the Bible there are a number of fire metaphors:

> See, **the LORD is coming with fire**, and his chariots are like a whirlwind; he will **bring down his anger with fury, and his rebuke with flames of fire.** (Isaiah 66: 15)
>
> When you appear for battle, **you will burn them up as in a blazing furnace.** The LORD will swallow them up in his wrath, and **his fire will consume them.** (Psalm 21: 9)

From such uses I can infer the concept: DIVINE PUNISHMENT IS FIRE. Of course, whether or not this is a metaphor or a statement of fact will depend on theological perspective and I would like to illustrate this with reference to an anecdote. Two friends, both of Irish Catholic origin, told me that when they were at school they were told that if they even put their foot in a Protestant church it would *burn*; one day they went to the porch of a Protestant church, opened the door and tentatively raised their foot over the threshold to feel the heat – only to be disappointed by the same cool dampness that they encountered in their own church. It was not clear whether the concept DIVINE PUNISHMENT IS FIRE was 'just' a metaphor or a literal statement about what would happen to them. The frames that were activated all depended on whether you were Catholic or Protestant. But it is precisely such a blurring of boundaries between fantasy and reality that illustrates how discourses of authority emanate from discourses of awe. It is certainly true that at various points in the history of Christianity discourses of awe, and the actual fires in which people were burned, were motivated by views as to how divine authority could best be imposed and how opponents could best be controlled.

## The fire Lexicon and fire concepts

In the previous section, I introduced a semantic approach to examining fire metaphors that forms the basis for the analysis that follows in the remaining chapters. It can facilitate linguistically based analysis to classify particular words according to conceptual criteria using the terms 'lexical field' and 'semantic field'. 'Lexical field' refers to the actual words that occur in a language, while 'semantic field' refers to a set of conceptually related meanings. So, in Figure 2.2, the semantic field of natural fire includes the words 'flicker' and 'flame'.

I propose a distinction between three semantic fields: Natural Fire, Functional Fire and Organic Fire. I will describe all the English fire terms shown in Figures 2.2–2.4 as the 'core fire lexicon' and organize them into these three semantic fields. Firstly, we may think of 'fire' in terms of its natural *properties* such as its appearance or its intensity. These are features over which humans have limited control; I will refer to this concept as NATURAL FIRE because these words refer primarily to fire as a phenomenon of nature. Secondly, we can think of fire in terms of its *effects* such as providing light or providing heat; I will refer to this concept as FUNCTIONAL FIRE because it implies a degree of human control over fire for a particular purpose such as providing light by a torch or candle or in the preparation of food. Words such as 'heat' and 'smoke' that could be nouns or verbs were difficult to classify because a natural fire produces heat or smoke (i.e. the nouns) without any human agency; however, heat and smoke can be used for specific purposes, as when a human agent applies heat or smoke for warming or cooking (i.e. the verb forms). I have therefore classified nominal uses of heat and smoke as 'NATURAL' and verbal uses of these words as 'FUNCTIONAL'. I have included 'meltdown' as functional (as well as 'melt') even though it is a type of fire that has gone out of control, because it can originally be attributed to human agency. Figures 2.2 and 2.3 summarize how the core fire lexicon is classified using these two fire concepts.

**Figure 2.2** Lexical and semantic field for NATURAL FIRE

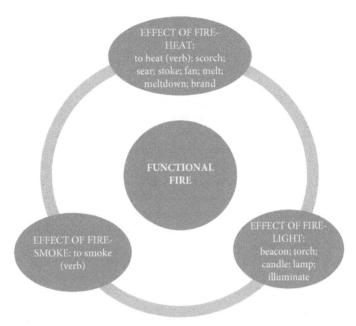

**Figure 2.3** Lexical and semantic field for FUNCTIONAL FIRE

Thirdly, we can think of fire as having a life cycle in which there is a temporal sequence of events from its start, and its growth through to its end; I will refer to this semantic field as ORGANIC FIRE because it conceives of fire as something that can be described as a process with a beginning, middle and end. Although some of the words classed in this category may have a human agency (such as 'ignite' or 'snuff out'), the meaning emphasis is on the degree in the stage of the fire cycle rather than on its function or purpose. ORGANIC FIRE is shown in Figure 2.4.

Since fire occurs quite independently of human agency – the universe may have originated from a big bang – it is definitively a natural phenomenon that operates quite independently of human agency as when a flash of lightening ignites flammable material. The burning flames that arise from this process of nature can be described as 'Natural Fire'. When fire arises from human agency, as when we ignite and kindle a flame, fan or stoke a fire, we have Functional Fire. This fire is used for human purposes such as heating, melting, scorching or producing smoke: the force of fire is controlled for human purposes. Fire may also be viewed as 'Organic' because, like living entities, it progresses through cyclical stages: commencing with 'birth', it grows and increases and, finally, 'dies' – metaphorically, it therefore has a 'life force'. The complex nature of fire is essential to its mystery and has had a dominant influence on human culture: the influence on human history has physical, social and psychological dimensions that will be explored in the next chapter.

Our experience of a particular fire may involve drawing on each of the fire concepts; for example the Olympic torch is ignited and extinguished, has a shape, and provides light – so it is organic, natural and functional. As mentioned earlier, 'heat' may be

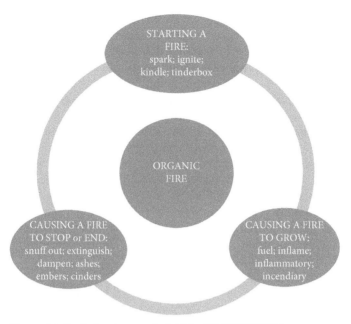

**Figure 2.4** Lexical and semantic field for ORGANIC FIRE

considered a natural attribute of fire when used as a noun; but it is also employed functionally as when heat is used for a purpose such as melting or cooking. It is only in context that we can see whether the primary reference of a fire word is to a natural phenomenon, to the application of fire for a purpose or to a stage in the process of fire generation or termination. My identification of these fire concepts offers a way of analysing fire terms in other languages – and I would expect there to be words corresponding with each of these fire-related semantic fields in other languages. There may also be words in other languages that offer additional concepts to the ones profiled in English. I hope readers will draw on their knowledge of other languages to test this hypothesis.

There were some difficult decisions to take in arriving at these lexical fields; for example I decided not to give separate entries for compound nouns related to 'fire' such as 'fireman' and 'firefighter' because there these words seemed to be used exclusively with their literal meaning. However, I did include the compound 'meltdown' as it is often used metaphorically. 'Light' was not included in the core lexicon for fire because, although it is commonly used as a metaphor, light does not necessarily depend on fire. The reflective properties of light as implied by words such as 'shine', or 'reflect', imply daytime light. However, I have included light terms when fire is viewed as a source of illumination at night – for example 'candle' 'illuminate' and 'glow'. For similar reasons I have included 'torch', 'beacon' and 'lamp' because the historical setting of many of the texts examined in this book was prior to the invention of electricity when nocturnal light required fire.

A highly problematic word that I eventually excluded from these lexical fields was 'consume' and its variations 'consumers' and 'consumption'. These words are not treated as part of the core fire lexicon though they surely belong to the semantic field of fire. This is because there is a metaphoric origin of all senses of 'consume' relating to fire. An earlier sense of 'consume' referred to the effect of illness on the human body and 'consumption' referred to the illness now known as 'tuberculosis', of which the major symptom was the wasting away of the body. This meaning was first extended to the effect of the action of fire, probably because it captured the idea of force of transmission and subsequently to the action of people when purchasing products or services. However, it seems that the cognitive frames for fire or illness are not necessarily triggered by this word with its current sense of using a service or a product, therefore 'consume' currently fits within a lexical field related to economics rather than to one for fire. However, it is a very good example of polysemy – that is a set of related meanings that have developed over time with the extension of a word to a new set of references – and in discussion of earlier historic senses I will include some discussion of 'consume' as it is part of the etymology of fire.

My method will be to examine patterns of use of each of the words shown in the figures in this chapter in various religious and political texts: discourses of awe and authority. Unless otherwise indicated, the reader can assume that I have searched for all morphological variations of a word – whether the inflection is for plural (e.g. 'spark' and 'sparks') or verbal (e.g. 'ignite', 'ignited', 'igniting'). This analysis will lead me to identify metaphors employing fire words, because these words refer to non-literal uses of fire such as emotional experience or experiences of the sacred and the sublime. The identification of various metaphors will enable me to propose some ideas that underlie such metaphors to arrive at so-called conceptual metaphors.

I am going to finish this chapter by comparing scientific and mythological answers to the question 'what is fire'? A scientific explanation might be as follows: 'fire is a sustained chemical reaction between a fuel and oxygen that occurs in a process known as combustion; this causes flames that give off heat and light'. Science may then go on to consider the cause of fire: 'for combustion to occur, there must be a source of ignition, a flammable material and the availability of oxygen'. It may also explain its effect: 'the matter that is burnt undergoes chemical transformation from a solid to a gaseous state'. A mythological explanation of fire would not be concerned with the process itself, but offers a story about how man obtained fire, for example 'fire belonged to Zeus, but it was stolen from him by Prometheus who was then punished for this theft'. The relative value of scientific and mythological explanations depends on the purpose for which they are created; a scientific explanation is designed to provide knowledge of a process that would enable the knower to produce and control fire – by providing ignition, fuel and oxygen, while a mythological explanation is designed to overcome fear of the unknown by accounting for what is unknown through narrative.

Fire offers a huge survival advantage for those who possess and control it by providing warmth, enabling cooking and providing protection from enemies. Cultural and social factors contributed to man gradually learning the functionality of fire. Control of fire entailed power and influence – both within the group since fire was at its centre as a hearth or oven – but also between groups: those that 'owned' fire were more powerful than those that didn't: it provided technological advantages and symbolized control over something inherently mysterious. Fire invites reverie, introspection, and activates the imagination, so that when we gaze into the embers of a fire, we have visions of how the world might be. It also forms a place around which people can gather – for reflection or to tell stories. I have also suggested that our understanding of the spreading of ideas that occur around a fire is modelled on how the fire itself spreads from one log or coal to another. Fire is inherently ambiguous, while it appears to be alive, it can also cause death: it is simultaneously safe *and* dangerous.

# 3

# Fire, Emotion and Cognition

## Introduction

In Chapter 1, I introduced some mythological and early religious accounts of the origin of fire by considering James Frazer's *Myths of the Origins of Fire*. Only by understanding how fire was transposed from the Gods to man, through the mediation of myth and then through ritual practice in religion, can we fully account for the 'carrying across' of meaning that occurs in metaphor. In this respect, metaphor itself is 'fire' at work in language: the transformational process in which one experience is understood in terms of another – just as fire transforms one material element into another, so metaphor transforms one meaning of a word into another. By understanding the cultural meanings attached to fire, we are in a better position to understand the social power of metaphor.

But as well as cultural meaning, there are also universal meanings that are attributed to fire; and it is these which have been examined in cognitive linguistics to provide accounts of how our deeply rooted experiences of the human body provide the basis for everyday metaphors. 'Fire' metaphors are typically used to describe human emotions – the nature of these emotions, their level of intensity and their cause and effect relationships. So, in this chapter I outline cognitive linguistic views on fire metaphors in relation to emotions such as love, desire, lust and anger; a central idea will be that the concept of force integrates knowledge of fire with knowledge of the embodied effect of the emotions and provides a more universal explanation of fire metaphors. This corresponds with ideas of the force of transmission that were introduced in the analysis of 'spread' in Chapter 1. Once both culturally based and 'universalist' theories of metaphor have been considered, we will be in a position to understand what motivates, or underlies, fire metaphors and why it is that they contribute to the discourses of awe and authority that underlie many power relationships.

## Fire and emotion in cognitive linguistics

In this section I explore the conceptual basis for fire metaphors by considering how cognitive linguists view fire as a means for modelling the emotions. I illustrate how fire is used as a way of understanding various aspects of the emotions: the nature of emotional states, their cause and their level of intensity or the force with which they are experienced. To assist with this I use further examples from the Corpus of Contemporary American English. But I will begin with some contemporary examples of fire metaphors:

> As concern over immigration mounts, public debate on the subject becomes ever more sensitive and controversial. *Passions* **are inflamed,** positions entrenched, tensions are palpable. (David Blunkett, *MailOnline*, 28 October 2014)

Here the strong emotions aroused by immigration are described as if they were a fire. The basis of these meanings is in our experience of our bodies and of fire: we know that when our passions are aroused, there is a rise in bodily temperature – this is metonymic as fire co-occurs with heat, and bodily warmth co-occurs with an emotion such as anger – but in both cases this co-occurrence is quite gradual. But we also know that fire can spread rapidly as a force and this is transferred to describe the emotional force of feelings. This is metaphoric because the force of fire is something outside the original frame of bodily warmth. Fire can be considered as something dangerous when out of control – so when passions are described as being 'inflamed', this implies a degree of danger. The metaphor describes the embodied experience of emotion for the person experiencing it, but also its impact *on others in the vicinity*. For this reason there is likely to be an effort to control the emotion of anger and Kövecses (2013: 77) summarizes these cause and effect relationships involved in anger as follows:

1) Cause → 2) Emotion (Person) → 3) Attempt at Control over Emotion (Person) → 4) Action (Person)

Stages 1 and 2 are essentially metonymic because they connect causes with effects based on embodied experience, but stages 3 and 4 are metaphoric because they express force. Fire metaphors are used to describe either the responses to social situations as in the example above or intimate personal relationships such as in the following examples:

> The temptation to cheat on their partner becomes strongest at the work Christmas do, with 51 per cent citing that occasion as the most likely time for an *illicit office romance* **to ignite.** (*The Sun,* 11 December 2014)

> The Science of Dating: why a box of chocolates **could spark** *first-date romance.* The box of chocolates used to be a first-date staple but has fallen out of fashion of late. (*Telegraph*.co.uk, 11 January 2015)

In these extracts the focus of the fire metaphor is on the cause of emotions related to 'romance' by using words such as 'ignite' and 'spark' that refer to the causes of fire. But our knowledge of fire tells us that once started, we can encourage it to grow or we can take actions to extinguish it; similarly, we know that when our passions are aroused, there is a choice between accepting and resisting the force of the emotion.

In other cases fire metaphors describe dramatic emotional responses of the type that occur when an emotion is left uncontrolled and here the metaphoric component becomes increasingly evident. After a left wing government was elected in Greece in January 2015, the *Daily Mail* ran an article entitled 'Greek Markets in Meltdown' (Jan 29th). The word 'meltdown' implies a very high level of intensity of heat as the author is implying that the economic effects on Greece will be very severe and the choice of a metaphor emphasizes *the effect* of an uncontrolled event. As Kövecses (2000) comments, fire metaphors typically specify the effect of an emotion, so that metaphors such as 'inflamed' or 'meltdown' describe emotional *responses* – this is also the case with metaphoric uses of words such as 'hot' or 'burning'. But it contrasts with other metaphors such as 'ignite' or 'spark' that describe the first stage of an emotion.

Metaphoric uses of 'fire' commonly describe human emotions; these include both positive emotions such as love and negative ones such as anger. Typically, love, affection, sexual desire and other emotional states involving the affects are conceptualized with reference to heat: someone can 'smoulder' with desire, or 'have the hots' for someone else, or we describe someone as being 'hot' to imply that they arouse our sexual desire. But how do they take on this meaning? A central tenet of cognitive linguistic approaches is that meaning originates in bodily experience. As Croft (1993: 336) notes: 'one of the central tenets of cognitive semantics is that the meaning of words is encyclopaedic: everything you know about the concept is part of its meaning. From this it follows that there is no essential difference between (linguistic) semantic representation and (general) knowledge representation; the study of linguistic semantics is the study of common sense human experience.' This encyclopaedic knowledge explains the basis for what Lakoff and Johnson refer to as 'metaphorical concepts', and have since become known as 'conceptual metaphors', that relate actual metaphors to a common underlying idea that they share (Lakoff and Johnson 1980). To illustrate this with a fire metaphor, consider the following two examples:

> Far from affecting the Dandy, however, he proclaimed the sporting Corinthian with every inch of his muscular frame. It was his eyes that must chiefly draw attention, however – brooding black eyes that fixed upon Fanny's with a **smouldering** *look*. She had excited a dangerous emotion in the young man's breast, I judged – one it should be as well, perhaps, to discourage before it caused general comment. (Barron, S. 2011, *Jane and the Canterbury tale*)

> One day they were disturbed by an Arab shepherd from the village in the wadi. He chased away the sheep which hemmed him in on every side, and unhesitatingly he approached the women sprawled under the ancient olive tree, fixed his **smouldering** *dark eyes* on Mazal's spotted eyes, weighed her breasts in his imagination and let his eyes wander to Geula's red hair. (Shifra, H. 1998, *Four Mothers*)

The writers here use 'smouldering' to describe the strength of the emotion arising from a protagonist's sexual desire. Cognitive linguists use the term 'target domain' to refer to what the metaphor describes – here 'sexual desire' – and the term 'source domain' to refer to the original literal sense of 'smouldering' – here a fire that burns slowly with no flame. They propose that there is a *systematic* transfer from source to target domains. Here our encyclopaedic knowledge of fire is transferred to sexual desire: for example a fire if left uncontrolled has a tendency to spread and can be dangerous; here it is the young women being looked at who are at risk, rather than the men who are looking at them. Experiential knowledge of fire can be transferred to how we understand desire when using or understanding a metaphor such as 'smouldering'. We could represent this transfer by a conceptual metaphor such as DESIRE/PASSION/LUST IS FIRE. Cognitive linguists describe this transfer of meaning as 'mapping' from a source to a target domain (Lakoff in Ortony 1993: 206).

But how can we know that all the knowledge we have of fire is mapped onto the target domain of desire in a way that permits us to propose a conceptual representation such as DESIRE/PASSION/LUST IS FIRE? One answer proposed by cognitive linguists is by finding further evidence from other instances where 'fire' metaphors are used to describe passions and desire. We can readily find these in large databases of language; consider the following:

> Serena had turned her head and their lips were inches from each other's. Antonio had expected her to turn her head away, but she'd pressed her lips against his and kissed him with a **scorching** *passion* that sent chills up and down his spine. He'd returned the kiss with fervor and zest that had allowed him to release years of pent up emotions, pent up desire and passion. **She had melted** *against his chest* and deepened the kiss. Their tongues danced against each other as Antonio had slipped his hand between her thighs. (Hodges 2011)

In this racy popular account, Serena's passion is described as if it were a fire; it is curious that the effect of her 'scorching' kiss is to 'send chills up and down his spine' – rather than to increase his body temperature! This is because in a conventional way of talking about sexual desire in popular, romantic fiction emotion is viewed as a force – emotions are described as 'pent up' (stage 3 in the above diagram). The overwhelming effect of desire that leads to Serena's sexual compliance is conveyed by the release of pressure and increase of heat implied by 'melted'. The use of diverse metaphors to describe passion and desire – 'smoulder', 'scorching' and 'melted' and so on – that are all related to fire provide further evidence of an underlying conceptual metaphor (also described as a 'root analogy' (Goatly 2007)). But since different emotions can lead to a rise in bodily temperature, the understanding of emotions as if they were fire can be represented using a more generic form as: EMOTION IS FIRE: this would include both sexual passion and anger.

For Lakoff (1993: 203) '... the locus of metaphor is not in language at all, but in the way we conceptualize one mental domain in terms of another'. He proposes that these metaphorical mappings derive from image schemas arising from everyday bodily interaction with the physical environment. As Gibbs (1999: 45) summarizes, 'Image schemas emerge throughout sensorimotor activity, as people manipulate objects, orient themselves spatially and temporally, or direct their perceptual focus for various purposes.' We may consider image schemas as a set of deep-level conceptual primitives that structure more complex concepts. Input for this conceptualizing ability includes schemas for containment (e.g. *in and out*) spatial orientation (e.g. *front-back, up-down, centre and periphery*) and motion (e.g. *source – path – goal*) (cf. Lakoff 1987: 269–307). Together with basic level domains and frames, image schemas constitute the raw material for conceptualization. As Lakoff (in Ortony 1993: 39) puts it, 'Experiential bases and realizations of metaphors are two sides of the same coin: they are both correlations in real experience that have the same structure as the correlations in metaphors.' The correlations in experience are essentially metonymic, so a spark can imply a flame, but they become metaphors when applied to something else, such as emotion.

Using Lakoff's conceptual metaphor theory, there are systematic correspondences between the topic of metaphor (the 'target') and the relations that exist in metaphor vehicles (the 'source'). In the above examples of 'smouldering look' and 'scorching passion', we can describe the correspondences (or mappings) between the entities in the source domain, FIRE, and those in the target domain, EMOTION using the mappings shown in Figure 3.1.

According to cognitive linguists, one explanation of fire metaphors is with reference to our basic experience of the warmth arising from another human body. Our image schema for bodily temperature originates in the experience enjoyed by a baby when cuddled by its mother, and is later extended to the heat generated from the intertwined bodies of two lovers. To consider the first of these: when a baby cries and is held to the breast, the bodily experience of warmth becomes closely associated with comfort, thereby creating a deep-rooted and embodied connection between bodily and emotional warmth that is based on the experience of physical proximity. Kövecses (2013: 81) argues that there is a metonymic basis for such correlational metaphors:

> There is a correlation between two events or states within the same frame, or scene, such that one of the events or states gives rise to the event or state that becomes the target domain.

In the case of bodily warmth, the heat of the body correlates with physical proximity (a metonym that provides a source domain for metaphor) and this then becomes affection when it is generalized. Metonymic experience of bodily warmth therefore provides the basis for the metaphoric understanding of affection. (Grady 1997: 24) describes basic level connections (such as those between warmth and physical proximity) as 'primary scenes':

> Primary scenes are minimal (temporally-delineated) episodes of subjective experience, characterised by tight correlations between physical circumstances

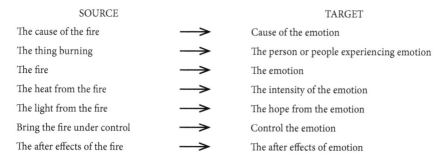

| SOURCE | | TARGET |
|---|---|---|
| The cause of the fire | ⟶ | Cause of the emotion |
| The thing burning | ⟶ | The person or people experiencing emotion |
| The fire | ⟶ | The emotion |
| The heat from the fire | ⟶ | The intensity of the emotion |
| The light from the fire | ⟶ | The hope from the emotion |
| Bring the fire under control | ⟶ | Control the emotion |
| The after effects of the fire | ⟶ | The after effects of emotion |

**Figure 3.1** Mappings for *EMOTION IS FIRE*

and cognitive response. They are universal elements of human experience, defined
by basic cognitive mechanisms and abilities, which relate in some salient sense to
goal-oriented interaction with the world. (Grady 1997 in Goatly 2007: 59)

Primary scenes therefore invite a link between a physical state and a cognitive response.
However, Grady and Johnson (2002) reject the view that these primary scenes are
metonymic, whereas Kövecses (2013) argues that 'correlation-based metaphors emerge
from frame-like mental representations through a metonymic stage' and explains how
this happens as follows:

> I proposed this happens when one of the elements of a frame-like mental structure
> is generalized (schematized) to a concept that lies outside the initial frame in
> a different part of the conceptual system. The generalization process leads to
> sufficient conceptual distance between the initial and the new frame on which
> metaphors can be based. (Kövecses 2013: 87)

I suggest that the element of bodily warmth arising from physical proximity in the
initial frame is generalized, so that warmth becomes generally associated with affection
and that fire metaphors such as 'scorching passion' provide evidence of this process.
It is therefore likely that a representation such as EMOTION IS FIRE derives from a
metonym WARMTH FOR AFFECTION. The claims made more recently by cognitive
linguists go back to the early development of the brain that Lakoff refers to as 'neural
learning':

> Primary metaphors are part of the cognitive unconscious. We acquire them
> automatically and unconsciously via the normal process of neural learning and
> may be unaware that we have them. We have no choice in this process. When the
> embodied experiences in the world are universal, then the corresponding primary
> metaphors are universally acquired. This explains the widespread occurrence around
> the world of a great many primary metaphors. (Lakoff and Johnson 1999: 56)

The conceptual metaphors and metonyms proposed by cognitive linguists seek to
provide explicit representations of the neural pathways that arise from correlations
between two types of experience: in the case of fire metaphors, between an increase
in temperature and an emotional response. So, expressions such as 'smouldering look'
or 'scorching passion' that may be conceptually represented as EMOTION IS FIRE
originate in WARMTH FOR AFFECTION because they weld together the experience
of high body temperature with intense sexual desire. I have argued that fire metaphors
describe emotions because of metonymic-embodied experience combined with fire as
a metaphoric model of force.

But fire metaphors are not used *exclusively* for the emotions: they are also used
to talk about physical pain. Further evidence for the experiential and neural basis of
metaphors occurs when fire-related expressions such as 'burning pain', or when a part
of the body being is referred to as being 'on fire' are used to describe physical suffering.
These metaphors describe physical damage *as if it were arising from fire being applied*

*to the body*: the pain feels as if that part of the body were being burnt. This is partially metonymic in that a *cause*, that is 'burning' is used to refer to an *effect* – 'pain'. We should also notice that it is only one of the attributes of fire – intense heat – that is profiled in such expressions. But if metaphors arise from embodied experience, then surely they would be the same in all languages?

We cannot answer such a question without considering the views of those who have challenged the idea that metaphors are based on universal embodied experience by emphasizing the role of cultural factors. For example Quinn (1991) proposes that, rather than originating in bodily experience:

> Particular metaphors are selected by speakers, and are favoured by these speakers, just because they provide satisfying mappings onto already existing cultural understandings – that is, because elements and relations between elements in source domain make a good match with element and relations among them in the cultural model. (Quinn 1991: 65)

This view would imply in the case of fire metaphors that their origin lies in preserving the cultural memories of the experience of fire by social groups rather than in universal experience of our bodies. There is some evidence of this cultural explanation of fire metaphors in descriptions of strategy as used by an enemy in war: metaphors such as 'scorched earth' seem to co-relate closely with actual historical experience more than with universal embodied experience. For example, if we examine the online Hansard, that includes all official spoken debates of the British Parliament, the first time the expression 'scorched earth' was used was in relation to the Chinese policy of destroying their own food supplies to prevent the advance of the invading Japanese army:

> and she certainly was not prepared for the measures which the Chinese Government have taken in the last 18 months – the '**scorched earth**' *policy* the plan of continual retreat – a retreat which has made the conquest of China quite impossible if, indeed, it was ever possible by any military force at all. (Sir John Ward Law-Milne, 31 July 1939)

Notice that the use of quotation marks implies that the metaphor was unfamiliar at the time. However, its popularity grew as this practice became a military strategy employed to prevent resources falling into enemy hands; it was used a total of seventy-five times in Parliament in the 1940s:

> The '**scorched earth**' *policy* has been…. and will continue to be pursued in the Far East to the maximum extent that is practicable, except for small supplies of food and water sufficient to meet the immediate necessities of the static native population in Malaya. (Sir E. Grigg, 8 January 1942)

However, once the war had ended, 'scorched earth' was used only six times in Parliament in the 1950s – and has never again been used with the same frequency as it was in the 1940s, indicating a strong influence of cultural and historical factors on fire metaphors.

When fire metaphors are used to describe the *destructive* effect of fire, this is influenced by cultural-historical factors rather than by the universal 'embodied experience' of cognitive linguists that account for its use for descriptions of emotional or physical pain. It may be that fire provides what cognitive linguists would refer to as a rich source domain – that is one that offers plenty of potential for elaboration through metaphor entailments – precisely because it does not rely *exclusively* on universal knowledge of embodied experience *or* on metonymic, cultural knowledge of how fire has often been used for destructive purposes. By incorporating *both* cultural *and* experiential aspects of human experience, fire metaphors have greater potential for creating discourses of awe and authority than they would have had, had they relied on either of these alone.

## The causes of, and responses to, emotion

I noticed in the previous section that an important aspect of fire metaphors is how they can describe both emotional responses and their causes and also that this is partially grounded in metonymy: an increase in body temperature correlates with some emotions, and fire correlates with experience of destruction. In the analysis of what I referred to as 'organic fire' in the previous chapter, I identified a group of words referring to how a fire is started that when used as metaphors emphasize the causes of an emotion; these include 'spark', 'ignite' and 'kindle'. Where there is already a strong emotion but actions are taken that cause it to grow or increase, we find words such as 'inflame'. Conversely, words such as 'extinguish' and 'dampen' that literally refer to actions that bring an end to a fire may refer metaphorically to a reduction or decrease in the intensity of an emotional state. There is also another group of words related to fire itself, such as 'burn', or 'scorch', that describe powerful emotional responses. In this section, I first consider fire metaphors for the *causes of* emotion and then those for emotional *responses*. In both sections I use the Corpus of Contemporary American English (COCA) to illustrate the evidence that metaphors provide of how the emotions are conceptualized.

### Cause of emotion

Fire metaphors such as 'kindle', 'spark' or 'ignite' are used to describe the causes and early stages of emotions. They are all semantically related in both literal and metaphoric senses by their common view of causation as correlated with force. They assume that the release of energy entailing a force leads to a change of state and therefore relies on the frame CAUSES ARE FORCES. However, 'kindle', 'spark' or 'ignite' all have different shades of meaning in their literal senses that transfer to their use as metaphors. The origin of 'kindle' is influenced by the Old Norse *kindill* 'candle' or 'torch', a small but constant fire: 'kindle' implies a gradual onset to a fire as compared to 'spark', where the onset is instantaneous, arising from the striking together of two hard surfaces. 'Ignite' originates from the Latin word for 'fire' *ignis* – the difference in meaning from 'spark' is that whereas a fire will not necessarily continue to grow from a spark, it will necessarily grow when it is ignited. These subtle meanings transfer when these words are used to refer to emotions, but they also take on affective meanings depending on whether the emotion that is caused is considered to be a positive or a negative one. And while all three verbs have the potential to imply that the speaker approves or disapproves of the behaviour arising from the emotion, there are interesting variations that go back to the literal senses of the fire words. Compare, for example the following:

> But there is little about public secondary schools themselves that **kindles** *an enthusiasm* among students for being in school or encourages a commitment to the work they do while they are there. (Toch, *Washington Post*, 1991)

Here the use of 'kindles' implies that the onset of the emotion is a gradual one that the reader expects will develop following the normal pattern of fire causation. Typically, 'kindle' implies a positive evaluation of the emotion that is caused, as in the following two examples:

> and Jamila suggested other solutions: narcissus to strengthen weak love, mandrake **to kindle** *flagging lust,* crab apple petals to assuage desire for another, and asphodel buds to focus scattered fidelity. (Shalev, M. 1994, *Esau*)

> Given to subterfuges on many subjects, he's brutally frank about her in Kora and the 1951 Autobiography: **she did not kindle** *his erotic imagination.* (Liebowitz, H. 2007, *Literary Review*)

Here, arousing sexual desire is something that is positively valued by the writer as can be proved by substituting alternatives; for example 'give rise to' implies a more rational and objective evaluation and 'ignited' would imply less control over sexual desire. Tables 3.1–3.3 summarize the sort of concepts that have an emotional cause expressed by 'kindle', 'spark' and 'ignite'; I included in this search the various inflections of each verb, so that 'kindle' includes 'kindles', 'kindling' and 'kindled'.

The examples suggest that 'kindle' would imply the onset of a force. We should note that responses such as 'imagination' and 'interest' can also be kindled, and these are not

**Table 3.1** Metaphorical collocates of 'Kindle' in COCA (4,4)

| Collocate | Example (collocates in bold) | Frequency of collocation |
|---|---|---|
| interest | Hillary Rodham Clinton began a tour of historic sites along the East Coast to **kindle** *interest* in sustaining such US legacies. | 37 |
| passion | Their kiss was slow, with a hesitancy born of the tension that had marked the recent weeks. But it **kindled** a *passion* that knew no bounds … | 19 |
| imagination | The device **kindled** *the imagination* of the writer, who used it in his new comic strip. | 10 |
| enthusiasm | Clinton's proposed energy taxes failed to **kindle** *the enthusiasm* of some environmentalists … | 8 |

**Table 3.2** Metaphorical collocates of 'Spark' in COCA (4,4)

| Collocate | Example (collocates in bold) | Frequency of collocation |
|---|---|---|
| interest | Select a word that could **spark** *interest* or provide focus for one of your lessons or presentations. | 432 |
| debate | The decision to charge the Libyan leader has **sparked** *a debate* among scholars, military officers and government officials over the role of such a politically sensitive prosecution in the midst of an armed conflict. | 313 |
| controversy | A Smartphone dog fighting game **sparks** *controversy* and condemnation. | 156 |
| protests | No one could have known that when a Tunisian fruit vendor set himself on fire in a public square in a town barely on a map, he would **spark** *protests* that would bring down dictators in Tunisia, Egypt and Libya. | 116 |
| outrage | And coming up, a new French law, banning Muslim women from wearing veils is **sparking** *outrage* across the European country. | 96 |
| imagination | Basically, children's literature promotes an appreciation for the wonder of language, **sparks** the *imagination*, re-lives everyday experiences and shares lives and information. | 72 |
| anger | McInturff backed McCain's decision to ignore the minister's inflammatory anti-America comments because it would have been seen as race-baiting and **sparked** *racial anger* and protests. | 61 |
| passion | Avoid unnecessary risks mid-month but expect the unexpected, which may be liberating. A **spark** *of passion* can light up your life. | 49 |
| curiosity | Julian deliberately chose a table in proximity to the dark-haired young woman who had **sparked** *his curiosity*. | 45 |
| fears | The housing market sputtered, **sparking** *fears* that the economy could slip into a recession. | 36 |

emotions, though they may have an affective component. There is evidence of a similar double activation of affective and cognitive responses in collocates of 'spark' as these also suggest that 'fire' metaphors overlap with 'light' metaphors to produce complex metaphors: those that rely on more than a single source domain. This evidence takes the forms of various words related to understanding, knowledge and language that follow 'spark' as summarized in Table 3.2.

Metaphoric uses of the verb 'spark' are much more frequent than 'kindle' – perhaps making them rather more clichéd stylistically. As well as referring to the onset of 'anger', many of these collocates also describe the cause of a *cognitive* response such as 'interest' and 'curiosity' – and the causes of forceful reactions related to communication: 'debate' and 'controversy'. These metaphors can be described using the frame THE CAUSE OF AN EMOTION IS THE CAUSE OF A FIRE. Fire metaphors such as 'spark' and 'kindle' are used when there is a strong affective component to what is caused – whether it is knowledge, understanding or intellectual debate. Fire metaphors often imply emotional states that lead to some form of action:

Two decades after his videotaped beating by four Los Angeles police officers, Rodney King died yesterday at the age of 47. His beating **sparked** *outrage* over police brutality. And after a jury acquitted the four police officers, that outrage erupted into riots that left some 55 dead, more than 1,000 injured and more than $800 million in damage in the city of Los Angeles. (*NPR TalkNat*, 2012)

The 'sparked' metaphor implies that emotionally driven behaviour is spreading rapidly from one location or group to another. Fire metaphors describe both emotions such as 'love' and 'anger' *and* affects: the responses arising from these emotions.

The contagious effects of fire are more fully conveyed by 'ignite' and are used to frame a forceful transition from cause to effect, irrespective of whether the emotion itself is a positive or negative one:

'We wanted to establish both teams as major presences in their respective leagues, **ignite** *the passion* of the fans, improve our business operations, and, of course, make the playoffs, and win a championship,' said Ted Leonsis. (La Canfora, J. and Wyche, S., *Washington Post*, 2002)

In 1992, perhaps the lowest point in recent memory, the brutal beating of unarmed black man Rodney King by four LAPD officers while 17 of their colleagues stood by. The four white officers were acquitted, **igniting** *a storm of anger* that tore apart Los Angeles and the nation. (Spoken *NBC*)

The idea of 'igniting a passion' implies that the force of an emotion is such that it will lead to behaviour that goes beyond the limits of what can be controlled; the entity that will grow may be something of value or something damaging. In a similar way, but using a different metaphor, when something is described as 'going viral' (on the internet) it can offer a positive as well as a negative evaluation. In the following the speaker is talking about the Olympic Games:

'They are kind of a spiritual event,' said Woody Thompson, senior vice president of consulting for Octagon, a sports marketing agency. 'They **ignite** *passion* in people across a much broader range, as simply evidenced by the gender equity in TV viewership.' (Leith S. 2004, business journal)

Evidently, Woody Thompson is praising the use of the Olympic Games because they arouse peoples' emotions; this is evident from other words that have a strong positive connotation such as 'spiritual' and 'gender equity'. His interest is in how marketing strategies around the Olympics can cause forceful positive feelings on the part of the people that his marketing strategy is directed towards. Table 3.3 summarizes the collocates of 'ignite'.

As was the case with 'spark', we see evidence of cognitive responses such as 'interest' and affective responses such as 'passion' and 'violence'; there are other responses that are both cognitive and affective such as 'debate' and 'controversy'. In terms of frequency these metaphors are less frequent than 'spark' but more frequent than 'kindle'. Although some of the affects arising from emotions are negative, they emphasize the *strength* of

**Table 3.3** Metaphorical collocates of 'Ignite' in COCA (4,4)

| Collocate | Example (collocates in bold) | Frequency of collocation |
|---|---|---|
| debate | Barack Obama has **ignited** *this debate* about whether you should support someone who is viable, whether you should let go of your fears. | 69 |
| passion | That insight **ignited** *her passion* for journalism, leading to positions with *The Washington Post* and *The New York Times*. | 49 |
| passion/s | Voice-over Fonda had mounted a North Vietnamese anti-aircraft gun, **ignited** *passions* at home that still burned when we sat down together two decades later. | 65 |
| controversy | And during the 2004 presidential election, outsourcing of jobs to India **ignited** *intense controversy*. | 49 |
| interest | 'So You Think You Can Dance' has **ignited** *more interest* in the art form than a decade's worth of shows by most dance companies. | 30 |
| anger | But it is the gay marriage issue that has **ignited** *the anger* and fear now including some racial tension. | 24 |
| violence | This act **ignited** *violence* between Hindus and Muslims in many parts of India. | 21 |

the emotion, so that writers are not necessarily condemning the cause of a powerful emotional response but emphasizing its intensity. The frame THE CAUSE OF AN EMOTION IS THE CAUSE OF A FIRE does not therefore imply that the resulting emotion is either good or bad since that will be determined by the wider verbal context and knowledge of the situation to which it refers.

## Effect of emotion

There is another group of words that refer to the results or effects of a fire and are used metaphorically to convey the effect of an emotion on the person who is experiencing it; these words include 'consume', 'scorch' and 'burn'. These fire terms are related to the effects and therefore are motivated by the frame EFFECTS ARE FORCES. I will consider some of the corpus evidence for the particular meanings that arise when these words are applied to the emotions. The origin of 'consume' is from the Latin *con* 'altogether' and *sumere* 'take up' so it emphasizes the completeness of the effect of fire. Although, as explained, it is not strictly speaking part of the lexical field of fire (see page 32), when used metaphorically it describes an emotion that is so powerful that it completely takes over someone's life.

A search of 'consume' produced many literal senses related to economics such as 'spending', 'demand', 'credit' and so on. However, a search of the adjectival form 'consuming' revealed a number of senses that are metaphoric because they do not refer to the physical action of wasting away but the intensity of an experience; these are illustrated in Table 3.4.

**Table 3.4** Metaphorical collocates of 'Consuming' in COCA

| Collocate | Example (collocates in bold) | Frequency of collocation |
|---|---|---|
| passion/s | Her experimentation with both colour and composition is laid bare in these works, which are a supreme manifestation of her **consuming** *passion* for Japanese prints. | 40 |
| interest/s | They chose Hero, who ended up writing the whole play while the two of them huddled together and whispered about their one **consuming** *interest*, a boy named Jeremy Alexander. | 28 |
| desire/s | His **consuming** *desire* to identify with blacks has led him to misrepresent his past. | 14 |

The metaphor 'consuming' refers to the force of the effect of an intensely experienced emotion on the person who is experiencing it: a consuming 'passion', 'interest' or 'desire' can arise from ideas, objects or people and in each case the metaphor refers to the force and totality of the effect – irrespective of whether it is emotional, cognitive or aesthetic. A consuming passion is a highly, and perhaps excessively, all-encompassing interest in something or someone that leads to the individual being completely absorbed by it – just as a flammable substance is completely absorbed by fire. Consider the following:

> But finding a pursuit that pushes your buttons can infuse anyone with sudden zeal for life. The secret about **consuming** *passions*, though, is that while they appear effortless, they require discipline and ability. If they were easy, they wouldn't be so rewarding....The Holy Grail comes in moments of 'flow', when you are so absorbed in what you're doing that you lose yourself. (McGowan, K. 2008, *Psychology Today*)

Here the writer also uses the metaphor 'lose yourself' to emphasize the effect of the consuming passion on the sense of individual awareness: the consuming passion is one that breaks down the sense of separateness experienced by individuals but implies a perspective of an objective self that views itself as 'lost'. In some cases the response of consuming passion has an effect over and beyond the person experiencing the emotion to include those towards whom the emotion is directed:

> Torn from her child-bed, Hannah Duston becomes an unstable, but resolved, devouring maternal avenger, who, with her **consuming** *passions*, poses a threat not only to Indians but to all of manhood. (Weiss, A. M. 1998, *American Studies International*)

Just as a fire can go out of control and burn more fuel than the original tinder, so passions can rampantly destroy whatever is in their vicinity. Typically, people are 'consumed by' 'grief' (7), 'hatred' (5), 'guilt' (5), 'anger' (5), 'rage' (4), 'anxiety' (4), 'fear' (3) and 'remorse' (2). All of these imply a negative evaluation of the forceful response

**Table 3.5** Metaphorical collocates of 'Scorch' in COCA (4,4)

| Collocate | Example (collocates in bold) | Frequency of collocation |
|---|---|---|
| hot/heat | The pavement was **scorching** *hot*, and the humid air felt suffocating; a swarm of mosquitoes instantly found me and started in on the bonanza. | 177 |
| earth | It is entirely possible that more civilians will be slain due to a **scorched earth** *policy*. | 152 |
| pain | Curious onlookers grace his bedside, sharing the **scorching** *pain* of being powerless to comfort or save his life. | 9 |
| passion | ... Paul Ryan, a conservative Republican congressman from Wisconsin, share little in common except their first names and a **scorching** *passion* for views they champion from opposite political poles. | 3 |

as 'out of control' – implying a loss of self-direction and well-being. To be 'consumed by' something implies that the effect of the emotion is so great that it incapacitates the person who is experiencing it, as if they were physically destroyed (as in the original disease sense). The effect and action of fire refers to a highly intense and potentially harmful emotional outcome; when a person is *consumed by* an emotion, he or she cannot continue functioning independent of this emotion. In such cases, the intensity of the emotion is likely to have the effect of destroying an individual as well as creating danger for those to whom the emotion is directed.

'Scorch' originates (probably) from the Old Norse *skorpna* 'be shrivelled' and is oriented to the outcome or effect of fire. When something is 'shrivelled', it affects its *entirety*, whereas if it is burnt, it may only be *partially* affected by fire. Scorch is therefore an intensifier: a scorching day is hotter than a very hot day. And a 'scorched earth policy' implies widespread destruction, and one that I have indicated could be influenced by cultural-historic factors. Table 3.5 shows the figurative collocates of 'scorch'.

On closer examination 'scorched' is generally used as a metonym in which the cause-effect relationship is one that *actually* occurs in the real world. So, the very commonly used phrase 'scorched earth' could refer to the actual policy of scorching the earth, but in practice this has a more general sense of destroying all resources rather than simply the 'earth' – so 'scorched' is a synecdoche for any form of destructive action and 'earth' is a synecdoche for 'resources'. 'Scorching heat' and 'scorching pain' can be described as metaphors that describe the level of intensity of the effect of heat, so that the temperature is as if fire were applied. Similarly, 'scorching passion' implies a very powerful emotional effect. This provides further evidence of how many metaphors originate in pre-existing metonymies that could be represented as EFFECT FOR CAUSE.

'Burning' refers to the chemical process of the interaction between fuel and oxygen. 'Burn' originates from the Old English *birnan* 'be on fire' and *baernan* 'consume by fire'. A number of collocates of 'burning' indicate that it is commonly used as a metaphor referring to the emotions, as summarized in Table 3.6.

**Table 3.6** Metaphorical collocates of 'Burn' in COCA (4,4)

| Collocate | Example (collocates in bold) | Frequency of collocation |
|---|---|---|
| desire | Some disappear down passages leading to buses or taxis, others that escape in two's rush into the nearest hotel, **burning** *with desire* for each other. | 202 |
| anger/angry | Her tongue darts in and out suggestively. He *eyes* are **burning** *with anger*. Her mouth poises itself over his nipple. | 130 |
| shame | … what strikes him as mysterious is that, in spite of his trembling hands and his *face* **burning** *with shame*, he's glad he helped Linscott. | 69 |
| rage | Her *ears* were **burning** *with rage*. It was a commingling of pride, anger, pain and frustration that determined what she was able to do in the next few moments. | 52 |
| hate | The cimanones, thirty dark men **burning** *with hate* for their former masters, seemed untouched by heat or rain. | 30 |
| embarrassment | … there she'd sat in her seat in the last row, her *face* **burning** *with embarrassment* as a horrible silence fell over the room and half the class turned. | 27 |

In contrast to 'consuming' and 'scorching' metaphoric uses of 'burning with' emphasize the physical, embodied nature of the emotion. If one is 'burning with' an emotion, this implies an overwhelming emotion that has an explicit effect on the body: the effect of the emotion is as if the body were burning. Again, this suggests a conceptual metonym EFFECT FOR CAUSE. Evidence of the embodied experience of this emotion can be found by the frequency with which a particular body part is described as 'burning' (see 'face', 'ears' and 'eyes' in Table 3.6).

Metaphoric uses of 'burning with' imply a physiological change arising from an intense emotion that involves the movement of blood and is therefore also associated with an appearance of redness such as blushing. Because a part of the body experiences a burning sensation, the body itself becomes a visible barometer of the emotion that is experienced. The embodied nature of the emotional response is highly evident in the collocation 'burning with embarrassment'. In every use of this phrase reference is made to the particular part of the body from which the emotional response is evident: cheeks, ear and face and so on. The rush of blood that arises from an intense emotion is also one that is physically visible to others, making explicit the circuitous and the complex chain of cause and effect that characterizes much intense emotional experience – especially negative ones such as embarrassment.

Anger provides a convincing example of fire metaphors that are motivated by the EFFECT FOR CAUSE and EFFECTS ARE FORCES conceptual frames and it is the emotion that has been identified by cognitive linguists as most strongly associated with fire. This is partly because the embodied nature of our experience of anger associates it with a heightened bodily temperature:

Milwaukee's discovery of a monster in its midst had also ignited **smoldering** *anger* and racial tensions in people still unused to seeing their once-tranquil city rent by drugs, murder, and gang wars. (Ullman, J. 1992, *Psychology Today*)

It occurred to Giselle that Lois might be afraid she was calling to berate her, to unleash the full force of her **smoldering** *anger* at long last. (Swick, M. 1999, *Evening News*)

These expressions describe the effect of anger on the people who are experiencing it: the smouldering is the effect of the anger and these metaphors imply a frame ANGER IS A FIRE. Other fire metaphors that describe anger are less related to different aspects of embodiment; for example 'boiling with anger':

But there were also old people and a young boy among the wounded. Iraqi estimates of the casualty toll are lower than the American figure, ranging from 20 dead to just six. But the city is **boiling** *with anger*. 'Is this freedom? Is this democracy?' This woman asked me. 'Is this what America has brought us?'(Spoken 2003, *PBS Newshour*)

And here I am, clenching, grinding my teeth, wondering how to save him from, how to hurt, how to savage, how to kill, the people who have called him a criminal. Rachel's letter goes on for three pages, **boiling** *with rage*. (Pincus, W. 1992, *Washington Monthly*)

It has been argued that these metaphors are based on the idea that anger is a liquid under pressure. Kövecses 2002 (95ff.) describes how liquid, heat and container metaphors are combined to form a schema: ANGER IS HOT FLUID IN A CONTAINER. In this model, anger is understood in terms of a liquid being heating in a container. There is evidence in certain phrases from COCA for this way of thinking and talking about anger; these are shown in Table 3.7.

In these phrases there is the idea of the effect of anger as equivalent to the effect of heating a liquid in a container to produce an increase in pressure that may lead to an explosion. However, it may be that since this concept was first proposed in Lakoff (1987), it has been rather exaggerated; consider the following:

Candace Garvey said that he was distant, that his anger was simmering, that he had this look of simmering anger. He was in a **slow burn** and the fuse was getting

**Table 3.7** 'Anger' phrases in COCA

| blood boil | 60 |
| --- | --- |
| blowing/letting off steam | 44 |
| simmer down | 37 |
| blew his/her/my stack | 13 |
| hit the ceiling | 11 |
| flipped his/her/my lid | 5 |

shorter. Something set him off and perhaps what set him off was his four-minute phone call at two in the afternoon. (CNN News, 1995)

> Pat felt the anger fuse begin its **slow burn** inside her. Her head told her to cool it. She didn't know this guy well enough to quarrel with him. (Booth, P. 1990, *Malibu*)

The 'slow burn' metaphor trigger the image of a fuse burning on a time bomb that is located within the body, and so anger could be represented conceptually as ANGER IS A TIME BOMB. Further evidence of this image schema is in the expression 'short fuse'; COCA shows that there are 103 instances of the metaphor 'short fuse':

> There was a suggestion that he had a temper, he had **a short fuse**.
> I exploded like **a short fuse** on a firecracker-quick, fast, in a hurry.
> But if he wins the Democratic nomination, **his short fuse** will become a liability.
> Like several of the others he has a **short emotional fuse**.

Here the fuse does not appear to be located within the body (as in 'feeling a slow burn inside oneself') but is something outside the body that is viewed from a distance by others – the possible victims of the time bomb. Evidence for this is that the pattern 'he', 'she' or some other third person + 'has a short fuse' occurs twenty-five times, whereas the pattern 'I' + 'have a short fuse' occurs only nine times; even then it is sometimes somebody viewing themselves from the perspective of other people as in the following:

> What I tell the patients and the obstetricians who talk to me is that I have **a short fuse** for going to a Cesarean section. In other words, if it is going to be a difficult delivery, or a long delivery, rather than taking the chance of stretching the anal sphincters or damaging the sphincters during delivery, it is better to do a Cesarean section. (SerVaas, C. 1994, *Saturday Evening Post*)

Here the speaker is viewing themselves from the point of view of mothers who are discussing childbirth options. So, while the focus of both the 'CONTAINER' model of anger and the 'TIME BOMB' model is on some aspect of the emotional response, the 'CONTAINER' model describes anger from the perspective of the person experiencing the emotion, while the 'TIME BOMB' model describes anger from the perspective of those who may experience the effect of the anger of others. It serves as a type of warning as in the following:

> That means you shouldn't tolerate name-calling or physical fights between siblings, or engage in hostile arguments or put-downs with your mate. And above all, try to keep **your own short fuse** in check. (Neifert, M. 1999, *Saturday Evening Post*)

> His wife, on the other hand, looked like a Bernini angel, but she had **a short fuse** and occasionally shot people with a pistol in disagreements. (Tanenbaum, R. 2001, *True Justice*)

These types of metaphors show evidence of the frames CAUSE FOR EFFECT, since the shortness of a fuse is a type of cause that in fact refers to its speed and danger, and CAUSES ARE FORCES since we know that a short fuse leads to a quick explosion. We can combine these frames to produce a metonymic frame CAUSE OF AN EXPLOSION FOR THE EFFECT OF AN EXPLOSION.

This shows the importance of empirical verification of expressions that are often derived from intuition and may well have fallen out of current use. It may be that the 'time bomb' metaphor is a topic or situation-triggered metaphor: this is one where a cognitive frame is provided by knowledge of the topic or situation that primes or triggers the use of a metaphor – giving it the effect of a pun (see Semino 2008: 104–106 for a fuller discussion). Consider the following uses of 'short fuse' that could occur in the context where actual violence was used:

> Baghdad has become a powder keg with **a short fuse**. Even the undertakers here are out of business. (Spoken CBS, 2003)

> Bobic, nicknamed 'Peca' pronounced pe-tsa, hasn't had any brushes with the law but he has a reputation for **a short fuse** and fighting and could easily be lost to the streets. (Lee, M. 2006, *Washington Post*)

These sorts of uses suggest that actual violence may be triggered by anger metaphors, once again suggesting the metonymic motivation of many metaphors.

## Intensity and force of emotion: EMOTION IS A FORCE

In this section I will answer the following questions:

- What does the level of intensity of how emotion is represented in fire metaphors tell us about their cognitive basis?
- How can the cognitive basis of this intensity be modelled?

Human emotions are known to be experienced at different levels of intensity. Metaphoric uses of 'scorch' and 'consume' both implied a high level of intensity of emotion, whereas 'kindle' and 'smoulder' imply a less intense force and a more gradual emotion. Similarly, a 'slow burn' is a less intense force than 'boiling with rage'. This can be analysed in terms of force, so that when someone has passed the stage in which anger is controlled and physically expresses their anger, this can be dangerous to the self and to bystanders. For example, it is much more problematic to be around when someone 'hits the ceiling' as compared to when they are just 'letting off steam'. Similarly, it might be quite pleasant to experience the kindling of a passion, but rather unpleasant to be consumed by one. Therefore, gradual emotions are more often more pleasant to experience than overwhelming ones. In this section I consider how metaphors that express the intensity of emotions are modelled on force dynamics.

As we saw at the beginning of the Section **Fire and emotion in cognitive linguistics**, a number of cognitive linguists (e.g. Kövecses 2005) have proposed a basic structure for anger and heat where there is a cause of anger (as with ignite, kindle etc.), the existence of anger (as with inflamed), an attempt at control (as with, simmering, smouldering) and the loss of control leading to an expression of anger (as with explode, erupt); these are displayed diagrammatically in Figure 3.2.

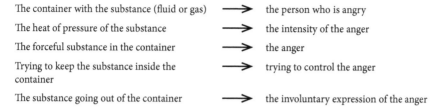

The container with the substance (fluid or gas) ⟶ the person who is angry

The heat of pressure of the substance ⟶ the intensity of the anger

The forceful substance in the container ⟶ the anger

Trying to keep the substance inside the container ⟶ trying to control the anger

The substance going out of the container ⟶ the involuntary expression of the anger

**Figure 3.2** The CONTAINER structure for 'anger' metaphors

Kövecses (2000) draws a distinction between 'hot' emotions such as anger, romantic love and sexual desire and milder kinds of emotions such as 'warmth' or 'affection'. We can use expressions relating to heat – such as 'a red-hot lover' – or expressions relating to fire – such as 'to be burning with desire' – to describe intense feelings associated with a physical force that is beyond our control. These could have positive meanings so that to be described as a 'red-hot lover' or to 'burn with enthusiasm' is a compliment. However, experiential knowledge of the dangers of extreme heat or fire – both to the person experiencing the emotion and to the target of their emotion – is more likely to make them negative. If someone is 'consumed by lust' or 'burnt their fingers' in a relationship we know that it is bad for them, and if your boss is 'breathing fire' or is 'consumed with rage' that it can also be dangerous for you because it implies an excess of force.

When emotions are experienced intensely they are frequently communicated by 'fire' or 'heat' metaphors. I will now try to explain the underlying cognitive basis for the modelling of the intensity of emotions with fire and heat metaphors. Kövecses (2008: 384) proposes that when we use physical force to describe emotions, this assumes 'the most deeply seated belief about emotions; namely, that we are passive and helpless in relation to them, just as physical objects are passive and helpless in relation to powerful natural forces acting on them'. He uses expressions such as being 'overwhelmed' by an emotion or 'swept off our feet' and goes on to suggest that 'Most (though not all) metaphors in the emotion domain can be characterized as an interaction of forces. We have seen in the previous section how CAUSES ARE FORCES and EFFECTS ARE FORCES. This leads to the conclusion that there exists a single master metaphor for emotion: EMOTION IS A FORCE' (Kövecses 2008: 385).

Both fire and emotion are highly salient entities, one is external and one is internal; they vary in intensity and can be controlled to varying degrees. The master metaphor EMOTION IS A FORCE is especially evident when intense states of emotion are expressed by metaphors that refer to extreme states of heat or fire and excessive force leads to the substance inside a container getting out. Moderate states of emotion are likely to be evaluated positively by metaphors that refer to moderate temperatures. So, a metaphoric use of 'warm' or even 'cool' is likely to express a positive state of emotion, whereas 'hot' or 'cold' (as in 'hot-headed' or 'cold-blooded') are more likely to express negative emotional states. Typically, 'hot' and 'cold' express an excess or deficiency of emotion, whereas 'warm' and 'cool' express a natural or normal level of emotion, as when we sign an email 'warm regards' or describe someone as 'cool': the level of force is appropriate to the situation. Conceptual metaphors AFFECTION IS

WARMTH and FRIENDSHIP IS WARMTH (Kövecses 2000: 93) have been proposed for emotion at this lower level of intensity. But I would like to propose two more general frames: CONTROLLED EMOTION IS MODERATE TEMPERATURE and UNCONTROLLED EMOTION IS EXTREME TEMPERATURE.

The origin of intensity in emotions is metonymic because they arise from an association between two entities that are adjacent to each other in experience. So, an expression such as 'to have warm feelings for someone' originates in the physical experience of an actual rise in body temperature that occurs when in proximity with a source of heat: a mother, or a lover. Since we develop good feelings for this other close body – one that offers comfort as well as warmth – the concept of affection is developed. I would like to suggest an additional metonymic frame for such 'warm'/'hot' and 'cool'/'cold' states: LEVEL OF TEMPERATURE FOR THE INTENSITY OF EMOTION. A good example of the positive and negative prosodies arising from these temperature schemes is by comparing two heat related metaphors: 'melt' and 'meltdown'. 'Melt' is motivated by a conceptual metonym LEVEL OF TEMPERATURE FOR THE INTENSITY OF EMOTION and implies a degree of emotion that is under control and is associated with the positive 'natural' experience of an empathetic other as in:

> She walked with unsteady steps to the front door, and her **heart melted** within her as she saw him standing there. (Wick, L. 1996, *Where the Wild Rose Blooms*)

Although such expressions occur across a range of discourse types, they typically occur in COCA in fiction and imply an increase in the level of emotion that does not necessarily imply sexual attraction but a less defined but positive emotional reaction. By contrast, 'meltdown' implies an excess of emotion that is damaging both to the person experiencing such passion and potentially to others in the vicinity – a meltdown is not selective and profiles a massive amount of destruction irrespective of who felt the original emotion:

> Jason's memories of Christmases past were so unsettling to him that he often had an **emotional meltdown** as the holiday approached, and his tears and discomfort made it impossible for him to accompany Odermatt and the other children on the family tree outing. (Olszewski, L. 1996, *San Francisco Chronicle*)
>
> Pollock asks fellow artist and long-time companion Lee Krasner (played by Marcia Gay Harden) to have a baby with him, only to send her into an **emotional meltdown** at the idea of bringing up a child with such an unstable man. (Lesko, A. 2001, *Bazaar*)

Here the force of the emotion has led to it exceeding the space over which an individual has control and seems to be clearly a metaphor. This can be explained as follows:

> metaphors derive from metonymies through the application of the cognitive processes of generalization (schematization) and specialization (elaboration).... the element inside the frame involves or is characterized by a particular frame-specific concept, which is, then, generalized, or schematized, into a concept that exists outside the frame (often in a different taxonomic hierarchy). When this happens, we

have to do with metaphor, i.e., where the initial frame, or domain, is conceptualized in terms of another, conceptually distant frame, or domain. (Kövecses 2013: 80)

With 'emotional meltdown' the metonym LEVEL OF TEMPERATURE FOR THE INTENSITY OF EMOTION has been elaborated by the idea that the effect of an emotion is so strong that the person is overwhelmed, so we have notions of excess and damage that are expressed by downward direction: and since spatial orientation is *outside* the initial frame of temperature, we have metaphor. I will suggest a conceptual metaphor THE LEVEL OF INTENSITY OF AN EMOTION IS THE LEVEL OF INTENSITY OF A FIRE to represent this; a further example of this frame is when passions are described as 'inflamed':

> It weakened the position of Palestinian leaders willing to negotiate with Israel. The announcement of new housing **inflamed** *anti-Israel passions* in the Arab world. (*Associated Press*, 2010)
>
> In normal times, men like Mr. Bin Laden or Samudra are frustrated in their quest to win more operatives to their cause. To almost everyone, their extreme views are too difficult to swallow. They make their greatest inroads when *passions* **are inflamed** by war and injustice. (Murphy, D. 2003, *Christian Science Monitor*)

The metaphor 'inflamed passions' refers to a destructive emotion that has the potential to go beyond control; the writer does not particularly approve or sympathize with those whose passions are aroused and 'inflamed passions' implies a degree of covert criticism of those experiencing these destructive emotions.

The primary reason for viewing fire and heat as the linguistic means for communicating intensity is because in experience fire was the element in the natural world that served as a very typical manifestation of *force* and – more importantly perhaps – of *changes in degree of force*. While physical force is also present in winds, in storms or in fast flowing rivers, the change in the force of wind from say a breeze to a gale, or in flowing water from a trickle to a rush are less salient than changes in the level of intensity of fire. Changes in the state of fire and heat have a very significant and direct effect on people leading readily from warmth and safety to death and destruction. As we have seen throughout human evolution, fire has been for socially shared purposes such as protection and warmth and later for manufacture and industry: fire therefore supplies a readily available situation for the social construal of the emotions that are dependent on force and heat.

The theory that Kövecses employs to explain the relationship between fire and emotion is that of force dynamics. This theory is based on our basic folk understanding of the physical world. Entities are connected by force relationships as one entity acts upon another. The two entities and their relationships can be described using the terms 'agonist' and 'antagonist'; these were explained as follows by Talmy, who originally developed force dynamic theory in linguistics:

> The primary distinction that language marks here is a role difference between the two entities exerting the forces. One force-exerting entity is singled out for focal attention – the salient issue in the interaction is whether this entity is able to manifest its force tendency or, on the contrary, is overcome. The second force

entity, correlatively, is considered for the effect that it has on the first, effectively overcoming it or not …. I call the focal force entity the Agonist and the force element that opposes it the Antagonist. (Talmy 1988: 53)

The two force entities act upon each other with the agonist either giving way to or resisting the force of the antagonist. The agonist is the person experiencing an emotion. The person can be viewed as the agonist and the emotion can be viewed as the antagonist (Kövecses 2000: 63). The agonist has an intrinsic tendency towards rest – that is, towards emotional equilibrium – but the antagonist has an extrinsic tendency to put force on the agonist. When the inertia of the agonist is strong enough to resist the antagonist, a stable emotional state is maintained, but when the antagonist overcomes the powers of resistance of the agonist, the person experiences a change in emotional state. This pattern can be classed as 'causative', because it explains the cause of emotion. Talmy suggests a general tendency in language to extend our knowledge of the physical to the psychosocial such as where an emotion is experienced. This can be represented in Figure 3.3.

FORCE A

ANTAGONIST:
emotion

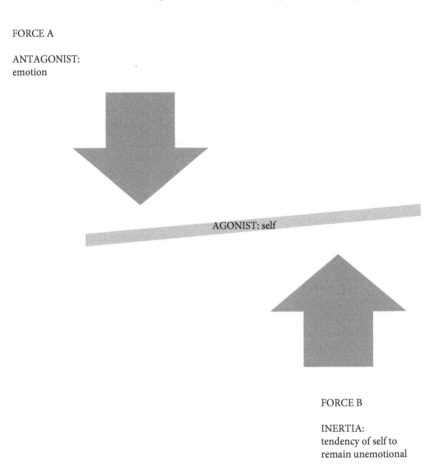

AGONIST: self

FORCE B

INERTIA:
tendency of self to
remain unemotional

**Figure 3.3** Force dynamic model for emotion

If force A, the emotion, exceeds force B, the tendency to remain unemotional, there will be a change of emotional state in the self, whereas if force B exceeds force A, the emotional state of the self will remain unchanged. The force dynamic approach is especially appropriate in relation to emotion because it explains the relationship between motion and emotion. A force is a concept in the physical world that gives rise to motion, and we know that the experience of emotion is also strongly associated with the physical experience of the motion of blood within the body. This inherently metonymic relationship is found in expressions such as 'having a rush of blood to the head' meaning 'angry' because there is embodied experience of blood motion within the body that correlates with the experience of anger. Motion also occurs in concepts such as 'flushing' – when a person becomes markedly red in the face or other parts of the body as a result of emotional or sexual arousal. One reason that force dynamics is especially relevant in our understanding of emotion is because it corresponds with embodied experience that is grounded in metaphors originating in bodily based metonyms.

But there are also models external to the body that can be used to model emotional causation as a physical force. If someone is 'bowled over' by a strong emotion, this is as a result of an external physical force. Consider the following in which the underlined phrases are physical actions, while those in bold are metaphors:

> A dark-haired, wildly handsome fellow with a full dark beard who would bow before her and, in a low, passionate voice, tell her how beautiful she was, how tempting, how much he adored her. And then, then, he would *leap up* from his low bow in an unrestrained fit of passion and *sweep her off her feet* and But no, she didn't want that. Not really. After all, what fun could there be in **being swept off your feet**, **bowled over** by someone else's strong will? As if she wasn't **pushed around enough already** by her own father and mother. (Matas, C. and Nodelman, P. 1995, *Of Two Minds*)

'Sweep her off her feet' and 'pushed around a lot' could be either literal or metaphoric and are best thought of as metonymic as the actions stand for a high level of passion on the part of their agents.

The behaviour of another external entity – fire – can also be employed to understand emotions using force dynamic concepts. Flammable material can be viewed as an agonist since it has a natural tendency to equilibrium – unless it is ignited. The cause of fire – the spark – can be viewed as the antagonist. The spark can either ignite the material and as a result a fire is kindled or if the conditions are such that fire is not possible (for example because the flammable material is damp), then there will be no fire and the material will remain in the same state rather than being combusted. Knowledge of the physics of natural fire therefore provides a readily available frame for change and stability as shown in Figure 3.4.

If force A exceeds force B, a fire will start, whereas if force B is equal to or exceeds force A, there will no fire and the material will remain unchanged. There are also correspondences in ideas of resistance, or inertia, between our experience of emotions and of fire. I proposed earlier that expressions such as 'passion are inflamed' and

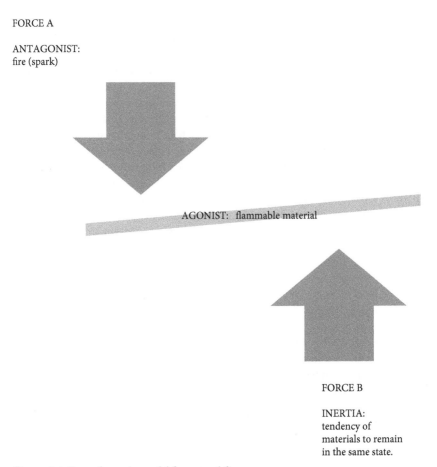

FORCE A

ANTAGONIST:
fire (spark)

AGONIST: flammable material

FORCE B

INERTIA:
tendency of
materials to remain
in the same state.

**Figure 3.4** Force dynamic model for natural fire

'emotional meltdown' imply a conceptual metaphor THE LEVEL OF INTENSITY OF AN EMOTION IS THE LEVEL OF INTENSITY OF A FIRE. We can now see how our understanding of the physical behaviour of natural fire provides the basis for this frame. In these expressions the inertia represented by force B is much weaker than that by force A. Similarly, an expression such as 'to spread like wildfire' implies a situation where the intensity of fire arises from force A being much stronger than force B.

Ideas of *controlling* the emotions are also explained by the force dynamic model. As evidence of this, consider the concept of resisting passion:

From then on, though she didn't reproach him again, **she resisted** *his advances* resolutely, her sense of virtue and honor preventing her from succumbing to his desire. **Her resistance kindled** *his passion*. Soon he told her that he couldn't help thinking of her all the time, as though she had become his shadow. (Jin, H. 2000, *Waiting*)

In the first metaphor we have a female agonist who resists the 'advances' of a male antagonist; the basis for her desire to remain emotionally uninvolved is her 'sense of virtue and honor'. The second metaphor however, indicates that her inertia itself contributes to further arousing the antagonist, and here a fire metaphor 'kindled' is introduced. These physical metaphors may be traced back to exogamy, where there was an evolutionary advantage to marrying outside one's tribe by forcefully carrying off women from other tribes. Both controlled and uncontrolled emotions are based on the underlying frames EMOTION IS A FORCE and THE LEVEL OF INTENSITY OF AN EMOTION IS THE LEVEL OF INTENSITY OF A FIRE.

Our understanding of the causation of fire can also be used to understand social causation because emotions also concern relationships between individuals as well as within an individual. As Talmy argues:

> Turning now to how language structures conceptions about the mind as a form of 'naive psychology', the main factor to note is that language largely extends its concepts of physical force interaction to behavior within the psyche and between psyches. That is, it largely physicalizes the psychosocial domain of reference. (Talmy 1988: 94)

Consider for example the following:

> Racial emotions can still be whipped up and *passions* **inflamed** by irresponsible rabble rousing. Once blood has been shed, many years of nation building and patient strengthening of inter-racial trust and understanding will come to naught. (Nagesan, N. 1992, *Asian Affairs: An American Review*)

Here a fire metaphor is used to describe the effect of 'rabble rousing' on multiple unnamed individuals to describe a social reaction. These systematic mappings between emotion – whether personal or social – and fire and force as a model for their causation are represented in Figure 3.5.

Using the relationships shown in Figure 3.5, we have a model for intensity that applies equally in relation to natural fire or emotion. Where force A exceeds force B, we have a model for loss of control in which the entity acted upon; the individual/social situation or the flammable material are overwhelmed or consumed by the intensity of the emotion or the fire. I will illustrate this situation first with a fire metaphor that describes an individual's emotional state and then a fire metaphor that describes a social emotion:

> Now she understood what he hadn't been able to tell her, that he had met **his old flame** again, and it was **a fire that was consuming** *his vacant moments* and the empty pockets in his life as it had before. There was nothing left over. Worst of all, she couldn't help liking the woman, who was sensitive and funny, even if by her own admission she was usually cranky and a bit of a slob. (Ackerman, D. 2001, *Hummingbirds*)

Here the narrator develops an extended fire metaphor to describe the emotion that is overwhelming her partner who is passive in resisting its force.

FORCE A

ANTAGONIST:
emotion
fire

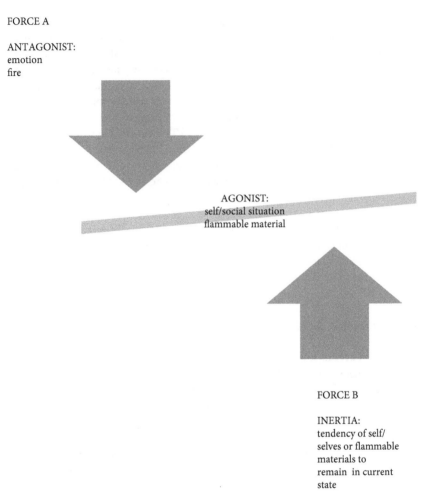

AGONIST:
self/social situation
flammable material

FORCE B

INERTIA:
tendency of self/
selves or flammable
materials to
remain in current
state

**Figure 3.5** Force dynamic model for fire metaphors of the emotions

> Absolute and relative deprivation stemming from population growth and environmental pressures can expand the breadth and depth of inter-group animosities. This creates a kind of **societal tinderbox** with ample opportunities for state elites to **spark** *violent conflicts* by playing on the fears, hatreds and desires of contending groups. (Kahl, C. 2002, *Journal of International Affairs*)

Here the antagonist is abstract – population growth and environmental pressures – and causes widespread emotional responses in multiple selves.

By contrast, when force B exceeds force A, we have a model for control in which the self/social situation (or the flammable material) though acted upon, remains unchanged either because of the lower intensity of the emotion or because of their greater resistance of inertia. In these cases, explicit fire metaphors are blocked because they would imply the greater force of the agonist. However, fire metaphors can be used to describe a related stage in force dynamics where an antagonist is overcome over time:

> Pete hated the useless beauty of the world and longed only for night and rest. When the shadows drew in at last, he and Sophie lay together and held each other close. So his fantasy came true, except that hunger had **extinguished desire** and all they could give each other was warmth. (Cowdrey, A. E. 2011, *How Peter Met Pan*)

Here hunger serves as an agonist whose force is greater than the desire of the antagonist (Peter's desire).

> The guilt around this issue is very unfortunate. If a woman doesn't understand her body and how it responds, showing a man what pleases her is that much more difficult. Women's traditional role as the 'receiving' partner may help **extinguish any desire** to experiment. 'One sexual should is that a woman always get her pleasure from a man'. But studies show that both women and men are more likely to masturbate if they have a partner than if they're celibate: lovemaking of any kind seems to breed a craving for more sexual pleasure. (Jacoby, S. 1996, *Cosmopolitan*)

Here traditional views of woman as sexually passive are the agonist that may eventually overcome the force of the antagonist: desire to experiment sexually. If people remain celibate, they are less likely to give in to sexual desire.

## Summary

In this chapter I have sought to extend the EMOTION IS FIRE frame by providing an account that incorporates notions of causation and intensity based on the frame THE LEVEL OF INTENSITY OF AN EMOTION IS THE LEVEL OF INTENSITY OF A FIRE. It may help to compare Figure 3.5 with Figure 3.1 that showed the mappings for the conceptual frame EMOTION IS FIRE. The mappings-based approach shown in Figure 3.1 originated in Lakoff's work and is rather static and, drawing on Kövecses (2000), I have tried to develop an approach to fire metaphors based on force dynamics as shown in Figures 3.3–3.5. Although emotions are viewed as a disturbing or even disrupting force when the antagonist has much greater force than the agonist, they can be countered by inertia (for example in the form of traditional values) and kept in check with reduced intensity. Both fire and emotion are highly salient entities, one is external and one is internal; they vary in intensity and can be controlled to varying degrees. These variations in intensity are grounded in metonymic-embodied experience and the experience of fire both of which can be integrated into force dynamics. In the case of emotion, the agonist can either be viewed as the individual self that is experiencing the emotion, as is typical for emotions such as romantic love, or as a social situation such as immigration or religious belief.

Table 3.8 summarizes the frames that depend on these pre-existing force relationships and their emotional resonance.

**Table 3.8** Resonance of 'Fire' and 'Heat' frames for emotions

| Fire frames with positive resonance | Fire frames with neutral resonance | Fire frames with negative resonance |
|---|---|---|
| WARMTH FOR AFFECTION | EMOTION IS A FORCE<br>EMOTION IS FIRE<br>WARMTH FOR EMOTION<br>PAIN IS FIRE | ANGER IS FIRE<br>LUST IS FIRE |
| FRIENDSHIP IS FIRE/WARMTH | THE CAUSE OF AN EMOTION IS THE CAUSE OF A FIRE<br>CAUSE OF AN EXPLOSION FOR EFFECT OF THE EXPLOSION | ANGER IS A HOT FLUID IN A CONTAINER |
| HOPE IS FIRE | THE EFFECT OF AN EMOTION IS THE EFFECT OF A FIRE | ANGER IS A TIME BOMB |
| CONTROLLED EMOTION IS MODERATE TEMPERATURE | THE LEVEL OF INTENSITY OF AN EMOTION IS THE LEVEL OF INTENSITY OF A FIRE<br>THE LEVEL OF TEMPERATURE FOR THE INTENSITY OF EMOTION | UNCONTROLLED EMOTION IS EXTREME TEMPERATURE |

We should remember that these are not the only ways to talk about emotions such as anger or friendship, as Kövecses (2000: 21) notes, anger can also be described as a captive animal or as an opponent in a physical struggle, as well as a hot fluid in a container, but at a more abstract level all these cases can be explained by the root concept EMOTION IS A FORCE. An illustration of this is provided:

> **Like a tuning fork,** Stewart begins to vibrate, caught between rage and desire. Mary's proximity has **ignited** *his banked passion* for her, but at this moment **she's just another trap to hold him** forever. When Stewart **finally explodes, he attacks like a cornered animal, teeth bared.** Shaking her ferociously, he sobs, 'Now, you listen to me, I don't want any plastics, I don't want in on any ground floor, and I don't want to get married ever to anyone!' Then, **raining hot** *kisses on her face,* this most native son surrenders. (Mortimer, L. 1995, *The Grim Enchantment of It's a Wonderful Life*)

Here we have at least seven distinct metaphor source domains – music, fire, containment, pressure, animals, weather and war – however, what all of these share in common is that they are construe Stewart's emotions as an antagonist that exerts a powerful force on their object. The focus is entirely on the antagonist and it is not always clear which of the metaphors are also potentially actual physical actions; for example he may *actually* have showed his teeth and certainly has physical contact with the target of his obsession with his hands and mouth. The use of 'surrenders' implies that whatever tendency there is to remain unemotional is completely overcome by the sheer force of emotion.

Part Two

# Fire in Religious Discourse

# Introduction: Sacred Fire

In the myths that I examined in Chapter 1, the original purpose of fire was not only with the practical functions of providing warmth and cooking but with making sacrificial offerings to a deity. It is likely that fire has become a common source for metaphors, and originates in embodied experience and also in its tendency to spread sometimes violently. Therefore, it is the force with which it can transmit that forms the basis of many of its metaphoric senses. The origin of fire festivals was the burning of an object or other materials (incense etc.) as an offering to God – so the mysterious or 'Sacred Fire' was integral to religious observance, and in Part Two I explore the symbolic meaning of fire in the Abrahamic religions, in Zoroastrianism and in Hinduism. Fire as a gift *from* God is returned *to* God by sacrifice, but it also became proof of the force and power of God.

'Sacred Fire' takes its origin in the recognition that fire was not originally created by man; as Fraser (1930: 2004–5) points out, 'Even when men have long been in possession of fire, they are apt to regard with peculiar awe and veneration a fire which has been kindled by a flash of lightening.' He illustrates this with reference to a story told by Sarat Chadra Roy concerning the Oraons of Chota Nagpur in India:

> Not very many years ago, at the village of Haril, a tree, on the branches of which an Oraon cultivator had stacked his straw, was struck by lightning and the tree caught fire. Thereupon all the Oraons of the village assembled and decided that, since God had sent this 'lightning fire', all existing fire in the village should be extinguished, and a portion of this 'Heaven-sent fire' should be taken and carefully preserved in every house and should be used for all purposes. And this was accordingly done.

This was in spite of the Oraons being perfectly familiar with the fire drill and illustrates how, in spite of technological progress, the mysterious appeal of Natural Fire re-emerges. Sacred Fire arises from the understanding that Natural Fire has an intrinsically divine quality, and that man's possession of fire is only temporary, as if on loan. It implies that at an unconscious level, even modern man can believe that, like Prometheus, he has stolen something that rightly belonged to the Gods – and risks some form of retribution for having done so.

There is an important distinction between the Sacred Fire, caused originally by lightning, which in the human mind attributes agency to a divine being in its quest for explanation, and the Functional or Profane Fire that is under human control. However, the psychological integration of Sacred with Profane Fire may require recognition of the *otherness* of fire: that it exists *apart* from man as well as *within* his fireplace and within his body. It is this celebration of the otherness of Sacred Fire, of the divine and mysterious fire, which is re-activated by fire-festivals, like the Scottish fires of Beltane, and has been resurrected by festivals like those in the Orkneys where a Viking ship is burnt and more recently in the Burning Man festival in the USA. The potential of fire to create spiritual meaning is based on the original practice of sacrifice – is still present in such ceremonies, as Goudsblom explains:

> In their religious practices the ancient Greeks and Romans differed greatly from the ancient Israelites. They had no sacred books; nor did they have a class of professional priests and prophets. They honoured many gods and they held numerous festivals throughout the year, with a great many local variations. Yet for them, as for the ancient Israelites – and for most other people in agrarian societies – the central act of worship was sacrifice, and most sacrifices were associated with meals and were made on a burning altar. (Goudsblom 1994: 119)

It is through the theme of sacrifice that we can explore fire in the hinterland between the mythologies of pantheistic religions, where natural fire inspired men with a sense of awe, and the powerful monotheistic religions that emerged as rivals to their predecessors. We will see in Part Two of this book how the awe inspired by natural fire gradually became replaced by a set of richly symbolic meanings that gave a particular role and status to the fire priest, the performers of the sacrifice, as the intermediary between nature, man and the divine.

# 4

# Fire in the Abrahamic Religions

## Fire symbolism

The Abrahamic religions (Judaism, Christianity and Islam) all believe in a single God. Their shared monotheism, by definition, required a rejection of the pantheistic religions that had preceded them. In such religions fire was created by a fire god and fire itself could be worshipped. In the monotheistic religions fire was a manifestation of God and so not something to be itself worshipped as a God. But in both monotheistic and pantheistic religions fire offered the possibility for reciprocal communication with God through sacrificial offerings: the awe that God had inspired through fire could be returned through the same medium.

In this chapter I propose that fire metaphors developed out of an understanding of fire as a symbol for God; fire was the element that stood for, or symbolized, divine inspiration. Fire was a means of transmission through which monotheists came to know about the power of God. As the forbidden idols of pantheists could be melted down, fire also had a practical function as a means of destroying the rival emblems of pantheism; fire therefore provided the believers with a divinely approved vehicle for action. By providing the means for enforcing monotheism by punishing non-believers, fire also became a symbol of divine anger. Once fire became a symbol for expressing the divine will – as implied by the concept of 'Sacred Fire' – this also created the potential for it to become a symbol of purity and eventually of knowledge. However, this worked differently in each religion; in Judaism fire has a broader meaning associated with its prophetic role as a symbol for maintaining tradition; Christianity largely replaced the symbolic system of fire in the Old Testament with the light metaphors of the New Testament, and with metaphors for fire as a vehicle for divine communication. However, in Islam the earlier sense of fire as a vehicle of divine retribution has survived and, at various times, been revived.

'Sacred Fire' develops a set of symbolic meanings that later form the basis of fire metaphors such as the following:

> Thus says the Lord God: 'behold, **I will kindle a fire in you**, and it shall devour every green tree and every dry tree in you; **the blazing flame shall not be quenched,** and all faces from the south to the north **shall be scorched by it.** All flesh shall see that I, the Lord, **have kindled it**; it shall not be quenched.' (Ezekiel 20: 46–48)

Here the action of kindling a fire is attributed to the agency of a single divine God, who kindles the fire and controls how long it will last. However, it is not fire in a literal sense because it is kindled 'in you' and it shall 'scorch' faces in all points of the compass implying that faith will spread in the same way as a physical fire spreads. Fire here is a divine force – a Sacred Fire – and metaphor is the natural language through which religious faith is communicated.

The symbolic meaning of fire was especially important in ancient Israel where acts of sacrifice at the altar and ways of sustaining holy fire eventually became part of religious ritual. The following extract from Leviticus emphasizes the need to keep the sacrificial fire burning:

> And the fire upon the altar shall be kept burning thereby, it shall not go out; and the priest shall kindle wood on it every morning; and he shall lay the burnt-offering in order upon it, and shall make smoke thereon the fat of the peace-offerings. Fire shall be kept burning upon the altar continually; it shall not go out. (Leviticus 6: 5–6)

The perpetuity of the fire became a symbol of the survival of the faith: as long as the fire kept burning the faith would survive because sacrifices could be offered. The flame became an important symbol of religious faith in Judaism to the extent that Jewish people ensured that it continued to burn throughout their wanderings in the wilderness. The flame was placed in a brazier while they were travelling across the desert and this is one of the possible origins of the pillar of fire that apparently guided the Israelites across the desert out of Egypt.[1]

The Christian Old Testament prescribes in detail the religious practices required for the use of fire in the offering of burnt sacrifices; a key element in correct observation of the ritual was that only the sacred altar fire could be used. Failure to observe the correct practices for Sacred Fire would be deemed 'profane' and the use of profane fire would meet with divine punishment:

> Then Nadab and Abihu, the sons of Aaron, each took his censer and put fire in it, put incense on it, and offered profane fire before the Lord, which He had not commanded them. *So fire went out from the Lord and devoured them, and they died before the Lord.* (Leviticus 10: 1–2)

We may wonder about the nature of this 'profane fire' and a clue to this is offered with the etymology of 'profane' which is from the Latin profanus – 'pro' meaning 'before' and 'fanum' meaning temple: they had ignited their incense from a source that was *outside* the temple – rather than using the sacred altar fire, as prescribed:

> Then he shall take a censer full of burning coals of fire from the altar before the Lord, with his hands full of sweet incense beaten fine, and bring it inside the veil. (Leviticus 16: 12)

Not only had Nadab and Abihu failed to light their incense from the sacred altar fire, they had also broken a second prescription:

> Then the Lord spoke to Aaron, saying: 'do not drink wine or intoxicating drink, you, nor your sons with you, when you go into the tabernacle of meeting, lest you die. It shall be a statute forever throughout your generations, that you may

distinguish between holy and unholy, and between unclean and clean'. (Leviticus 10: 8–10)

So, the two offenders suffered instant combustion because their drunkenness had led them to ignore the distinction between the sacred temple fire and the profane fire. This illustrates the origin of the symbolic meaning of fire in the Abrahamic religions. Survival of the faith was dependent on the observation of holy practice, and the use of the Sacred Fire was integral to this.

In Judaism fire has retained its deeply symbolic meaning through various iconic forms and forms of religious observation. For example, the seven-branched candelabrum known as the Menorah has become an important symbol (and is included in the coat of arms of the modern state of Israel). In the Judaic calendar a major festival, Hanukkah, is observed by the kindling of a nine-branched menorah, with an additional candle being lit on each day of the eight-day festival. Fire has become part of Jewish ritual because of its role in announcing the new moon – since the appearance of the new moon signalled the start of the year. According to The Mishnak (the earliest Jewish legal code) two witnesses of the new moon were required; once their testimonies had been examined and approved by judges in Jerusalem, the knowledge of the new moon would be transmitted by lighting bonfires around Jerusalem and would trigger off the lighting of similar beacons around the surrounding mountaintops. Some Jewish groups commemorate the new moon (Rosh Chodesh) festival with the practice of a single participant lighting her candle from a central flame. The flame is then passed on to all the other participants until everyone has lit a candle and the ritual enforces group identity.

The Christian Orthodox tradition believes in a miraculous Holy Fire that ignites at the Holy Sepulchre in Jerusalem on the day preceding Orthodox Easter. A light shines from Christ's tomb and forms a column of fire that is then used to light the Patriarchs candles, which in turn are used to light the candles of all those present in the Church. The Patriarch testifies to the supernatural origin of this fire:

> It is emitted from the Holy Sepulchre with a hue completely different from that of natural light. It sparkles, it flashes like lightning, it flies like a dove around the tabernacle of the Holy Sepulchre, and lights up the unlit lamps of olive oil hanging in front of it. It whirls from one side of the church to the other. It enters some of the chapels inside the church, as for instance the chapel of the Calvary (at a higher level than the Holy Sepulchre) and lights up the little lamps. It lights up also the candles of certain pilgrims. In fact there are some very pious pilgrims who, every time they attended this ceremony, noticed that their candles lit up on their own accord! This divine light also presents some peculiarities: as soon as it appears it has a bluish hue and does not burn. At the first moments of its appearance, if it touches the face, or the mouth, or the hands, it does not burn. This is proof of its divine and supernatural origin.[2]

While critics have argued that the fire is caused by chicanery and magic – the covert use of naphtha[3] – this is unlikely to influence the symbolic meaning of the Holy Fire to its attendants. In the modern and post-modern periods, a distinction can be made between religions that articulate a clear role for the divine origin of fire by establishing fire rituals, and a broader spiritual sensitivity in which many believers and non-believers alike feel are drawn to bonfires to revive a sense of the mystery of being alive. Those who are reluctant to endorse the power structures of established religions, their rituals and textual cannons may still recognize and respond to the appeal of fire: but this is *not* the Sacred Fire of the Hebrew Bible or the Holy Fire of Eastern Christians, but fire as a means of establishing a focus around which a social group can establish relationships. This is closer to the early primitive experience of fire as a means of destroying the forest to establish settlements – before fire became 'colonized' by religion. Awe may have been present but there were not yet discourses of awe. It is similar to Canetti's idea of fire as a symbol of the crowd; I will refer to this as 'Group Fire'.

We should remember that Judaism was not the only monotheistic religion whose set of symbolic meanings required that a divine fire be kept continually burning. In Christianity there was a long period when an altar fire was kept within the home and that fire continued to have that broader social role of bringing people together in shared spiritual experience:

> Like the ancient roman temples, all Christian houses of worship contained a perpetually burning altar fire – as a tacit reminder of the times when fire was a precious group possession. (Goudsblom 1994: 132)

The Group Fire contributes to social identities by integrating the instinctive appeal of Natural Fire, originating in the pantheistic mythologies that predated the Abrahamic religions, with some of the symbolic meanings of Sacred Fire. These monotheistic religions originally depended for their legitimacy on the concept of Sacred Fire, and the fate that befell the sons of Aaron for their use of profane fire was proof of this. The fire priests who observed the textual rubrics became the original mediators of the divine force who offered a bridge between Fraser's Fireless Age and an Age of Light. Within the natural world fire served as a metonymy for this divine force: God gave them fire and they gave fire back to God.

In this chapter, I explore both the symbolic meaning of fire through its use in sacrifice and its metaphoric meanings, where words from the lexical field of fire are used in sacred texts to communicate the divine. The monotheistic religions sought to extend their reach beyond mere ritual by spreading the word and metaphor played a crucial role in this. I examine language evidence in the holy texts of the Abrahamic religions for a transition from Sacred Fire – fire as a means of sacrifice, ritual and power – to fire as a metaphor for the survival and extension of the faith. These transitions do not occur in the same way in each religion. In Judaism, candles continue to play an important part in Jewish ritual with the use of Hanukkah and Shabbat candles and this serves as a vehicle for maintaining traditions. In Western Christianity, the symbolism of fire in the Old Testament is largely replaced by metaphors of light in the New Testament. This corresponds with a shift in understanding from fire as a vehicle of divine wrath to a set of metaphors based around the concept JESUS IS THE LIGHT. In Eastern Christianity, the concept of Holy Fire retains a stronger symbolic role for fire and some branches of Western Christianity, such as Pentecostalism, have revived fire as a symbol for divine communication. In the Qur'an, there is a resistance to metaphor and Sacred Fire retains its symbolic meaning as a force for the divine punishment of non-believers. There are, then, important divergences in the extent and direction of fire symbols and metaphors that are indicative of underlying theological differences between the three Abrahamic religions, and fire metaphors provide insight into the nature of these differences.

## Fire and sacrifice in the Torah and Old Testament

The primary purpose of a sacred text such as the Torah,[4] Bible or Qur'an was to establish a monotheistic faith, or ideology, based around a set of core beliefs that would displace those of the pre-existing pantheistic religions: discourses of awe. Sacrifice – how it was performed, what was burnt, how fire was obtained and what was done with the ashes – provided proof of the authenticity of the one God and his prophets. This explains why the majority of fire terms in the Torah refer to practice and guidance about sacrifice. It accounts for the high frequencies of 'fire' and 'burn' in the books of Exodus, Leviticus and Numbers. In primitive societies the power of fire to transform the material into the immaterial through performing ritual sacrifice by a trained priestly cast was the predominant means for religious participation. As reward for his specialist knowledge of the correct methods for religious observation the priest had the right to keep the skin of the animal that he sacrificed. Given the value attached to animal hide, there was probably little incentive for priests to be too hasty in giving up this ritualistic aspect of worship. As Pyne (1992: 75) notes:

> The perennial problem centred round just who was allowed or obliged to offer what to whom; in order to reach a solution it was necessary also to settle where and when sacrifice was to be made. All these issues were potential sources of conflict, and the texts show that they sometimes lead to fierce clashes.

The opening of Leviticus prescribes in some detail the ritual practice surrounding burnt offerings and can be understood as an attempt to resolve disputes and conflicts between rival priests and rival tribes:

> Now the Lord called to Moses, and spoke to him from the tabernacle of meeting, saying, 'Speak to the children of Israel, and say to them: when any one of you brings an offering to the Lord, you shall bring your offering of the livestock – of the herd and of the flock. If his offering is a burnt sacrifice of the herd, let him offer a male without blemish; he shall offer it of his own free will at the door of the tabernacle of meeting before the Lord. Then he shall put his hand on the head of the burnt offering, and it will be accepted on his behalf to make atonement for him. He shall kill the bull before the Lord; and the priests, Aaron's sons, shall bring the blood and sprinkle the blood all around on the altar that is by the door of the tabernacle of meeting. And he shall skin the burnt offering and cut it into its pieces. The sons of Aaron the priest shall put fire on the altar, and lay the wood in order on the fire. Then the priests, Aaron's sons, shall lay the parts, the head, and

the fat in order on the wood that is on the fire upon the altar; but he shall wash its entrails and its legs with water. And the priest shall burn all on the altar as a burnt sacrifice, an offering made by fire, a sweet aroma to the Lord'. (Leviticus 1: 1–9)

The importance of following these practices was demonstrated by the fate that befell Aaron's sons: it was their failure to observe the correct practices that led to their punishment by divine fire.

There was also the crucial question of *what* was to be burnt as an offering. In some primitive religions, priests would argue that a God would be displeased if anything less than the most valued and loved entity was sacrificed – hence typically this would be a firstborn child as suggested in the following: 'you shall not delay *to offer* the first of your ripe produce and your juices. The firstborn of your sons you shall give to Me' (Ezekiel 22: 29). However, these are the only verses in the Bible that appear to condone human sacrifice and elsewhere human sacrifice is strictly prohibited as a practice associated with pagan followers of Molech or Baal: 'and you shall not let any of your descendants pass through *the fire* to Molech, nor shall you profane the name of your God: I *am* the Lord' (Leviticus 18: 21). This prohibition implies that human sacrifice was condemned: it was a boundary marker between acceptable and non-acceptable forms of worship:

> You shall not worship the Lord your God in that way; for every abomination to the Lord which He hates they have done to their gods; for they burn even their sons and daughters in the fire to their gods. (Deuteronomy 12: 31)

In the book of Genesis when God tests Abraham's faith by asking him to sacrifice his son, replacing a human victim with some form of substitute was a necessary part in the evolution of Abrahamic thought. The account is worth quoting because it illustrates exactly *how* sacrifice would have been carried out in the early phases of the Abrahamic religions:

> Now it came to pass after these things that God tested Abraham, and said to him, 'Abraham!'
>
> And he said, 'Here I am.'
>
> Then He said, 'Take now your son, your only son Isaac, whom you love, and go to the land of Moriah, and offer him there as a burnt offering on one of the mountains of which I shall tell you.' So Abraham took the wood of the burnt offering and laid it on Isaac his son; and he took the fire in his hand, and a knife, and the two of them went together. But Isaac spoke to Abraham his father and said, 'My father!'
>
> And he said, 'Here I am, my son.'
>
> Then he said, 'Look, the fire and the wood, but where is the lamb for a burnt offering?'
>
> And Abraham said, 'My son, God will provide for Himself the lamb for a burnt offering.' So the two of them went together.
>
> Then they came to the place of which God had told him. And Abraham built an altar there and placed the wood in order; and he bound Isaac his son and laid

him on the altar, upon the wood. And Abraham stretched out his hand and took the knife to slay his son. (Genesis 22: 1–9)

This passage reveals that the offering would be ritually slaughtered prior to the igniting of the fire. Fortunately, however, for Isaac (and Abraham) there is a divine intervention that stops the human sacrifice by the substitution of an animal:

Then Abraham lifted his eyes and looked, and there behind him was a ram caught in a thicket by its horns. So Abraham went and took the ram, and offered it up for a burnt offering instead of his son. (Genesis 22: 13)

This is a literal use of fire as a recognized means for offering sacrifice to Gods, and what seems strange to later readers is that Abraham seems quite prepared to go along with sacrifice of his firstborn; this suggests that human sacrifice was quite normal in pre-Abrahamic religions and that termination of this practice was crucial in establishing monotheism. It indicates how remarkable it was that burning at the stake became the standard form of punishment for heretics from the thirteenth to the seventeenth centuries (Tyndale met such a fate for daring to translate the Bible into English). Followers of the Abrahamic religions should view such uses of fire as a return to the practices of Molech: fire as a form of human sacrifice.

The laws of Moses specified the appropriate non-human sacrifices at a properly consecrated altar and gave rules for the correct form for the slaughter and burning of an animal such as a lamb, calf or bull. Perhaps the best illustration of how fire sacrifices worked in the society of ancient Israel is in 1 Kings 25–39, where Elijah challenges the prophets of Baal to an 'Ignition Combat' in a sacrificial offering where the challenge is to ignite a fire that has been previously drenched. This illustrates how the symbolic meanings of fire emerged from its role in resolving struggle between competing ideologies. Goudsblom (1994: 84) suggests that Elijah may have secretly used a combustible liquid – a petrol compound made from neftar or naphtha – which was then ignited by a piece of obsidian as it became heated by the midday sun. This liquid could have been concealed in one of the 'waterpots' that were emptied over the sacrifice. Perhaps this was a case where a sacred end justified a magical means. The story of Elijah shows how fire integrated pre-existing emotions of awe within a powerful monotheistic ideology. Fire no longer *was* God but had become a means of divine validation. God's choice to ignite *only the believers'* fire convinced doubters that *theirs* was the one and true God. Fire therefore became a symbol that demonstrated divine reality. Ideologically, this divine manifestation contributed to the Israelites' social cohesion and group identity and gave rise to a set of meanings emerging from Sacred Fire.

## Fire and divine display

The role of Sacred Fire in establishing an ideology raises two crucial questions: Is the fire an actual fire or is it a sign of something else? And if it is a sign, what does it signify? The answer provided by the fire lexicon of the Torah and Old Testament is that fire announces a divine presence. As we saw in the previous chapter, there are many mythological accounts of how mankind first came to obtain fire from the Gods, by contrast, in the Abrahamic religions the perspective is reversed and fire is integral to divine revelation. The divine origin of fire shows in two contrasting ways in the Bible: fire is the primary means through which God displays his reality (known as 'theophany') and fire is also the primary means through which he exerts his authority by punishing those who offend him; both of these contribute to an understanding of Sacred Fire. In this section, I consider theophany and in the following section the issue of divine wrath.

The first use of fire as a means of divine display is when Moses is instructed to lead his followers out of the oppressive land of Egypt into a land flowing with milk and honey:

> Now Moses was tending the flock of Jethro his father-in-law, the priest of Midian. And he led the flock to the back of the desert, and came to Horeb, the mountain of God. And the Angel of the Lord appeared to him in a flame of fire from the midst of a bush. So he looked, and behold, the bush was burning with fire, but the bush was not consumed. Then Moses said, 'I will now turn aside and see this great sight, why the bush does not burn.'
>
> So when the Lord saw that he turned aside to look, God called to him from the midst of the bush and said, 'Moses, Moses!'
>
> And he said, 'Here I am.'
>
> Then He said, 'Do not draw near this place. Take your sandals off your feet, for the place where you stand *is* holy ground.' Moreover He said, 'I *am* the God of your father – the God of Abraham, the God of Isaac, and the God of Jacob.' And Moses hid his face, for he was afraid to look upon God. (Exodus 3: 1–5)

The episode of the 'Burning Bush' is the precursor for God's instructions for Moses to deliver his people from Pharaoh. The concept of a Chosen People underlies the growth and emergence of both Judaism and Christianity and takes its origin in a narrative of exceptional, or sacred, fire: that does not follow the laws of nature because it burns but does not consume. This Sacred Fire does not have an apparent source of ignition and does not appear to require fuel. Fire is therefore the predominant natural feature that develops a religious meaning through its rich set of symbolic meanings. If fire were not the natural symbol of religion, why else, we may ask, did the Angel of the Lord appear to Moses from the midst of a burning bush? Presumably fire was the closest that man became to something that did not have an obvious explanation, something that was dangerous, exciting and inspired feelings of awe. Sacred Fire became the purest manifestation of a monotheistic being – the archetypal theophany, or 'divine showing' – and can be represented conceptually as DIVINE DISPLAY IS FIRE.

It is against this background that we are able to account for the extensive occurrence of natural fire terms in the lexicon of the Old Testament. It was because natural fire was the most evident force in the natural world that it was adopted as a symbol of divine power. This is evident from Table 4.1 that compares fire terms in translations of the Old Testament, the New Testament and the Qur'an.

**Table 4.1**  Core fire lexicon in New King James version of the Bible and the Qur ͏a.

| NATURAL FIRE | | | | |
| --- | --- | --- | --- | --- |
| **Fire concept** | **Fire term** | **Old Testament** | **New Testament** | **Qur'an** |
| FORM & ACTION | fire(s) | 438 | 79 | 80 |
| | burn | 578 | 36 | 26 |
| | flame(s) | 32 | 6 | 10 |
| | fiery | 23 | 6 | 1 |
| INTENSITY | blaze/ablaze | 2 | 0 | 25 |
| TOTAL | | 1,073 (81%) | 127 (67%) | 142 (79%) |
| **FUNCTIONAL FIRE** | | | | |
| EFFECT OF FIRE: HEAT | heat | 17 | 9 | 7 |
| | scorch | 3 | 4 | 0 |
| | seared | 1 | 1 | 0 |
| | melt | 31 | 2 | 1 |
| | brand | 2 | 0 | 2 |
| EFFECT OF FIRE: LIGHT | torch | 10 | 2 | 0 |
| | lamp | 67 | 26 | 0 |
| EFFECT OF FIRE | smoke | 28 | 11 | 4 |
| OUTCOME OF FIRE | ashes | 37 | 4 | 8 |
| TOTAL | | 196 (15%) | 59 (31%) | 22 (11%) |
| **ORGANIC FIRE** | | | | |
| STARTING A FIRE | spark | 6 | 0 | 2 |
| | kindle | 40 | 4 | 8 |
| | tinderbox | 1 | 0 | 0 |
| CAUSING A FIRE TO GROW | fuel | 7 | 0 | 5 |
| | inflame/ inflammation | 5 | 0 | 0 |
| CAUSING A FIRE TO END | extinguish | 3 | 0 | 2 |
| TOTAL | | 62 (4%) | 4 (2%) | 17 (10%) |
| OVERALL TOTAL | | 1,331 (100%) | 190 (100%) | 181 (100%) |

The table only shows fire terms that occurred in the Bible (New King James version) and in a translation of the Qur'an since there were a number of words from the core lexicon for fire that did not occur at all; these included: 'smoulder', 'glow', 'flare', 'ignite', 'cinders' or 'embers'. An explanation of the predominance of *natural* fire terms in all three texts is in the strong association of fire with force that it naturally took on an association with divine punishment. The manifestation of force in the natural world served as the basis for power and authority in the social world. Some functional fire terms also convey this symbolic meaning, for example all the uses of 'smoke' in the

New Testament occur in the book of Revelations as predictions of the end of the world: where divine punishment becomes a form of divine display.

Moses guides the children of Israel out of the oppressive lands of Egypt with the aid of a 'pillar of fire':

> And the Lord went before them by day in a pillar of cloud to lead the way, and by night in *a pillar of fire* to give them light, so as to go by day and night. He did not take away the pillar of cloud by day or the pillar of fire by night from before the people. (Exodus 13: 21–22)

The fire has a function, to provide light, but to fulfil a sacred purpose: the survival of the Chosen People. This divine guidance is referred to subsequently in the Bible:

> Even when they made a molded calf for themselves,
> And said, 'This *is* your god
> That brought you up out of Egypt,'
> And worked great provocations,
> Yet in Your manifold mercies
> You did not forsake them in the wilderness.
> The pillar of the cloud did not depart from them by day,
> To lead them on the road;
> Nor the *pillar of fire* by night,
> To show them light,
> And the way they should go.
> You also gave Your good Spirit to instruct them,
> And did not withhold Your manna from their mouth,
> And gave them water for their thirst.
> (Nehemiah 9: 18–20)

Fire provides the light that shows the way, but it is also shows God's support for his followers. In the New Testament the metaphor of light becomes the predominant metaphor. It may be that symbolic meaning of a pillar of fire originated in experience of fire whirls: a natural phenomenon in which fire causes a whirlwind leading to the fire being sucked up into the atmosphere in the search for oxygen to consume. But, whatever their cause, the pillar of fire took on symbolic meaning and implies a frame DIVINE DISPLAY IS FIRE. Another suggestion (Pyne 1992: 81) is that the pillar of fire was the holy fire that was kept burning at all times and was transported at the front of the caravan to provide the temple fire at whatever new site was chosen. Like the fire that ignited Elijah's sacrifice and the burning bush witnessed by Moses, the pillar of fire is an example of theophany: the extraordinary revelation of the divinity. There are various other instances of divine display through fire such as the following:

> For it came to pass, when *the flame went up* toward heaven from off the altar, that the angel of the Lord ascended in *the flame of the altar*. And Manoah and his wife looked on *it*, and fell on their faces to the ground. (Judges 13: 20)

Such divine manifestation through fire is significant because it marks the transition from fire as an inseparable part of a ritual sacrifice to a more symbolic meaning as something that *stands for* the divine. This prepares the way for metaphoric uses of 'fire' such as the following:

> The Light of Israel will become **a fire**, their Holy One **a flame**; in a single day **it will burn and consume** *his thorns and his briers*. (Isaiah 10: 13)

The destiny of the Israelites is bound up with divine symbolism as God's agents, his Chosen People. However, the most frequent and widespread metaphors in the Old Testament, the Hebrew Bible and the Qur'an are where fire metaphors frame divine displeasure and it is these metaphors that I explore in the next section.

## Fire metaphors in the Hebrew Bible/Old Testament and the Qur'an

### Causes and effects of divine wrath

Fire as an expression of divine anger is the most widespread of the fire images in the Hebrew Bible/Old Testament and in the Qur'an. I suggest that once God is framed as a person, then it follows that fire may be used as a metaphor for divine displeasure; this is because, as we have seen in Chapter 3, the embodied experience of anger entails force and metonymically fire is connected with destruction. Fire becomes a metaphor for divine displeasure once the meaning of 'disapproval' is personified by attributing the human emotion of wrath to a divine being. The first metaphoric use of a fire metaphor for divine anger in the Bible is the following:

> Then Judah came near to him and said: 'O my lord, please let your servant speak a word in my lord's hearing, and do not let **your anger burn against your servant**; for you are even like Pharaoh.' (Genesis 44: 18)

Tables 4.2 and 4.3 give a brief summary of how often various anger terms (in the columns) occur in close proximity to words related to fire (in the rows) in the Hebrew Bible and in the Qur'an; these correspond with a frame that associates fire with anger.

**Table 4.2** DIVINE ANGER IS FIRE in the Hebrew Bible/Old Testament

|        | fire | burn | kindle | melt | TOTAL |
|--------|------|------|--------|------|-------|
| anger  | 21   | 20   | 9      | 1    | 51    |
| wrath  | 10   | 10   | 5      | 1    | 26    |
| fury   | 9    | 5    | 2      | 2    | 18    |
| TOTAL  | 30   | 35   | 16     | 4    | 85    |

**Table 4.3** DIVINE ANGER IS FIRE in the Qur'an

|        | fire | burn | kindle | melt | TOTAL |
|--------|------|------|--------|------|-------|
| anger  | 11   | 4    | 0      | 0    | 15    |
| wrath  | 13   | 4    | 2      | 0    | 19    |
| fury   | 3    | 0    | 1      | 0    | 4     |
| TOTAL  | 27   | 8    | 3      | 0    | 38    |

Charteris-Black (2004) proposed DIVINE ANGER IS FIRE as a conceptual metaphor that is specific to religious discourse. A phrase that occurs ninety-one times in the Bible is 'The anger of the Lord', and approximately a quarter of these are expressed by fire metaphors. An equivalent expression of divine wrath occurs in the Qur'an where the words 'Allah' 'fire' and 'punishment' occur sixty-one times in close proximity with each other, as in the following:

> This is because they defied and disobeyed Allah and His Messenger. And whoever defies and disobeys Allah and His Messenger, then verily, Allah is Severe in punishment. This is the torment, so taste it, and surely for the disbelievers is *the torment of the Fire.* (The Spoils of War 13–14)

An expression that occurs twenty-seven times in the Qur'an is 'dwellers/inmates of the fire' – a periphrasis for non-believers:

> Verily, We have sent you (O Muhammad Peace be upon him) with the truth (Islam), a bringer of glad tidings (for those who believe in what you brought, that they will enter Paradise) and a warner (for those who disbelieve in what you brought, they will enter the Hell-fire). And you will not be asked about *the dwellers of the blazing Fire.* (The Cow 119)

Punishment by fire is a fate that awaits those who do not heed the words of the Prophet, as fire is the appropriate punishment for non-believers. The image of 'dwelling' in the fire emphasizes the permanence of this punishment, it also implies a degree of agency on the part of the 'dwellers of the fire' – as if they had *chosen* this fate, rather than having it imposed on them. This strong, assertive style characterized by making predictions about the punishments that await those who disobey Allah can be described as 'prophetic discourse'. The role of fire is to elaborate on these punishments by various forms of rhetorical embellishment as in the following:

> Woe to every slanderer and backbiter.
> Who has gathered wealth and counted it,
> He thinks that his wealth will make him last forever!
> Nay! Verily, *he will be thrown into the crushing Fire.*
> And what will make you know *what the crushing Fire is?*

**The fire of Allah, kindled,**
Which leaps up over the hearts,
Verily, it shall be closed in on them,
In pillars stretched forth (i.e. they will be punished in the Fire with pillars, etc.).
(The Slanderer 104: 1–9)

Here fire becomes a physical force with the power to crush, and also takes on a three-dimensional form so that it closes in and is formed of 'pillars'. Fire is conceptualized as a solid and permanent structure around the damned.

The first occurrence of fire as an actual instrument of divine punishment in the Bible occurs in Genesis:

The sun had risen upon the earth when Lot entered Zoar. Then the Lord *rained brimstone and fire* on Sodom and Gomorrah, from the Lord out of the heavens. (Genesis 19: 23–25)

A similar association of divine anger with the use of fire to punish non-believers is described in Deuteronomy:

The whole land *is brimstone*, salt, and *burning*; it is not sown, nor does it bear, nor does any grass grow there, like the overthrow of Sodom and Gomorrah, Admah, and Zeboiim, which the Lord overthrew in His anger and His wrath. All nations would say, 'Why has the Lord done so to this land? What does **the heat of this great anger** mean?' (Deuteronomy 29: 23–25)

The 'heat of this great anger' seems to be a metaphor-based metonymy because the emotion of anger causes actions associated with punishment by fire. It is based in CAUSES ARE FORCES and the LEVEL OF TEMPERATURE FOR THE INTENSITY OF EMOTION. Because God is angry, he uses fire as a means of punishing the inhabitants of Sodom and Gomorrah as we found in the analysis of 'scorched earth' in Chapter 1. So, there is a cause and effect relationship in which corrupt behaviour by offenders leads to divine anger, that leads to the desire to punish the offenders, which in turn leads to the use of fire. It would be typical to lay waste to an enemy's property and assets by burning them as the quickest and most reliable way to completely destroy them – both materially and morally. The destruction of food supplies such as livestock and the previous year's harvest would also lead to famine. Evidence of the metonymic basis of divine anger metaphors is in the inclusion of other words from the semantic field of warfare such as 'chariots' and 'battle' as in the following:

Their appearance is like the appearance of horses;
And like swift steeds, so they run.
With a noise like chariots
Over mountaintops they leap,
Like **the noise of a flaming fire that devours the stubble,**
Like a strong people set in battle array.

Before them the people writhe in pain;
All faces are drained of color. (Joel 2: 4–6)

The expression of intense emotion, with belief and divine punishment occurs most expressively in a debate between Moses and God over issues of theological discipline after the Israelites have made a golden idol in the shape of a calf:

> And the Lord said to Moses, 'I have seen this people, and indeed it is a stiff-necked people! Now therefore, let Me alone, that **My wrath may burn hot against them and I may consume them.** And I will make of you a great nation.' Then Moses pleaded with the Lord his God, and said: 'Lord, why does **Your wrath burn hot** *against Your people* whom You have brought out of the land of Egypt with great power and with a mighty hand?' (Exodus 32: 9–11)

The personalized God experiences embodied emotion. As well as being a metaphor for divine displeasure, fire is also the means for destroying the evil practices that are associated with fire sacrifice. Eventually, it is the human Moses who shares divine wrath when he punishes the idolatry of his followers:

> So Moses' **anger became hot**, and he cast the tablets out of his hands and broke them at the foot of the mountain. Then he took the calf which they had made, **burned it in the fire,** and ground it to powder; and he scattered it on the water and made the children of Israel drink it. And Moses said to Aaron, 'What did this people do to you that you have brought *so* great a sin upon them?' So Aaron said, 'Do not let the anger of my lord become hot. You know the people, that they are set on evil.' (Exodus 32: 19–22)

Here it is Moses' anger that 'becomes hot' just as earlier in the chapter it was the Lord whose 'wrath had burnt hot' – so there is an interdependency of divine and human emotion; it is as if the heat of the anger metaphorically ignites a fire that is also the actual fire transferred from pagan fire sacrifices. Again, there is a blending of metonymy and metaphor, so the indignation shared by God and by Moses (conveyed by metaphor) expresses itself by the use of fire to melt the idols of the non-believers (metonymy). Emotion and actions arising from the emotion together constitute divine purification and moral legitimacy may be framed as: THE CAUSE OF DIVINE ANGER IS THE CAUSE OF A FIRE.

There is particular evidence for this in the sixteen phrases relating to the 'kindling' of 'anger/wrath' of which the following are representative:

> Therefore the wrath of the Lord **was kindled against His people,** So that He abhorred His own inheritance. (Psalms 106: 40)

> And I will make you cross over with your enemies
> Into a land which you do not know;
> For **a fire is kindled in My anger,**
> **Which shall burn upon you.** (Jeremiah 15: 14)

But we should also be aware that metaphoric uses of 'kindle' are not used exclusively with the target of anger but can also describe faith, as in the passage from Ezekiel at the start of this chapter.

Divine anger can also be framed as THE EFFECT OF DIVINE ANGER IS THE EFFECT OF A FIRE; these metaphors are indicated by lower frequency words such as 'smoke', 'melt', 'fuel' and 'extinguish':

> But the wicked shall perish;
> And the enemies of the Lord,
> Like the splendor of the meadows, shall vanish.
> **Into smoke** they shall vanish away. (Psalm 37: 20)
> *As* **smoke is driven away,**
> So drive them away;
> **As wax melts before the fire,**
> So let the wicked perish at the presence of God.
> (Psalm 68: 2)
> They shall mount up **like rising smoke.**
> Through the wrath of the Lord of hosts
> The land **is burned up,**
> And the people shall be as **fuel for the fire;**
> of his own arm. (Isaiah 9: 18–19)
> They shall lie down together, they shall not rise;
> **They are extinguished, they are quenched like a wick.** (Isaiah 43: 17)

These metaphors evoke the effect of actual war, as it is the end point of a conflict that is profiled in the use of words such as 'smoke' and 'extinguished'. Metaphors that describe the cause and effect of divine anger can also be analysed using the force dynamic model introduced in the previous chapter. Figure 4.1 (p.82) shows such an analysis.

The figure represents followers of one of the Abrahamic religions as the agonist. They may accept their religion but there is also a force for them not to accept it by becoming lapsed believers since inertia or apathy may lead them to revert to earlier pagan beliefs and practices. The counter force – the antagonist – is the force of fear of divine punishment; if this fear is greater than their tendency to give up religion, they will continue to follow the religion. The conceptual frame shown here may be summarized as FEAR OF DIVINE PUNISHMENT IS A FORCE.

Clusters of fire metaphors that are oriented to the effect of fire occur in the form of prophecies. These utterances are directives: language that aims to change behaviour – in this case, warnings about the consequences that will arise should behaviour not change. Predictions about God's anger serve the rhetorical and ideological purposes of warning those who are considering rejecting the monotheism of Judaism. Note the future forms of the verb:

> By the wrath of the LORD Almighty the land **will be scorched** and the people **will be fuel for the fire**; they will not spare one another. (Isaiah 9: 19)

FORCE A

ANTAGONIST:
fear of divine punishment: fire

AGONIST: followers of Abrahamic Religions:
flammable material

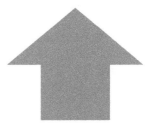

FORCE B

INERTIA:
tendency of believers to revert to
earlier beliefs and pagan practices.
Tendency of material to remain in
same state

**Figure 4.1** Force-dynamic model for divine punishment

The LORD Almighty will come with thunder and earthquake and great noise, with windstorm and tempest and **flames of a devouring fire**. (Isaiah 29: 6)

The LORD will cause people to hear his majestic voice and will make them see his arm coming down with raging anger and **consuming fire**, with cloudburst, thunderstorm and hail. (Isaiah 30: 30)

See, the LORD is **coming with fire**, and his chariots are like a whirlwind; he will bring down his anger with fury, and his rebuke **with flames of fire**. (Isaiah 60: 16)

I will enslave you to your enemies in a land you do not know, for my anger **will kindle a fire that will burn** against you. (Jeremiah 15: 14)

Linguists analyse these claims using the concept of modality: the potential for language to express levels of probability, necessity or desirability. Here fire metaphors contribute to prophetic discourse: there is a high level of modality in describing the fatal consequences of not heeding God's word. A predominant feature of prophetic discourse is that it removes any doubt as regards their certainty that their prophecies will be realized and their commitment to the necessity and desirability of these prophecies. The prophets draw on force dynamics to guarantee the absolute certainty that God will punish those who do not follow him and are convinced that it is right that he should do so. As upholders of the divine will, their position as authorities is dependent on the certainty with which their views are expressed: it is strong language to express a level of conviction that is appropriate to their sense of destiny and divine validation. In prophetic discourse, making a prediction is equivalent to ensuring that it will happen. The Prophets' legitimacy as enforcers of the divine will was dependent on their ability to eliminate doubt among potential followers.

It is a question of interpretation as to at what point a fire term shifts from being a symbol of the divine will to a metaphor. In these divine predictions fire is best thought of as a symbol because (from the perspective of theological hermeneutics) the fire here is an actual fire that expresses the divine will, rather than a metaphoric fire. In symbol, the meaning is intrinsic to the symbol, so that what the symbol represents *is* its meaning; metaphor evolves from symbol when there is either some linguistic signalling of two separate concepts between which the metaphor mediates. Metaphor relies on some cognitive distance between the original and the implied meaning of the metaphor vehicle. As we have seen, one way this is done is when an abstract divine entity such as a God is attributed with emotions such as anger that are normally human.

Metaphor can also arise from when a milder language develops out of the discourse of divine punishment. This occurs when fire is used to describe emotions other than anger. The expression 'their hearts melted with fear' occurs twelve times in the Bible; these are metaphors because there is cognitive distance between physically melting and when human feelings are described as 'melting'. It is based on the conceptual representation: THE EFFECT OF AN EMOTION IS THE EFFECT OF A FIRE. Unlike divine anger, the powerful emotion of fear is human rather than divine:

Then even the bravest soldier, whose heart is **like the heart of a lion, will melt** with fear, for all Israel knows that your father is a fighter and that those with him are brave. (2 Samuel 17: 10)

I am poured out like water, and all my bones are out of joint. **My heart has turned to wax; it has melted** within me. (Psalms 22: 14)

However, when divine emotion is expressed the metaphoric meaning of 'melt' is intensified. The following account of divine anger draws on the industrial image of furnaces:

Therefore thus says the Lord God: 'because you have all become dross, therefore behold, I will gather you into the midst of Jerusalem. As men gather silver, bronze, iron, lead, and tin into the midst of a furnace, to blow fire on it, to melt it; so I will gather you in My anger and in My fury, and I will leave you there and **melt you.** Yes, I will gather you and **blow on you with the fire of My wrath,** and **you shall be melted in its midst.** As silver is melted in the midst of a furnace, **so shall you**

**be melted in its midst**; then you shall know that I, the Lord, **have poured out My fury** on you. (Ezekiel 22: 19–21)

These intense metaphors draw on the functional sense of 'melt' as in smelting down metal. In the smelting frame, the status of humans is reduced to that of inanimate entities and the metaphor emphasizes the intensity of heat and is framed as: THE LEVEL OF TEMPERATURE FOR THE INTENSITY OF EMOTION and THE LEVEL OF INTENSITY OF AN EMOTION IS THE LEVEL OF INTENSITY OF A FIRE. The smelting image blends the intensity of divine anger with the intensity of the suffering that will be inflicted on the non-believer.

An indicator of metaphor is the word 'like' – although technically this indicates a simile – it may also indicate that a symbol has become a metaphor. Emotional state metaphors based on intensity are frequently expressed by the phrase 'burn *like* fire' which occurs eighteen times in the Bible, as in the following: 'circumcise yourselves to the LORD, circumcise your hearts, you people of Judah and inhabitants of Jerusalem, or my wrath will flare up and burn like fire because of the evil you have done – *burn with no one to quench it*' (Jeremiah 4: 4). What is noticeable is a shift from symbol to metaphor in the writing of the Prophets, who, by the use of the predictive future were rhetorically motivated to influence their audience through the scare tactics shown in Figure 4.1. Their use of fire metaphors for intensity enhances the status of their own voice and contributes to the awe in which they would be held as mediators between divine anger and a fearful humanity. These fire metaphors associate the outcomes that would arise from divine displeasure with the results of defeat in war – in both cases the effect will be the same: annihilation. Some of these metaphors constitute exhortations, or verbal forces, for their audience to modify their behaviour – or risk the consequences. However, in other instances fire metaphors occur in the context of describing communication itself – that is the processes through which the divine message is spread; in these cases it is the action of fire, that is its tendency to spread, that becomes salient.

## Speaking in tongues

The ongoing influence of prophetic voice is in communities where it continues to satisfy a psychological need. Particular insight into this is provided by the religious phenomenon associated with Pentecostalism, known as glossolalia or 'speaking in tongues'. This occurs when individuals are empowered to speak in diverse language of which they had no previous knowledge; for believers such vocal expression is viewed as a manifestation of the divine.[5] Typically, communities where Pentecostalism flourishes are those where there is a stronger need to forget, if only temporarily, the mundane social and economic pressures of everyday life – finance, health, family concerns and so on. It is perhaps no coincidence that Pentecostalism thrived originally in poorer areas of Western industrial cities and subsequently in African American communities in the USA and in the African Independent Church. The charismatic appeal of the messianic myth of Martin Luther King was greater in communities experiencing social and economic difficulties. Christians who believe in this exceptional use of human sound are known as 'charismatics' and Pentecostal Christianity is an influential force within the Evangelical movement. The Pentecostal movement was originally inspired by an event recorded in the Acts of the Apostles:

> And suddenly there came a sound from heaven, as of a rushing mighty wind, and it filled the whole house where they were sitting. Then there appeared to them **divided tongues, as of fire,** and one sat upon each of them. And they were all filled with the Holy Spirit and began to speak with other tongues, as the Spirit gave them utterance. (Acts 2: 2–4)

Here the onset of the Holy Spirit is symbolized by the tongue 'as of fire' that ushered in the ability to overcome the barrier of language. Subsequent testimonies to the phenomena of speaking in tongues satisfy the yearning for a return to the time of the prophets, the sense that the Holy Spirit is immanent and present – rather than condemned to ancient history. It is closely related to prophecy:

> But now, brethren, if I come to you **speaking with tongues**, what shall I profit you unless I speak to you either by revelation, by knowledge, by prophesying, or by teaching? (1 Corinthians 14: 6)

The conceptual basis for the expression 'tongues of fire' which metaphorically associates language with fire, arises from associations both between the physical shape of the human tongue and the physical shape of flames and between the effect of fire and that of language. There is some precedent for this association in the Old Testament:

> Behold, the name of the Lord comes from afar, **Burning with His anger**, And His burden is heavy; His lips are full of indignation, And His tongue **like a devouring fire.** (Isaiah 30: 27)
> **'Is not My word like a fire?'** says the Lord, 'And like a hammer that breaks the rock in pieces?' (Jeremiah 23: 29)

In these metaphors language is associated with fire ('his tongue' and 'my word') with the idea being that those who spread the word of God have the same force as the divine will. Just as fire is a symbol of God's power, so the frame DIVINE LANGUAGE IS FIRE connects the power of fire with the influence of language. In such prophetic language, the speaker is *compelled* to speak as a vehicle of God:

> Then I said, 'I will not make mention of Him, Nor speak anymore in His name.' But His word was in my heart **like a burning fire** Shut up in my bones; I was weary of holding it back, And I could not. (Jeremiah 20: 9)

Just as fire comes from God, so fire metaphors are the weapons with which the Prophets overcome non-believers. The language that connects the voice of God with the voice of his self-appointed prophets is characterized by fire metaphors:

I was mute with silence, I held my peace even from good; And my sorrow was stirred up. **My heart was hot** within me; While I was musing, **the fire burned.** Then I spoke with my tongue: 'Lord, make me to know my end, and what is the measure of my days, that I may know how frail I am. (Psalms 39: 2–4)

Metaphors that are limited to the semantic field of fire alone are relatively rare in the New Testament and the majority refer to fire as a symbol of divine anger. This is because New Testament metaphors are predominantly based on the source domains of light and plants (see Charteris-Black 2004: 181) and Table 4.1 (see p.75) showed twenty-six instances of 'lamp'. They draw on fire only when one of the attributes of fire, its ability to produce light, is profiled – as for example in the following:

Nor do they **light a lamp and put it under a basket, but on a lampstand**, and it gives light to all who are in the house. (Matthew 15: 5)

  If then your whole body is full of light, having no part dark, the whole body will be full of light, **as when the bright shining of a lamp gives you light**. (Luke 11: 36)

Light-based metaphors – with images of lamps that would have contained fire – are quite extensive in the New Testament and I have previously summarized them using the conceptual representations: SPIRITUAL KNOWLEDGE IS LIGHT and JESUS IS THE LIGHT (ibid.: 189).

  However, if we restrict analysis to the core fire lexicon, and treat 'light' as a separate semantic field from fire, then we find that it is another attribute of fire that is profiled in New Testament metaphors: its tendency to spread. As we found at the start of this section, the most important fire symbolism in the New Testament was the onset of glossolalia – the experience of early Christian Communities of speaking a range of sounds, apparently from other languages, that is often referred to as 'speaking in tongues':

'Phrygia and Pamphylia, Egypt and the parts of Libya adjoining Cyrene, visitors from Rome, both Jews and proselytes, and Arabs – we hear them *speaking in our own tongues* the wonderful works of God.' So they were all amazed and perplexed, saying to one another, 'Whatever could this mean?' (Acts 2: 10–12)

This linguistic experience of the Holy Spirit has led to the growth of the Pentecostal movement that takes its origin and inspiration from this Biblical account. As we saw earlier, the reference in Acts is to 'divided tongues, as of fire' (Acts 2: 3). If we think of this image, we realize that it is partly an appearance-based metaphor: the shape of a flame resembles that of a human tongue in that it has wide base and becomes more pointed towards one end. But there is also a deeper meaning based on our conceptualization of fire: that it is simultaneously unitary and unifying – when fire is burning it divides into flames in its extremities. A flame can be solitary – as in a candle – but is also a dynamic unifying phenomenon: though flames have a separate individual shape, they are made of the same fire. The use of a candle to ignite another in the ceremonies of Hanukkah and the Holy Fire symbolizes the unifying role of religion. Similarly, language is something that both occurs individually – as in thought and reflection – and socially to bring people together. It is fire as a means of making the solitary flame into something unifying that is taken up when fire is used as a metaphor for religious communication drawing on the frame DIVINE LANGUAGE IS FIRE. This is then less dependent on the force dynamic language of the prophets implied by FEAR OF DIVINE PUNISHMENT IS A FORCE.

The powerful appeal that speaking in tongues has for Pentecostal movement can be compared with an earlier narrative in the Bible: the Tower of Babel:

> Now the whole earth had one language and one speech .... But the Lord came down to see the city and the tower which the sons of men had built. And the Lord said, 'Indeed the people *are* one and they all have one language, and this is what they begin to do; now nothing that they propose to do will be withheld from them. Come, let Us go down and there confuse their language, that they may not understand one another's speech.' So the Lord scattered them abroad from there over the face of all the earth, and they ceased building the city. Therefore its name is called Babel, because there the Lord confused the language of all the earth; and from there the Lord scattered them abroad over the face of all the earth. (Genesis 11: 5–9)

Here linguistic diversity is a form of divine punishment, a confusion that sets people apart from each other and prevents them from sharing a common purpose. So the image of fire as something that spreads and unifies disparate elements became symbolized by speaking in tongues. Here language replaces fire as a means for communication of a divine presence. Glossolalia is a form of second layer of meaning where meaning arises from the interpretation placed on a 'real' event by those who are present, sometimes relying on other experts to interpret the signs. We could infer that the attribution of meaning to language-like behaviour is a semantic extension of the same signification that was originally attached to fire symbolism in the stories of the Burning Bush or the Pillar of Fire, and that the notion of tongues of fire became an image that blended together these earlier symbolic appeals of fire with later metaphor-based interpretations.

## Summary

In the Abrahamic religions fire was originally employed in relation to the practice of sacrifice. As this practice gave special powers to the fire priests, it developed a rich set of symbolic meanings that can be framed as DIVINE DISPLAY IS FIRE. But a prophetic voice also developed in the Abrahamic religions around the central concept of divine punishment: this was conveyed as a certain outcome for the non-believer and those who offended God; it can be framed as EMOTIONS ARE FORCES and DIVINE ANGER IS FIRE, FEAR OF DIVINE PUNISHMENT IS A FORCE and more generally as THE LEVEL OF INTENSITY OF AN EMOTION IS THE LEVEL OF INTENSITY OF A FIRE. We have seen how this prophetic discourse was characterized by the making of predictions about the future, by powerful imagery as well as with the spreading of the faith. However, this took different forms in each of the religions, so that in Judaism the symbolism of fire carried over to the concept of fire as a symbol of the Chosen People, and there has been an ongoing role for fire in ritual practice of Hannukah. In the Qur'an, this type of symbolic extension was rejected, and fire retained its status as a symbol of divine punishment of the non-believer.

In Christianity the earlier meanings of fire as an instrument of punishment were initially replaced by a set of fire metaphors framed as THE CAUSE OF DIVINE ANGER IS THE CAUSE OF A FIRE; these metaphors imply a God who has the human-like capacity for emotion. Once human emotional responses were attributed to the divine, the experience of the divine could give rise to metaphors expressing feelings of awe framed as THE EFFECT OF AN EMOTION IS THE EFFECT OF A FIRE, as in expressions such as 'their hearts melted'. The emergence of a prophetic voice was characterized by metaphoric expressions of emotional intensity such as 'wrath/fire will burn like fire' based on the frame THE LEVEL OF INTENSITY OF AN EMOTION IS THE LEVEL OF INTENSITY OF A FIRE and metonymies based on THE LEVEL OF TEMPERATURE FOR THE INTENSITY OF EMOTION. The prophetic voice later developed into a system of light metaphors framed on SPIRITUAL KNOWLEDGE IS LIGHT – so that a forgiving and loving God was better understood as a means of illumination rather than as a source of divine punishment. The imagery of fire as a source of inspiration was adopted in some Christian communities that yearned for a return to the prophetic voice framed as DIVINE LANGUAGE IS FIRE. These conceptual frames are summarized in Table 4.4:

**Table 4.4** Fire-based Conceptual Frames in the Abrahamic Religions

| |
|---|
| DIVINE DISPLAY IS FIRE |
| DIVINE ANGER IS FIRE |
| THE CAUSE OF DIVINE ANGER IS THE CAUSE OF A FIRE |
| THE EFFECT OF DIVINE ANGER IS THE EFFECT OF A FIRE |
| THE LEVEL OF INTENSITY OF AN EMOTION IS THE LEVEL OF INTENSITY OF A FIRE |
| FEAR OF DIVINE PUNISHMENT IS A FORCE |
| DIVINE LANGUAGE IS FIRE |

Moving beyond the Abrahamic religions, there were links between Zoroastrianism and Judaism. In 586 BCE, the Babylonian Empire had conquered the Jews and taken their leaders into exile. They were liberated from exile by the Persian King Cyrus; some returned to their homeland while others continued to live in Persia and undergo further exposure to Persian religious influences. A similarity with the Abrahamic religions is the underlying dualism between good and evil that originates in the cosmic division between good and bad angels. As Rose (2011: 88) notes, 'The Talmud states that the names of the angels come from Babylon' and so the distinction between the angels of Light and Good and the angels of Darkness and Evil came from the East. This throws up the possibility that the complex system of light metaphors that distinguishes the Bible from the Qur'an may have originated in Zoroastrianism. There are parallels in the seven days that it took to make the world in Genesis and the seven stages of the Zoroastrian creation narrative. The Day of Judgement and the apocalypse are equivalent to the Last Days of Zoroastrianism.

The Jewish practice of enclosing fire within some type of container for transportation may have been influenced by the Parthian cult of fire. But perhaps the best evidence of contact between Judaism and Zoroastrianism is in the linguistic etymology of the term for a Sacred Fire that was kept enclosed in the temple:

> When the matter (restoring the fire) became known and the king of the Persians heard that in the place where the exiled priests had hidden the fire a liquid had appeared, with which Nehemiah and his people had purified the materials of the sacrifice, the king, after verifying the facts, had the place enclosed and pronounced sacred. (2 Maccabees 1: 33–34)[6]

The liquid referred to here is petroleum, known as 'naphtha', a word arising from a combination of the Persian and Hebrew words for petrol. This shows that Jewish writers were aware of the Zoroastrian concept of Sacred Fire and that there were equivalent fire rituals in both religions.

However, there are differences between Judaism and Zoroastrianiam, as Rose (2011: 89) notes: 'In Jewish ideology, however, Satan and his minions, although adversarial to God, are subordinate to him … unlike Angra Manyu (evil), who is completely separate from Ahura Mazda'. 'In Zoroastrianism fire had a more elevated status as it protected mankind from pollution and – as a force within *all* the creations – symbolized the dominance of good in the struggle with evil. The special symbolic status of fire in Zoroastrianism can best be understood through the distinction between symbol and metaphor, in Judaism, and even more in Christianity, there was a drift from symbol to metaphor, while in Zoroastrianism fire retained its status as a symbol. It is to the Iranian and Indian religions that I now turn.

# Fire in Zoroastrianism

## Introduction: Symbol and metaphor

My main argument in this chapter is that the symbolic role of fire in Zoroastrianism constrains, and even blocks, the use of fire terms as metaphors in Zoroastrian religious texts. This is in contrast to Hinduism where, as we will see in the next chapter, fire terms are often used metaphorically. The symbolic status of fire is a precondition for it being revered in Zoroastrian religious observance, so metaphoric senses of 'fire' in the Avesta, though not impossible, are rare *because fire has an essentially sacred status*. This status is in contrast to early Hinduism where there is extensive use of metaphor in the Rig Veda to describe Agni the God of fire, and even more extensively in the Upanishads. But for Zoroastrians, fire is the *predominant expression of the sacred in daily life* – present in the ever-burning hearth fire in the home, the temple and in the sun. Its role as a potent symbol therefore constrains its use as a metaphor because fire is an actual manifestation of Ahura Mazda, it is no longer simply 'like' God it *is* God and *symbolizes* God. It is the manifest form of 'fire' that provides the most direct access to Ahura Mazda and explains the importance of praying in the presence of fire, offering gifts and sustaining the Sacred Fire.

The argument that Zoroastrianism relies on fire as a symbol while Hinduism develops fire metaphors invites a discussion of the distinction between the terms 'metaphor' and 'symbol' and the implications of this difference for religious viewpoints. A symbol is a 'thing that represents or stands for something else, especially a material object representing something abstract' (OED). It is important to note that the second part of the definition refers to a physical entity, rather than a linguistic form. Although it is a sign because it has meaning by referring to something external to itself, it is a material sign, or 'a thing'. By comparison, a metaphor is a *linguistic* sign that shifts its reference from a more to a less basic entity; it is therefore a word or phrase that changes its sense. In language the term 'sense' refers to meaning that is internal to the language system. The primary distinction between metaphors and symbols is that metaphors represent concepts by using the abstract system of language that includes sets of related senses; by contrast, symbols represent concepts by using material artefacts or icons with an entirely intrinsic meaning that is not dependent on language. However, this does not prevent us from having words that refer to symbols, but these words do not shift meaning; so that if the meaning of a symbol changes, this is not as a result of language and the new meaning would eliminate any previous one; by contrast metaphors retain echoes of earlier senses.

I can illustrate this distinction between symbols and metaphors with reference to the conceptual field of gender. A phallus is a symbol of male potency that has an intrinsic meaning because it represents the part of the male anatomy associated with potency. Evidence of the importance of this symbol as a signifier is that many different cultures have used the phallus as a symbol of male potency: Priapus was an Ancient Greek God of fertility symbolized by an exaggerated phallus and Shiva was worshipped in Ancient India and was symbolized by the Lingam or phallus. But if, colloquially, I refer to someone (male or female) as 'a prick', this is partially a metaphor because it shifts the reference to a person who I dislike – it therefore has reference. I say 'partially' because 'prick' is also a metonymy in which a body part stands for the person: if I refer to someone as 'a prick', I am commenting on the whole person with reference to a part of the body – so the earlier sense of 'prick' is retained. But this use is combined with a metaphor because some negative attributes of masculinity associated with shame are applied to the person unfortunate enough to be referred to in such a way. Proof that the abusive use of 'prick' is a metaphor is because the male sexual organ can be used equally accurately to refer to a man *or* to a woman.

A further point about senses is that they exist in semantic relationships, so the sign 'male' is semantically the opposite of 'female'; the notion of 'opposition' is a sense relationship. However, the use of the phallus as a symbol in a culture does not entail that the culture necessarily has a symbol representing the female sexual organ. The meaning of a symbol is entirely intrinsic: a symbol for male potency does not presume the existence of a corresponding symbol for female fertility.

In contrast to language-based concepts, symbols can have a tendency to *become* the thing they represent. For example, symbols are similar to metonyms as they have a 'stands for' relationship with the entity they refer to – 'The White House' refers to the American government. Here a material entity – a building refers to ('stands for') something more abstract: government. However, this is just shorthand for a concept because nobody thinks that a building actually is the American government. However, for their adherents, religious symbols *become* the entity that they represent and therefore are not simply metonyms. For Muslims, the Qur'an represents the Word of God but it also actually *is* God's word. For Catholics, unconsecrated bread and the wine represents Christ's flesh and blood, but when consecrated in the ceremony of the Eucharist, they actually *become* the flesh and blood of Christ and therefore cease to be metonyms. Catholics do not worship the bread and the wine, but transubstantiation gives these entities an existential holy status. This merging together of the symbol and its referent so that they become *indistinguishable* is crucial to understanding fire in Zoroastrianism: some types of fire do not simply *stand for* God nor do Zoroastrians worship fire itself, but for believers a Sacred Fire may become indistinguishable from the divine.

There is considerable evidence that Hinduism was strongly influenced by Zoroastrianism and in this and the next chapter I undertake a study of fire terms in translations of the surviving core texts of Zoroastrianism and Hinduism. The Indo-Aryan and Iranian language groups diverged during the later third millennium BCE, with the Indo-Aryans moving towards present day India and the Iranians moving towards the Iranian plateau. The earliest Zoroastrian *Gathas* were contemporaneous with the Hindu Rig Veda and both texts formulate a view of paradise that is based on the Airyana Vaejah or 'Aryan expanse' – an area now associated with eastern Uzbekistan, Turkmenistan and other Central Asian Republics. More importantly, they share a common mythology expressed in oral religious poetry characterized by meter, metaphor, poetic syntax and imagery based on the rich common ancestry of pastoralism.

Further evidence of the links between Zoroastrianism and Hinduism is that they revered the same sacred entities; in the relatively short surviving Zoroastrian text known as the Avesta, the sacred plant *haoma* is referred to 125 times, while its equivalent in the Indo-Aryan tradition – *soma* – is referred to 1,544 times in the much longer Rig Veda. In both texts the plant symbolizes endurance, strength and fertility and the imagery of the priestly bards originates in cultural memory of the 'Aryan expanse'. In both texts there is reverence for *haoma/soma* as a plant that symbolized the life force. Both texts also make extensive reference to the sun God Mithra. In Zoroastrian iconography, Mithra is depicted as a solar deity in a two-wheeled chariot pulled by four white horses – the same means of warrior transportation used by the Aryans as they spread to the pastures of the south. There is also considerable evidence in both religions that the functions of an earlier sun deity became divided between two Gods – one higher in status than the other: Ahura Mazda and Mithra in Zoroastrianism and Varuna and Mitra in Hinduism (Varuna was the guardian of the cosmic and moral order and therefore equivalent to Ahura Mazda). In both religions the 'higher' God (Ahura Mazda and Varuna) is referred to first and the 'lower' God – Mithra/Mitra – comes second. Mithra is a significant sun deity and iconography typically depicts him with a solar nimbus around his head and as a bearded warrior holding a spear and a sword. There is therefore highly persuasive textual and iconographic evidence of cultural contact between early Hinduism and Zoroastrianism. It is against a backdrop of shared ancestral memories sustained and transformed by the religious poetic forms of the bards that I now hope to interpret the symbolic and metaphoric meanings of fire in Zoroastrianism and Hinduism.

## Zoroastrianism: Introduction

Zoroastrianism is the ancient religion that takes its name from Zoroaster,[1] who lived around 1200 BCE, and became practiced in the geographical areas now known as Iran and also, after migration from Persia to India following the Arab Muslim incursion towards the end of the seventh century, among the Parsi community of India. It was the religion of the First Persian (Achaemenid) Empire (c.550–331 BCE) founded by Cyrus the Great. Evidence for it comes from an ancient oral tradition, from Ancient Persian monuments and inscriptions and from references in Greek texts. It was also the state religion of the Parthian (Arsacid) Empire (247 BCE–224 CE) and the second Persian (Sasanian) Empire (224–651 CE), so its survival as the religion of Iran extended for a period of around 1,000 years. The Arab conquest from 651 CE onwards led to the replacement of Zoroastrianism by Islam in the latter part of the tenth century. Many fire temples were converted into mosques and many books of the Avesta were 'lost' during this period, but survive in Indian translations. Some of the Avesta was apparently translated into Arabic. Zoroastrianism continues to have a number of adherents in Iran, but, due to the establishment of Islam as the state religion of Iran, has historically enjoyed greater freedom of practice among the Parsi Community in India, which is now much larger than its Iranian equivalent; more recently the religion has migrated to England, Europe, Australasia and North America.

Much of what we know about the early forms of Zoroastrianism has been filtered through Ancient Greek sources from the so-called Hellenistic period, partly because there was a fascination with Zoroaster as the founder of astrology and magic. The Roman historian Pliny the Elder names Zoroaster as the founder of magic. There was an etymological link between the Greek version of the name 'Zoroaster' (as 'Golden Star' or 'living star'; etymology; 'living' zo-; 'star' -astr-) and the mythic belief that he met his death as a victim of a star invoked in magic. Diogenes Laertius calls him 'astrothutes', or 'star-diviner'.

Because of the vagaries of oral transmission and the effect of the Arab incursion and later Turkic and Mongol conquests on written sources, only part of the Avesta survives. The earliest Zoroastrian texts were written in the Avestan language of eastern Iran and are divided into 'Old' and 'Young' Avestan. The Old Avestan texts include a collection of poems known as the Gathas or 'songs' that were orally transmitted for many centuries and whose authorship is attributed to Zarathushtra. These describe the harmonious co-existence of animals (cows, bulls) with humans (herders) within a rich pastoral setting that is often described using metaphor. In the Young Avestan texts, the semi-nomadic pastoral metaphors are augmented by agricultural metaphors as virtuous activities are likened to 'the person who sows the grain, sows Asha' (Vd. 3.30–2). (Rose ibid.). However, since fire has a particular theological and ritual significance, metaphoric uses such as these are relatively rare and this, I suggest, is because of the highly symbolic meaning of Sacred Fire in Zoroastrianism.

## Sacred Fire

There is no living religion for which fire (Av. Atar, MP. Adur/Adar or Ataxsh, NPers. Ātaš) has a greater symbolic meaning than Zoroastrianism. Although Zoroastrians themselves do not always use the term 'Sacred Fire', it is a term that I employed earlier to refer to the feelings of awe and reverence for the divine that are evoked by fire in religious contexts and settings. These include fire temples, religious texts such as the Avesta and ritual ceremonies that require the specialist knowledge of the priests (OPers. 'magi'). The symbolic meanings of Sacred Fire therefore play a vital role in Zoroastrian belief, practice and ritual. As the source of life, fire symbolizes the order (asha) of the universe and fires are kept perpetually burning in many fire temples in Iran and India, where they are maintained by priests and guarded from pollution. Priests have an elevated social status because of their knowledge of what type of fire is required, the appropriate means for igniting, and maintaining a fire, their ability to guard against fire contamination and dealing with fire if it gets 'polluted'. As well as formal religious rituals, there are popular customs based on respect for the creation of fire, for example a flame cannot be blown out but is allowed to 'die' naturally. In the home, great care must be taken not to pollute the Sacred Fire by spilling anything on it, and if this happens accidentally, a penance must be performed.

The veneration of fire involves priestly offerings. This veneration originated in Indo-Iranian culture, but the construction of specific fire temples may have begun later as a counter-move to an alternative temple-cult.[2] Zoroastrian practice involves praying five times a day facing the sun or in the presence of fire (or a *divo*, or electric light) as the symbol of asha/order/right – and of Ahura Mazda; in Persepolis there is an icon showing attendants praying in the presence of fire. The fire temples in Iran (*ateshkadehs*) and in India (*agiaries*) are the primary location of priestly religious observance: some of these fires have been burning for centuries (Rose 2011: 81ff.). There is a fire in the temple of Yazd believed to have been burning continuously since the Arab incursion in the early seventh century. The fire was rescued by priests and kept in their homes until instated in the fire temple that was built in the late nineteenth century, then reconstructed in the 1930s (Rose 2011: 122). The most ancient fire temples in Iran were said to be located on hills in Parthia, Persia and Media. A special status is given to priests, religious experts known as 'magi' in the Greek texts (the origin of the word 'magician'[3]) who, equipped with their knowledge of the appropriate rituals for each type of fire, were intermediaries between mankind and Ahura Mazda and the *yazatas*. The priests then are viewed as an essential force in the maintenance of the religion as is evident in the following invocation:

> And I invoke the most imposing forces of the Mazdayasnian Faith, and the fire-priests I invoke, and the charioteers, the warriors, and the thrifty tillers of the soil. (*Invocations and Dedication*, 3)

Correct observation of fire ritual is viewed as essential to the strengthening of humanity in the struggle between the forces of good and evil. As an element associated with physical force in nature, fire became the means for understanding metaphysical forces. Boyce (1968) offers probably the most detailed account of these rituals:

> By a tradition which is first recorded in post-Sasanian times such a fire is created from embers taken from many fires, including lightning fire, which are purified over and over again before being combined and consecrated …. The Sacred Fire is then carried in procession to be installed in its sanctuary *pad wahrāmīh* 'victoriously'….

The value placed on fire originated in the connection between the sun and fire as conjunct symbols of purity and, because symbols tend, magically, to *become* what they represent, Sacred Fire therefore needed physical protection from contamination by impure entities. The magi would wear a mouth cover, or *padan*, to prevent their breath coming into contact with the fire and menstruating women were required to avoid the fire temple altogether (Rose 2011: 54). Contamination could also arise from incorrect practice of the fire rituals and the following passage refers to the punishment for offenders:

O Ahura Mazda, Thou most bounteous Spirit! W*ho brings pollutions to this (Thy flame) him wilt Thou cover with pollutions (in his turn)*. (Yasna 36.1)

The principle of reciprocity operates – so that whoever pollutes the fire will be polluted. However, those who are 'friendly' to Sacred Fire will be rewarded with extra spiritual strength. Showing respect to fire by offering appropriate sacrifices will also protect the worshipper from death:

To his undoing Grehma, and the Kavis, have long devoted their purpose and energies, for they set themselves to help the liar, and that it may be said, '*The Ox shall be slain that it may kindle the Averter of Death to help us*.' (Yasna 32.14)

Funerary practices further reflect the need to avoid contaminating the fire through cremation and the traditional Zoroastrian practice was to avoid such risks by carrying the body of the deceased on an iron bier to a stone tower where the flesh would be devoured by vultures and the bones bleached by the sun and wind. However, in contemporary Zoroastrianism, cremation is permitted by the use of electric fire. There were also complicated rituals known as 'exalting the fire' to restore purity to polluted fire:

There was further the general ritual of rescuing embers from fires which had been actually polluted (in smiths' shops and the like), purifying them by lighting nine successive fires from these embers, each intermediate one being allowed to go out, and then taking the ninth fire, consecrated by prayer, to a temple fire.[4]

The ritual of multiple successive kindling to purify fire followed by uniting the purified fire with a Sacred Fire brings rewards for the performer of the ritual. Performance gives a theatrical dimension to Zoroastrian fire ritual; the interaction of sound, visual effects and actions contributes to symbolic meaning. Concern about the risk of polluting Sacred Fires explains why nowadays fires, such as the *Atash Bahram* ('Victory Fire') in Yazd, can only be viewed through glass by non-Zoroastrians and in some fire temples, there is a 'hidden' ever-burning fire that is kept separate from the ceremonial fire holder on public display. Boyce describes the limits to which Zoroastrians went during the period when Muslims were seeking to replace their religion by destroying fire temples and extinguishing their Sacred Fire:

Like all the Sacred Fires which survive, these were kept during the centuries of oppression in small mud-brick buildings, looking outwardly like any poor man's house. Moreover, for safety's sake the Iranian Zoroastrians abandoned the custom (maintained by the Parsis) of enthroning a Sacred Fire conspicuously in a central sanctuary, with open grills, and instead hid it away in a small side-room, entered by a tiny cupboard-like door. Priests crept through this door to serve the fire, but the laity gave up entirely the joy of seeing it, for the better chance of its survival. If Muslims broke into the temple, all that they saw in its main hall was an empty fireholder, so that it seemed as if the Sacred Fire were already extinguished.[5]

The symbolic power of Sacred Fire was also because it was the prime symbol of authority and power in Ancient Persia. Middle Persian and New Persian texts recount the use of fire judicially – for example in the story of *Vis and Ramin*, or that of Siyavash, the accused passes through fire to prove his innocence; other texts mention the pouring of molten metal on the chest, such as was said to be the case of the high priest under Shapur II (309–379 CE), Adurbad-I Mahrasapndan. If the accused died, this proved he was guilty; if he survived, this proved innocence by protection from Mithra. On the cosmic scale, the perfecting/renewal of the world will be marked by fiery judgement, when the metals in the mountains will melt to create a flowing river that will only punish the wicked: the righteous will not be burnt.

There is iconic evidence of the cognitive association between fire and authority in many symbols connecting 'fire' with 'authority'; these include the symbol of a king alongside a winged sun disc and were inherited from the Assyrian and Babylonian cultures; they imply that the king inherited his authority from the sun. Offerings made to the fire were a symbolical re-enactment of the homage that was due to the king: fire as the embodiment of divine power was therefore the basis for force on earth. Among the earliest evidence of sites of worship are at Pasargadae where there are two, three-stepped fire-holders. As Rose (2011: 47) notes, 'The three-stepped fire-holder from the Ancient Persian period is the most enduring icon of the Zoroastrian religion, being continuously illustrated down to the present age.' It is significant that the king is depicted standing before a fire-holder and both the king and the fire-holder are located on three-stepped plinths (for example, at Naqsh-e Rostam and Persepolis). But the head of the king is higher than the fire-holder, and the subject peoples are depicted on a horizontal rank *below* the king and the fire-holder. Above them is a winged sun disc and crescent moon, implying that king and fire are mediators between ordinary humanity and 'Ahura Mazda' (the 'Wise Lord'), and that fire is the source of divine order that transmits to the king. Later, iconic evidence of the link between fire and authority is found in the fire holder depicted on the reverse of the coins of the Sasanian kings.

The equivalence between Sacred Fire and divinely based dynastic authority is re-enacted in ritual. From Parthian times onwards, it seems that a fire known as 'the regnal fire', was ignited on the king's accession and kept burning for the full duration of his life and then extinguished at his death; similar fires were sustained for the duration of a whole dynasty. The status of fire as a symbol of divine authority/presence and cultural identity explains why in 1742 an original Sacred Fire known as the *Iran Shah*, said to have been carried by the Parsis from Iran, was relocated to Udwada in Gujarat, where it continues to symbolize the connection of the Parsi community with Iran (Rose 2011: 191).

## Fire in Zoroastrian cosmology

In most versions of the Zoroastrian creation myth the world was created in seven stages: a sky made of stone, water, earth, the original Plant, the Bull, the First Man and finally the source of fire – the sun. As the last creation, fire was present as a life-force in the other six creations (Boyce 1997: 241). Fire was believed to be the gift of the Lord of Wisdom – Ahura Mazda – one of three great ethical beings Ahuras ('Lords'). Its position as the dominant symbol for the religion is indicated by the occurrence of the expression 'Fire, O Ahura Mazda's son' twenty-eight times in the surviving Avesta and there are nine further instances of 'Fire of Ahura Mazda'. The use of vocative forms to address a divinity characterizes both early Vedic and Avestan religious poetry, in which rhythmic incantation communicates the sacred status of fire.

In Zoroastrianism Ahura Mazda (good) is engaged in a cosmic struggle with Angra Maniyu (evil). The social origin for the ambiguous role for fire as a force for both creation and destruction was probably in the conflict between Zaruthushtra's own people and neighbouring groups that became projected into a struggle between good and evil. Repeated disputes between 'us' and 'them' became symbolized in a belief system characterized by a never-ending struggle between the forces of good and evil. Within this dualism Ahura Mazda became God, but not a fully omnipotent God, because existing alongside was his evil twin – Angra Mainyu with whom he is engaged in a cosmic struggle. Ahura Mazda has the advantage of assistance from his Holy Spirit, Spenta Mainyu, and six other great Amesha Spentas. Each of the Spentas inhabits and protects one of the seven creations. Good will eventually overcome evil, but only after a final cosmic battle when fire will melt the metals in the mountains and a flood of molten ore will destroy the wicked; only then will the orderly rule of Ahura Mazda be fully established again in the spiritual and material realms. The status of fire in Zoroastrian Cosmology is summarized in Figure 5.1:

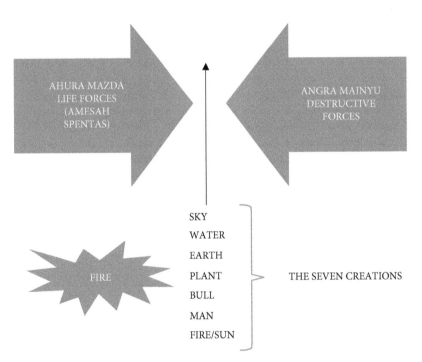

**Figure 5.1** Dualist forces in Zoroastrian cosmology

## Sacred Fire in the Avesta

The meaning of fire in Zoroastrianism arises from language and symbol. I have already provided a brief overview of the symbolic meaning of fire and in this section I develop this further by describing some of the fire-based Zoroastrian rituals. But first I will undertake a linguistic and conceptual analysis of 'fire' in the surviving collection of holy texts known as the Avesta. The Avesta is comprised of the Old and the Young Avestan texts – a collection of writings originally in the language known as Avestan. Old Avestan is relatively uncommon, comprising the five Gathas (now divided into seventeen sections), the Yasna Haptanhaiti and two holy manthras; these texts were composed orally around the later second millennium BCE at about the same time as the Sanskrit Rig Veda. The much longer Young Avestan includes the Videvdad and the Yashts (hymns) and a compilation of interpretations and explanations of the Old Avestan by poets and scholars. The surviving Avesta is therefore a mixture of these sources and consists of liturgies, hymns and prayers and has been translated into English to produce a translation of 41,125 words; this English translation is employed for the analysis of the fire lexicon.[6] My procedure was to compile a single text containing the surviving Avesta and to analyse the core fire lexicon.

There are only a few fire terms from the core lexicon in English translations of the Avesta; the terms that occur more than four times are 'fire' (87) and flame (5). There is no translation equivalent of 'fiery', 'torch', 'spark' or 'extinguish'; as a result the only type of fire present to any extent in the Avesta is what I have termed 'natural fire' and which, for the reasons given earlier, is better described as 'Sacred Fire'. What is remarkable is the absence of metaphor. Because fire symbolizes truth and righteousness, metaphoric uses of 'fire' would detract from this symbolic role. Consider how, in an expert's account of the struggle between good and evil, fire *becomes the entity that it symbolizes*:

> Spenta Mainyu (Holy Spirit) & six other great beings assist God in battle with Evil. One of these is Asha Vahishta, 'Best Truth/Righteousness' and is fire. All those who seek to live according to Asha should try to bring the great Amesah Spentas into their hearts and bodies by caring for their physical creations by philanthropy. (Boyce 1997)

Here 'Best Truth/Righteousness' is not just *likened* to fire but actually *is* 'fire'. The status of fire as a symbol is explained in the following:

> Then shall I recognize thee as strong and holy, O Mazda, when by the hand in which thou thyself dost hold the destinies that thou wilt assign to the Liar and the Righteous, *by the glow of thy Fire whose power is Right*, the might of Good Thought shall come to me. (Yasna 43.4)

Here 'the glow of thy fire whose power is Right' is not a metaphor for Mazda but equates divine power with fire; as we saw earlier, fire inherits the divine authority that in turn transfers to the ruler. Until the appearance of Mazda at the Last Judgement, fire symbolizes the actual triumph of good and the promise of immortality and is invoked to assist followers to be truthful in the struggle against evil. Fire is the ultimate symbol of goodness and virtue – it is not a metaphor because it is actual fire that has this meaning, rather than any linguistic representation of fire (since metaphor is by definition a linguistic phenomenon).

Although spiritual meaning is only directly accessible from the presence of fire as a divine symbol rather than from fire metaphors, frames can be proposed that capture this symbolic meaning; I suggest that it is preferable to rely on the metonymic 'stands for' frame for these symbolic meanings as follows:

FIRE FOR TRUTH
FIRE FOR JUSTICE
FIRE FOR GOODNESS

These three concepts – truth, justice and goodness – are all translations of the concept of 'Asha'. Other frames are

FIRE FOR LIGHT
FIRE FOR PURIFICATION
FIRE FOR KNOWLEDGE

Since in Zoroastrianism fire is the primary material means for bringing reverence into ordinary live, the symbolic meaning of fire is therefore strongly oriented to awe. Unlike the Abrahamic religions, the categories of natural, functional and organic fire cannot fully convey the symbolic meaning of fire. As with the Christian 'burning bush' narrative, Zoroastrianism is better understood through the concept of 'Sacred Fire': fire as it is enacted and performed in Zoroastrian ritual.

Zoroastrians pray five times a day in the presence of fire and the principal act of worship is known as the 'Yasna' (this is also the name of the primary liturgical collection of Avesta texts). The Yasna is a lengthy ceremony that is now performed daily by two Zoroastrian priests only in certain fire temples in India. Its purpose is to strengthen both the spiritual and material dimensions of the world; it is therefore a form of cosmic regenerating ceremony, to assist in the overcoming of evil (Angra Mainyu); it guards the world against chaos. As well as chanting the Avestan manthras, the priests make offerings to the fire. Although the Yasna is viewed as literally saving the world, it is performed with reference to a set of symbols: the fire symbolizes the orderly/true/right way of Ahura Mazda, the metal accoutrements represent the divine creative power/sky and the sacred area (pavi) upon which the Yasna takes place symbolizes the earth. Milk, butter and the sieve made out of hair from a white bull symbolize the animal kingdom – and good thought. haoma/hom – a sacred drink made from a plant – symbolizes the original Plant – and 'immortality'. Consecrated water symbolizes the waters of the world (and 'wholeness') and the priests represent humanity ('beneficent spirit').

As Boyce (1997: 246) explains, 'The temple cult of fire was, it seems, instituted as late as the fourth century BCE. It, too, centres on an ever-burning wood fire, set either in the top of an altar-like pillar or in a metal vessel.' The grade of Sacred Fire reflects in the level of attention required in its preparation. There is not a single Sacred Fire but *three* types of fire. The highest grade of a fire is called the *Atash Bahram* ('Fire of Victory'); this is the only grade that can be placed in a Zoroastrian fire temple and therefore requires the most attention in its preparation. The rituals are so detailed and involve so many people that they can take as long as a year to complete. The fire has to be generated from sixteen different sources including lightning (natural fire) and fire as used by trades that require fire ('functional fire'), as well as fire used in cremation. These different fires need to be purified by the appropriate priests, of whom at least thirty-two are required for the satisfactory consecration of the *Atash Bahram*. The fire is consecrated in a ceremony of enthronement in which four priests carry it while others hold a canopy over it, and once enthroned it is 'served with royal ritual and deep reverence' (Boyce 1968: 53).

The second grade of fire is known as the *Atash Adaran* ('Fire of Fires') and the third grade of fire – the *Dadgah* fire ('Court Fire') – is one that is kept in the home and does not require special priestly consecration. What is significant about the Zoroastrian typology of fire is that it shows how key concepts are evident from naming practices. The grades of fire are lexicalized and those who are members of the speech community would be fully aware of the meaning and signification of each grade and its position within a community of religious practice. But within this symbolic system of fire each grade of fire retains its distinct symbolism: 'once a Fire of any grade is consecrated, it has its own entity, and must be maintained, as far as is possible, for ever. It is indivisible; and each new Sacred Fire must therefore be consecrated separately and individually' Boyce (1968: 55). The meaning of symbols is intrinsic.

The Avesta provides textual evidence of the sacred status of fire; for example in the following vocative address in which fire terms are in italics:

TO THE FIRE.
I offer my sacrifice and homage to *thee, the Fire,* as a good offering, and an offering with our hail of salvation, even as an offering of praise with benedictions, to thee, *the Fire,* O *Ahura Mazda's son!* Meet for sacrifice art thou, and worthy of (our) homage. And as meet for sacrifice, and thus worthy of our homage, may'st thou be in the houses of men (who worship Mazda). Salvation be to this man who worships thee in verity and truth, *with wood in hand,* and Baresman ready, *with flesh in hand,* and holding too the mortar. (Yasna 62.1)

The vocative form implies that fire is alive and can hear; animacy is reinforced by the description 'O Ahura Mazda's son!' There is no reason to interpret this as a metaphor any more than when Jesus is referred to as 'the son of God'. Clearly, the fire is to be venerated through the practice of supplying it with fuel in the form of wood. The nurturing of the fire is facilitated by the use of twigs (often tamarisk or pomegranate), which are used to 'feed' the fire. The priests will also hold 'baresman/ barsom' (bundles of metal rods) which are iconographic symbols of fire offerings and serve as metonyms for the magi, so that when a figure is depicted in a sculptured relief as holding a 'baresman', this implies his status as priest. Possession of the knowledge of the prescribed way of making offerings to Sacred Fire was a defining feature of the magi, and the dependency of fire on their attention is emphasized by the use of metaphor in descriptions of the intricate fire rituals:

> And may'st thou **be (ever) fed with wood** as the prescription orders. Yea, may'st thou *have thy perfume* justly, and *thy sacred butter* without fail, and *thine andirons* regularly placed. **Be of full-age as to thy nourishment, of the canon's age as to the measure of thy food,** O Fire, Ahura-Mazda's son! (Yasna 62.2)

References to 'fed' and other human-related attributes such as age imply that this is an extended metaphor – a personification of fire; this might remind us of the Anglo-Saxon riddle 'He will meekly serve both men and women, if they know the trick of looking after him and feeding him properly' – although of course there is a crucial difference in the speech act, since praising God is different from entertaining humans. The status of fire as something alive and requiring nurturance is reinforced by 'nourishment' with valued entities (perfume, butter) leading to the maturity of a 'full-age'. Similarly, the ritual care of fire requires the adjustment of the iron supports known as 'andirons'.

The use of an imperative form throughout is a form of positive politeness in that it reflects the solidarity of the poet-worshipper with the subject of his supplication. The attributes of fire are invoked so that they magically transform the supplicant's capabilities:

> Give me, O Fire, Ahura Mazda's son! A speedy glory, speedy nourishment, and speedy booty, and abundant glory, abundant nourishment, abundant booty, an expanded mind, and nimbleness of tongue for soul and understanding, even an understanding continually growing in its largeness, and that never wanders, and long enduring virile power. (Yasna 62.4)

Fire is requested to grant the same powers to the supplicant as those that he has provided it with. There is shift of transitivity so that whatever is done by the supplicant, will magically be returned to him. Just as the fire has been fed with honour, so fire will provide honour, abundant food as well as spiritual advantages such as intellectual attributes ('an expanded mind'), communicative gains ('nimbleness of tongue') and sexual prowess (a 'virile power'). This inversion of agency is at the core of magical thinking. Sacred Fire is

> an offspring sure of foot, that never sleeps on watch [not for a third part of the day, or night], and that rises quick from bed, and likewise a wakeful offspring, helpful to nurture, or reclaim, legitimate, keeping order in men's meetings, (yea,) drawing men to assemblies through their influence and word, grown to power, skilful, redeeming others from oppression, served by many followers, which may advance my line (in prosperity and fame), and (my) Vis, and my Zantu, and (my) province, (yea, an offspring) which may deliver orders to the Province as (firm and righteous rulers). (Yasna 62.5)

The authority of the king, and those to whom he delegates, is legitimized through a figure of speech that equates the attributes of fire with the attributes of those in authority. The authority inherited from fire provides the legitimacy for keeping order, delivering orders and rescuing 'others from repression'. The authority that originates in the Sacred Fire is enforced by hyperbolic religious invocation:

> And may'st thou grant me, O Fire, Ahura Mazda's Son! That whereby instructors may be (given) me, now and for evermore, (giving light to me of Heaven) the *best life of the saints, brilliant, all-glorious*. And may I have experience of the *good reward, and the good renown*, and of the *long forecasting preparation of the soul*. (Yasna 62.6)

As well as the vocative address to Fire, there is an appeal formed in superlatives and an isocolon: 'the good reward, and the good renown'. Agency dramatically shifts to the Sacred Fire so that it becomes an active agent who makes provision for the spiritual and material needs of followers:

> The Fire of Ahura Mazda addresses this admonition to all for whom he cooks the night and morning (meal). From all these, O Spitama! he wishes *to secure good care, and healthful care* (as guarding for salvation), *the care of a true praiser*. (Yasna 62.7)

The needs of the material bodies of worshippers for food and health are made prominent and Sacred Fire is requested to make provision for these. In this switching of agency, the needs of Zoroastrian followers now become the passive entity that is observed by the Sacred Fire:

> At both the hands of all who come by me, I, the Fire, keenly look: what brings the mate to his mate (thus I say to him), the one who walks at large, to him who sits at home? We worship the bounteous **Fire, the swift-driving charioteer.** (Yasna 62.8)

'The swift-driving charioteer' is a metaphor that also occurs in the Rig Veda. This 'war' metaphor relates to a ritual practice symbolizing spiritual struggle that is described in this account of the transporting of a Victorious fire: 'the priests escorting it carry swords and maces; and after the ceremony some of these weapons are hung on the sanctuary walls, to symbolise the warrior nature of the fire, and its ceaseless fight against all that is opposed to aša "truth"'.[7]

An appropriate state of mind and attention to ritual are equally important as preconditions for prayers to be answered:

> And if this man who passes *brings him wood brought (with good measure that is) with sacred care*, or if he brings the Baresman *spread with sanctity*, or the Hadhanaepata plant, then afterwards Ahura Mazda's Fire will bless him, contented, not offended, and in (its) satisfaction (saying thus). (Yasna 62.9)

It is not any wood that can be cast on the fire but only wood 'brought with sacred care' and the bundles of twigs need to be 'spread with sanctity' for prayer to be efficacious.

It is also worth noting that the purpose of ritual practice is to obtain the blessing of the Sacred Fire:

> As a blest soul may'st thou live through thy life, the nights which thou shall live. This is the blessing of the Fire for him who brings it wood (well) dried, sought out for flaming, purified with the earnest blessing of the sacred ritual truth. (Yasna 62.10)

Sacred Fire exists in symbiosis with its worshippers: it is the recipient of the spiritual energies of Zoroastrians and in return blesses them for these efforts. As recipient and benefactor, as taker and giver, target and source, Sacred Fire is all encompassing.

The practice of fire worship permeates Zoroastrianism and is perhaps the best example in any religion of the special sacred status that can be attached to fire in the creation of discourses of awe. As well as the equivalences between Ahura Mazda and Sacred Fire that permeate the Avesta in vocative supplications and religious observance through fire rituals, there is also extensive iconographic and archaeological evidence of the sacred status of fire. As the prototypical symbol of force in nature, it became an archetype for the expression of metaphysical forces. This is further supported by social practice; for example the major fire celebrations include No Ruz ('New Day') celebrating the seventh creation (i.e. fire) and the triumph of good. The demise of the Persian Empire in AD 642 led to a migration of the survivors to India and so at this point I will turn to Hinduism.

# 6

# Fire in Hinduism

## Introduction

One of the distinctions between discourses of awe and authority is that discourses of authority adopt the symbols of awe for the purpose of self-legitimacy; this phenomenon is best understood as a process by which symbols – with their intrinsic meanings distinct to a particular ritual system – are transformed into metaphors which enable them to be transported to other discourses, carrying with them the magical power that has accrued to them through their sacred status. The symbols and rituals associated with discourses of awe emerge when religions are geographically isolated and become inward looking, but metaphor facilitates the transfer of meaning between different religions and enhances their potential to spread. In Chapter 4 we saw how the light metaphors that were present in Judaism were taken up in the New Testament and served a vital role in spreading the word. In this chapter we see how many of the symbolic meanings of fire in Zoroastrianism are also evident in early Hindu symbolic ritual practice but then how they became transformed through metaphor in the latest of the Vedas: the Upanishads.

Hinduism is best viewed as a religious tradition as practiced in India rather than as a single coherent religion; as Weightman (In Hinnells 1997: 261) points out:

> Hinduism displays few of the characteristics that are generally expected of a religion. It has no founder, nor is it prophetic. It is not creedal, nor is any particular doctrine, or dogma or practice held to be essential to it. It is not a system of theology, nor a single moral code, and the concept of god is not central to it. There is no specific scripture or work regarded as being uniquely authoritative. Finally, it is not sustained by an ecclesiastical organization. Thus is difficult to categorize Hinduism as a 'religion;' using normally accepted criteria.

For the purpose of understanding the meaning of 'fire' metaphors and symbols in Hinduism I have focused on the Vedas, a corpus of religious literature written in the period 1500–500 BCE. The Vedas were written in Indo-Aryan, which is a subfamily of the Indo-European languages. In this chapter I will consider the earliest Veda, known as the Rig Veda, and the latest Veda, the Upanishads, to identify differences and similarities in how fire metaphors are used in these two texts. The Rig Veda was concurrent with, and influenced by, Zoroastrianism; we have seen that there is common reference to a sacred plant known as haoma/soma, and a Sun God known as Mithra/Mitra, so I will also compare references to fire in the two Hindu texts with the Avesta. The influence of fire originates in the spread of the Indo-Aryan branch of the Indo-European language that moved from Europe into India via West Central Asia. The Indo-Aryans were pastoral nomads and warriors who migrated from the steppes of eastern Europe in the second millennium BCE; they were one of a number of Indo-European tribes that spread out from the steppes, some entering northwest India through the upper reaches of the Indus river, while others migrated into Iran.

As in Zoroastrianism, fire has a vital role in Hindu symbolic ritual, for example in purification rituals when the body of a deceased person is cremated on a funeral pyre. This symbolism is also evident in Hindu iconography; for example statues of Vishnu show him holding a quoit in one hand and a conch in the other: both are decorated with flames. When depicted as Nataraja, king of the dancers, Shiva is depicted within a circle of fire that represents the universe and his left hand holds fire. Fire is the symbol for the cyclical pattern of divine creation and destruction that is also symbolized by the movements of the dancer: fire and dance together represent the alternating forces of order and chaos. However, there is a dramatic shift during this period from elaborate metaphors to describe the fire god Agni in the Rig Veda, to more abstract fire metaphors in the Upanishads: in these metaphors language and spiritual knowledge, rather than a fire god, become the topic of metaphor.

## The Rig Veda

The Rig Veda is a collection of 1,028 hymn-poems probably written during the period 1500–1200 BCE (known as *sūkta* from *su-ukta* 'well said') for use in religious fire rituals conducted by priest-poets while they offered sacrifices to the gods. Its English translation[1] is approximately 306,416 words long. The hymn-poems are addressed to various gods to grant favours such as 'long life, riches, sons, cattle and victory in battle' (Staal 2008: 4). Agni, the god of fire is among the most important to whom invocations are made; there are 1,970 references to 'Agni' – and he is addressed in about 200 or 20 per cent of the hymn-poems. The early Aryans who migrated into the area of the Indus in their two-wheeled, horse-drawn chariots brought with them a set of beliefs and myths in which offerings to a Sacred Fire was the primary form of religious practice:

> At its simplest and probably earliest level, the Indo-Iranian sacrifice was a hospitality rite to the gods. Gods of special concern to the worshipper were invited to a celebration in their honour centred around a fire built on a special altar. The attendant gods seated themselves on grass strewn around the altar as a place of honour, and there received offerings as guests. The most important offerings were placed in the fire and were conveyed to the other gods by Agni, the god of the fire. It was around these offerings that the Vedic ritual developed. The divine guests were honoured not only with food and other gifts but with hymns of praise recited by a poet-priest …. A typical sacrificial hymn contained an invocation in a tone of friendliness, reverence, or fear depending on the god and the poet's relation to him; praise of those great qualities and actions of the god called to mind by the

occasion; and a request, either implicit or direct, that the god used his powers for the benefit of the sacrificer. Within this general framework, the poet demonstrated his skill in combining mythical reference, figurative or symbolic allusions, and metrical form to create a statement that captured both the truth about the god and the spirit of the occasion. (Hopkins 1971: 14)

The eloquence of these priest-poets, or bards, is evident in the rhetorical homage that is paid to Agni, the fire God, in the following hymn addressed to him. The whole passage is structured around a complex extended metaphor that depicts the fire god as a powerful and benevolent ruler:

NE'ER waxeth faint the Immortal, Son of Strength, since he, the Herald, hath become Vivasvan's messenger. On paths most excellent he measured out mid-air: he with oblation calls to service of the Gods. (1)

Never decaying, seizing his appropriate food, rapidly, eagerly through the dry wood he spreads. His back, as he is sprinkled, glistens like a horse: loud hath he roared and shouted like the heights of heaven? (2)

Set high in place o'er all that Vasus, Rudras do, immortal, Lord of riches, seated as High Priest. Hastening like a car to men, to those who live, the God without delay gives boons to be desired. (3)

Urged by the wind he spreads through dry wood as he lists, armed with his tongues for sickles, with a mighty roar. Black is thy path, Agni, changeless, with glittering waves! When like a bull thou rushest eager to the trees. (4)

With teeth of flame, wind-driven, through the wood he speeds, triumphant like a bull among the herd of cows. With bright strength roaming to the everlasting air: things fixed, things moving quake before him as he flies. (5)

The Bhrgus established thee among mankind for men, like as a treasure, beauteous, easy to invoke. Thee, Agni, as a herald and choice-worthy guest, as an auspicious Friend to the Celestial Race. (6)

Agni, the seven tongues' deftest Sacrificer, him whom the priests elect at solemn worship, The Herald, messenger of all the Vasus, I serve with dainty food, I ask for riches. (7) (Hymn LVIII, Agni)

Agni is attributed with a range of attributes of a powerful ruler such as riding on a horse (verse 2); rapid motion (verses 3 and 4); masculine power and potency (verse 5) and friendship (verse 6). The hymn also includes several other stylistic characteristics that are typical of the Rig Veda, including the use of syntactic fronting: the making more prominent of Agni's attributes by positioning them at the front of the sentence – rather than in their normal position following the main verb. For example, the following phrases are put at the start of the sentences: 'never decaying' (verse 2); 'with teeth of flame' (verse 5); 'with bright strength roaming' (verse 5); 'the seven tongues' deftest Sacrificer' (verse 7). The rhetorical effect of bringing Agni's ruler-like qualities to the front of the sentence is to provide emphasis, or markedness; this is an alternative to leaving them in an unmarked position *after* the main verb of the sentence which would have been another option for author and translator alike.

But it is perhaps extended metaphor that best characterizes the style of the Rig Veda; in the hymn above Agni is referred to as 'son of strength' (verse 2), as 'herald' (verses 1 and 6), as 'messenger' (verses 1 and 7), special 'guest' or 'friend' (verses 6). This implies the metaphor frame FIRE/ AGNI IS A PERSON. Although normally the use of the adverb 'like' is associated with a simile, in this passage 'like' (as in 'like a horse' (2); 'like a car' (3); 'like a bull' (4 and 5); 'like as a treasure' (6)) indicates that we are dealing with metaphor rather than with symbol. As we saw in the previous chapter, symbol merges with its referent so that they become *indistinguishable* but the presence of the adverb 'like' highlights that this is a language-based image that is being created – a metaphor. There are of course other simile-based metaphors in which the two elements are fully merged in the metaphor, for example 'teeth of flame' (5) and 'seven tongues deftest Sacrificer' (7).

Some stylistic features of the hymn to Agni characterize the whole Rig Veda; for example 'Thee, Agni' (6) is a vocative form and 'thee O Agni' occurs twenty-five times in the text. This way of explicitly addressing the recipient of a sacrifice or offering is found in a range of similar vocative forms: 'O Agni' occurs 330 times; 'thou O Agni' or 'O Agni thou' (thirty-three times). But it is perhaps the extended personification that best characterizes the style of the Rig Veda. Similar personifications to the ones identified above permeate the Rig Veda; for example Agni is referred to as 'Son of strength' seventy-nine times; 'Herald' fifty-nine times; 'Messenger' forty-eight times and 'Guest' forty-six times. As with the Greek gods, Agni is made more accessible to worshippers by framing him as human, with human qualities. These personifications are further sustained by motion verbs that could be used to describe either human movement or the motion of fire; Agni is typically a forceful agent that is 'hastening', 'rushing' or 'speeding', leading the hearer to think of fire as a forceful person. Indeed, rapid motion verbs and travel-related metaphors are very common throughout the Rig Veda, as summarized in Table 6.1. The frequency column shows the overall frequency

**Table 6.1** Fast motion and travel metaphors for 'fire' in the Rig Veda

| Mode of transport/ motion verb | Example of 'fire' metaphor | Frequency |
|---|---|---|
| Car | Great, high, auspicious, Agni, is thy shelter. **Ascend today thy splendid car, o Agni**, in splendour, with the holy ones around it. | 571 |
| Swift | **Keen and swift Agni,** thousand-eyed, chaseth the Raksasas afar … | 362 |
| Chariot | Let us not in thy friendship, Agni, suffer harm. When to **thy chariot thou hadst yoked two red steeds and two ruddy steeds,** wind-sped, thy roar was like a bull's. | 266 |
| speed | Let songs of ours **speed Agni forth like a fleet courser in the race** … | 223 |
| travel | Fair, **Agni, is thy long-known path to travel:** yoke for the juice thy bay, thy ruddy horses, Or red steeds, Hero-bearing, for the chamber. | 101 |
| rush | **Like Agni's blazing rush** he may not be restrained, whomever Brahmanaspati takes for his friend. | 78 |
| hasten | Singers with Soma pressed have made thee, **Agni, hasten to the feast** … | 61 |

of the root form of the word shown and the middle column illustrates how it is used poetically as a metaphor to describe the fire god Agni.

Here, among the tropes we find a complete frame of cultural reference for the physical actions and material world that were typical of the life and culture of the nomadic Aryan tribes: moving across the mountains and plains by horseback, travelling with massive carts towed by oxen and fast horse-driven chariots. They also suggest another frame: FIRE/AGNI IS A FORCEFUL TRAVELLER. Invading and conquering as they went, it is little wonder that there are also numerous metaphors that refer to Agni as a powerful male animal: typically a bull or a steed, since these were the prototypical symbols of masculine strength and power, as shown in Table 6.2.

These animals are dynamic active agents and, following a similar cultural trope, worshippers of Agni are described as cows or 'milche-kine'. The cow is a symbol of a valued but passive entity that would follow and obey rather than lead. So, worshippers of Agni are positioned in typically feminine roles in relation to a dynamic masculine god. Table 6.3 summarizes these.

In the Rig Veda, rather than being a source domain of metaphor, we find that the fire god Agni is the primary *target* (or topic) of metaphor, so that other culturally valued entities in the Aryan world view – steeds, chariots, bulls and 'milch-kine' – are used as metaphors to pay homage to Agni. These, along with continued use of honorific forms of address, show evidence of the frame FIRE/AGNI IS AN HONOURED PERSON. However, I will present later evidence that the priests also attributed to themselves a dynamic role as active leaders.

The final group of metaphors to describe Agni relate to appearance, and these typically profile physical attributes such as colour and light, as summarized in Table 6.4.

These metaphors imply the frame FIRE/AGNI IS A BRIGHT COLOURFUL LIGHT. What is poetically significant in the discourse of these metaphors is how they accumulate through repetition and interact with each other to produce an exceptionally high metaphor density: metaphor is stacked upon metaphor, like bouquets of flowers

**Table 6.2** Masculine animal metaphors for 'fire' in the Rig Veda

| Animal | Frequency | Example as fire metaphor |
|--------|-----------|--------------------------|
| steed | 557 | Agni the Priest, they glorify with homage. Him who spread out both worlds by Law Eternal they balm with oil, **strong Steed who never faileth.** |
| bull | 261 | **The oil-anointed Bull,** Agni who hears, who sends as God full hero strength to him who freely gives. |

**Table 6.3** Domestic animal metaphors for 'fire' in the Rig Veda

| Animal | Example as fire metaphor | Frequency |
|--------|--------------------------|-----------|
| cow | My praises, Agni, go to thee, **as the cows seek the stall to meet,** The lowing calf that longs for milk. | 334 |
| milch-kine | At night and morning, Agni, have they called to thee, **like milch-kine in their stalls lowing to meet their young.** | 42 |

**Table 6.4** Light metaphors for 'Fire' in the Rig Veda

| Descriptive attribute | Example as fire metaphor | Frequency |
|---|---|---|
| light | So thou, O Agni **rich in light, beaming like Surya with thy rays** Boldly demolishest the gloom, | 487 |
| bright | Bright Agni **with the bright car**, Lord of green domains, Vaisvanara dweller in the floods, who *finds the light*, | 370 |
| dawn | Agni **hath shone forth when the dawn is breaking**. Yea, he hath been acknowledged as most mighty, the joyous Priest of men, the youthful Agni. He, spreading o'er the earth, *made light around him*, and grew among the plants with blackened fellies … | 319 |
| shine | **Agni shines far and wide** with lofty splendour, and by his greatness makes all things apparent. | 222 |
| golden | Him let us worship, set within the dwelling, **the red, the golden-hued, the all resplendent.** | 127 |
| red | The Son of Strength, the Child of Heaven, the signal of sacrifice, **red Agni** will I worship. Unlike in form are **the Red God's two Daughters:** one is the Sun's, and stars bedeck the other. | 122 |
| resplendent | Upward, O Agni, rise thy flames, pure and **resplendent, blazing high**, Thy lustres, fair effulgences. | 73 |

being offered as sacrificial offerings to the listener. In the following hymn the basic metaphor of FIRE/AGNI IS AN HONOURED PERSON is then elaborated with animal metaphors, transport metaphors and appearance-based metaphors such as light metaphors:

> WITH sacrifice exalt **Agni who knows all life**; worship him 'with oblation and the song of praise, **Well kindled, nobly fed;** heaven's Lord, Celestial Priest, who **labours at the pole where deeds of might are done.**
>
> At night and morning, Agni, have they called to thee, **like milch-kine in their stalls lowing to meet their young. As messenger of heaven thou lightest all night long** the families of men. **Thou Lord of precious boons.**
>
> Him have the Gods established at the region's base, **doer of wondrous deeds, Herald of heaven and earth; Like a most famous car,** Agni **the purely bright,** like Mitra, to be glorified among the folk.
>
> **Him have they set in his own dwelling,** in the vault, **like the Moon waxing, fulgent,** in the realm of air. **Bird of the firmament,** observant with his eyes, **guard of the place as 'twere, looking to Gods and men.**
>
> May he **as Priest** encompass all the sacrifice, men throng to him with offerings and with hymns of praise. **Raging with jaws of gold among the growing plants, like heaven with all the stars, he quickens earth and sky.** (HYMN II. Agni)

The effect of these cumulative metaphors is hyperbolic, as there is an excess of imagery and colour. As was the case in the use of metaphors in the Anglo-Saxon poem Beowolf, the intention of the priestly bards in the use of these extended and elaborate metaphors was surely to enhance their own status as skilful rhetoricians whose services were in much demand. These poetic invocations made their role as bards necessary for the successful outcome of a sacrifice. The patron seeking a priest would be doing so with the purpose of gaining the usual desirable outcomes of health, wealth, family (especially sons) and cattle. Agni was therefore himself endowed with the qualities that patrons would be hoping to *gain for themselves* through sacrifice force and power. The most common adjectives occurring before Agni are shown in Table 6.5.

Taken together, these personifications imply the frame FIRE/AGNI IS A POWERFUL LEADER. The worship of Agni therefore brought considerable benefit both to patron and animator of the sacrifice since it is likely that no effort would be spared in seeking out these skilled bards and rewarding them appropriately:

> It was most common practice for at least the most renowned priests to travel long distances to serve such patrons. Other priests gathered at their sacrifices to observer and occasionally participate, and priests often competed for honours in the skill of their sacrificial performances. Innovations in the sacrifice, additional details and embellishments, and new ritual skills were readily adopted by fellow professionals to increase the effectiveness find value of their services ... Acquired bodies of hymns, details of ritual procedure, and training in performance of sacrifices passed in this way from one generation to another, creating normative patterns for the priestly community as a whole. (Hopkins 1971: 15)

As a result of the influence and power a distinction emerged between the *Shrauta* rites that involved the extensive use of Vedic hymns chanted by priests and the *Griah* or domestic rites that could be performed by any Aryan householder. It was in the more elaborate *Shrauta* rites that three different types of fire evolved and sacrificial rites became increasingly complex (and reminiscent of those of the Zoroastrian fire temples). As both the God of fire and the sacrificial fire itself, Agni had a special status as the means through which communication was made with all the other gods. Agni

**Table 6.5** Powerful human attributes in metaphors for 'Fire'/'Agni'

| Positive attribute | Example | No. |
|---|---|---|
| victorious | THY blessed majesty, **victorious Agni, shines brightly** in the neighbourhood of Surya. | 7 |
| immortal | **Immortal Agni, shining far, enrobed with oil**, well worshipped, bears the gifts of sacrifice away. | 6 |
| youthful | The Gods, most **Youthful Agni, have made thee, inflamed,** the bearer of oblations and the messenger. | 6 |
| mighty | Whoso with toil and trouble brings thee fuel, **serving the majesty of mighty Agni, He, kindling thee at evening and at morning,** prospers, and comes to wealth, and slays his foemen. **Agni is Master of sublime dominion, Agni is Lord of strength and lofty riches.** | 5 |

came to have a ubiquitous presence that permeated the belief system as indicated by both the high frequency of references in the Rig Veda and the numerous extended and elaborated metaphors.

However, we need to see these metaphors within the context of their use in ritual. The purpose of ritual is to control the world and metaphors contributed to the enactment of priestly power. Priests were required for the highly ritualized *Shrauta* rites; they would require three fire altars constructed of earth, sand, pebbles and wood that were constructed, each in a particular shape and in a particular location that had a symbolic meaning: the three fires symbolized the heaven, the earth and the atmosphere between them. The *Āhavanŷa*, or celestial fire, was square to represent the sky and located to the East of the sacrificial zone; this fire was for making the sacrificial offering. The *Gārhapatya*, or terrestrial fire, was round to represent the earth and located to the west of the *Āhavanŷa*; this fire was used to prepare food for the sacrifice. The *Dakṣina*, or atmosphere fire, was semi-circular in shape to represent the atmosphere between heaven and earth and located to the south of the sacrificial zone was; its function was both to ward off hostile spirits and to make offerings to the ancestors.

This complex fire ritual required more than one priest since Agni was present in each of the celestial, the terrestrial and atmosphere fires and it is likely that the growing status of the priesthood went hand-in-hand with an expanded role for Agni – who came to stand for many of the other Gods because even when a particular sacrifice was not made to Agni, fire was the medium through which it was made. The multiplicity of fires therefore reinforced priestly authority leading to the emergence of a super-deity. Agni is referred to as a 'Leader', a 'Director' and as a 'ministering Priest' as well as overruling other gods such as Indra, Vishnu and Mitra. Given the representation of Agni as a forceful being, the implication is that the wealthy should not stint when making offerings, since if they do it is unlikely that their prayers will be answered; as the hymn says:

> We dare not stint the sacred food of Mitra and Varuna upon the back of Agni.
> **Agni is Sovran Lord of wealth, Agni of great prosperity:**
> May he bestow these gifts on us.
> Hither to us, rich pleasant Dawn, bring many things to be desired,
> **Thou who hast ample store of wealth.** (HYMN LV, 7–9)

The implication of exhorting the wealthy to be generous to Agni is that they should *pay equal respect to his priests*: there are many such exhortations to respect the authority of the priesthood in the Rig Veda. This is typically by using a metonymy in which just as the priest stands for the God, so that God stands for the priest:

> **Thou shonest forth, O Agni**, after former dawns, all visible, O rich in light. Thou art our help in battle-strife, **the Friend of inan, the great high priest in sacrifice.**
>     Like Manu, we will stablish thee, **Agni, performer of the rite**, Invoker, **ministering Priest,** exceeding wise, the swift immortal messenger.
>     When as the **Gods' High Priest**, by many loved, thou dost their mission as their nearest Friend, Then, like the far-resounding billows of the flood, thy flames, **O Agni, roar aloud.** (HYMN XLIV, 10–12, Agni)

This implies a frame FIRE/AGNI STANDS FOR THE FIRE-PRIEST. At times, it is not clear whether the hymns are paying homage to the Gods *or to the priests who conduct the rituals of fire sacrifice.* In the following, it is not really clear whether it is the priests or Agni who the people are being exhorted to make friends with:

> Let us not in thy friendship, Agni, suffer harm.
>
> We will bring fuel and prepare burnt offerings, reminding thee at each successive festival. Fulfil our thought that so we may prolong our lives. Let us not in thy friendship, Agni, suffer harm.
>
> His ministers move forth, the guardians of the folk, protecting quadruped and biped with their rays. Mighty art thou, the wondrous herald of the Dawn. Let us not in thy friendship, Agni, suffer harm.
>
> Thou art Presenter and the chief Invoker, thou Director, Purifier, great High Priest by birth. Knowing all priestly work thou perfectest it, Sage. Let us not in thy friendship, Agni, suffer harm. (HYMN XCIV, 3–6, Agni)

The frame FIRE/AGNI IS A FRIEND seems to blend with FIRE-PRIEST FOR FRIEND. The following appears to be as much a prayer to priests as it is to the great fire god Agni:

> **Agni is Priest, the great High Priest of sacrifice,** most swift in act: **He knows the rite in constant course.**
>
> **Oblation-bearer, deathless, well inclined, an eager messenger,** Agni comes nigh us with the thought.
>
> Ensign of sacrifice from of old, Agni well knoweth with his thought to prosper this man's aim and hope.
>
> **Agni, illustrious from old time, the Son of Strength** who knows all life, The Gods have made to their Priest.
>
> **Infallible is Agni,** he who goes before the tribes of men, A chariot swift and ever new.
>
> Strength of the Gods which none may harm, subduing all his enemies, **Agni is mightiest in fame.** (Hymn Xl, 1–6, Agni)

Hymns such as these pay tribute to Agni as a force and emphasize the need for knowledge of the correct sacrificial rites, so that the efficacy of prayers to the Gods is dependent on the priesthood and their knowledge of the fire rituals. By invoking Agni, priests are in reality asserting their own power as his medium. Through such means the boundary between awe and authority slips away so that the divine message is articulated through the human voice in the form of the priestly hymn:

> The priest as ritualist clearly had both enormous power and a great responsibility. By his knowledge of *brahman* and by his supervision of the ritual he preserved the universal order. Knowledge and purity were essential for his role. He was under obligation to speak the truth, since his very words has creative power. As a participant in the great ritual drama that reproduced the order of the cosmos, he largely defined man's place in the cosmos. Set apart from other men, he alone had

access to the means by which all men might obtain their desired goals. (Hopkins 1971: 34)

However, the focus on the fire God Agni gradually diminishes because of a gradual realization that a sacrificial culture alone would not satisfy man's aspirations for immortality. The practice of sacrifice on a literal fire was an engagement in a material phenomenology in which an object was transformed into another state using ritual practice: but what if this other state offered by priestly sacrifice provided no guarantee that man's desires would be satisfied? The Brahmans advocated an internalization of the cult of ritual actions so that spiritual knowledge could be accessible to the individual without reliance on the specialist knowledge of priests; this new understanding is found in the Upanishads.

## The Upanishads

The body of texts known as the Upanishads demonstrate intense philosophical speculation about the nature of the self, the cosmos and the relation between self and cosmos. They originate from around the sixth century BCE and are considered to be the final part of the Vedas and are concerned, broadly speaking, with the mystical experience of cosmic unity. According to Staal (2008: 174) they reject ritual and mantras as an encumbrance and embrace pure knowledge. The English translation of the Upanishads is 357,478 words in length and therefore slightly longer than the Rig Veda. They describe an inner journey that involves a rejection of, and even a turning away from, the world to explore the potential of the human self (known as *ātman*) to experience itself as a single cosmic power, or Brahman. Originally this retreat involved withdrawal to the forests, and the earlier Upanishads, the Āranyakas, were known as the 'Forest Books' because they were taught and practiced in the forests. A key feature of the Upanishads is the emphasis on a spiritual reality that underlies appearance.

Through meditation and ascetic practices such as yoga, the ego can be liberated to attain liberation from *samsara* – the cycle of birth and rebirth. But individual existence continues as long as the effects of individual actions remain. The universal law of cause and effect, or *karma*, can only be broken through good actions and knowledge. The rejection of the world that is described in the Upanishads precedes the period of classical Hinduism in which spiritual beliefs became prescribed by religious laws and were reflected in the duties and obligations of the four classes ('*varnas*') headed by the Brahmans (teachers or priests). The early Vedic definition of Brahman was not associated with a particular social group but with the power of sacrifice, sacred speech and knowledge of ritual, but this was gradually replaced by a concept of Brahman as the understanding of pure essence. In some texts Brahman is conceived as a supreme deity while in others he is a more abstract impersonal force referred to as 'the One' (an expression that occurs 238 times in the Upanishads) as in the following:

The sage fulfils his duty with the realization, 'I am *the one* Brahman';
(Brahman is) the ground of all, non-dual, supreme, eternal, of the essence

of being, intelligence, and bliss, beyond the range of word and mind. There shine not the forms of the moon and the sun; the winds blow not; and none of the gods are there. This divinity alone shines forth as being, pure by itself, free from rajas. (Annapurna Upanishad IV-30-31)

The Upanishads frequently represent speech itself as a form of spiritual practice with references to breath and speech; speech-related verbs in the Upanishads are compared with those in the Rig Veda in Table 6.6.

References to speech occur in the Rig Veda but their frequency is much higher in the Upanishads, where there is emphasis on solitary meditation and the chanting of mantras – typically 'Om' – as well as an emphasis on the importance of breath and breathing, rather than priestly ritual, as a means to enlightenment. The connection between language and the divine is evident in the following:

O Emperor. *The organ of speech*, O Emperor, is the supreme Brahman. The *organ of speech* never leaves him who, knowing thus, meditates upon it, all beings eagerly come to him, and being a god, he attains the gods. (Brihadaranyaka Upanishad IV-i-2)

The fire of ritual sacrifice becomes less important and fire becomes the predominant trope for language itself:

This deity after taking away death, the evil of these gods, next carried them beyond death. *It carried the organ of speech*, the foremost one, first. *When the organ of speech got rid of death*, **it became fire. That fire, having transcended death, shines beyond its reach.** (Brihadaranyaka Upanishad I-iii-11-12)

Although fire retained its earlier symbolic meaning, in the Upanishads the fire of ritual sacrifice becomes less important and fire becomes the predominant trope for language through fire metaphors:

**Fire entered into the mouth** *taking the form of the organ of speech.* (Aitareya Upanishad I-ii-4:)

This deity after taking away death, the evil of these gods, next carried them beyond death. It carried *the organ of speech*, the foremost one, first. When *the organ of speech* got rid of death, **it became fire. That fire, having transcended death, shines beyond its reach.** (Brihadaranyaka Upanishad I-iii-11-12)

**Table 6.6** Frequency of 'speech' verbs in Upanishads and Rig Veda

|  | breath | speak | speech | mantra | chant | om | tell | utter |
|---|---|---|---|---|---|---|---|---|
| Upanishads (357,478 words) | 320 | 150 | 419 | 434 | 64 | 1,075 | 124 | 63 |
| Rig Veda (310,904 words) | 22 | 128 | 65 | 0 | 9 | 1 | 36 | 37 |

Through *the organ of speech* – **through fire,** which is the (real) priest called Hotr. The sacrificer's *organ of speech* is the Hotr. *This organ of speech* **is fire; this fire is the Hotr; this (fire) is liberation; this (liberation) is emancipation.** (Brihadaranyaka Upanishad III-i-4)

*The divine organ of speech from the earth* **and fire permeates him.** That is *the divine organ of speech* through which whatever he says is fulfilled. (Brihadaranyaka Upanishad I-v-18)

The earth is the body of that *organ of speech*, **and this fire is its luminous organ.** And as far as *the organ of speech* extends, so far extends the earth and **so far does this fire.** Heaven is the body of this mind, and **that sun is its luminous organ.** (Brihadaranyaka Upanishad I-v-11-12)

In these extracts it seems that fire is a metaphor for both speech and language, and that language, in turn, serves as a metonymy for spiritual knowledge. It is possible to infer the underlying frames LANGUAGE FOR SPIRITUAL KNOWLEDGE and SPEECH IS FIRE. The word that translates as 'fire' becomes a root metaphor for the cosmic principle of Brahaman – the universe:

**This world, O Gautama, is fire, the earth is its fuel, fire its smoke, the night its flame, the moon its cinder, and stars its sparks.** In this fire the gods offer rain. Out of that offering food is produced. **Man, O Gautama, is fire, the open mouth is its fuel, the vital force its smoke, speech its flame, the eye its cinder, and the ear its sparks.** In this fire the gods offer food. Out of that offering the seed is produced. **Woman, O Gautama, is fire.** In this fire the gods offer the seed. Out of that offering a man is born. He lives as long as he is destined to live. Then, when he dies they carry him to be offered in the fire. The fire becomes his fire, the fuel his fuel, the smoke his smoke, the flame his flame, the cinder his cinder, and the sparks his sparks. In this fire the gods offer the man. Out of that offering the **man emerges radiant.** (Brihadaranyaka Upanishad VI-ii-15)

Here there is the frame MAN IS FIRE. As in Zoroastrianism, fire is the element in the natural world for accessing metaphysical experience because it is a force that acts on man. The basis for this elaborate metaphor that represents impregnation as a fire is that sexual desire is a force – one that acts on man and woman alike. So, fire is the element in nature that comes to symbolize the mysterious origins of life because, like desire, it is an overpowering force. Fire is also the intermediary for how man communicates with God: speech is the fuel for a fire, language is the flame and hearing is metaphorically the spark; this implies that the frame SPEECH IS FIRE can be generalized to SPIRITUAL COMMUNICATION IS FIRE.

This extended fire metaphor frame is a means for understanding the cyclical relationship between God, man and the Universe: their co-existence in harmony with each other is expressed by equating them all with fire. When the body is burned at death, the human spirit – metaphorically represented as fire – is returned to the actual fire of the funeral pyre. The merging of fire as a metaphor for the spirit with the fire of the funeral pyre symbolizes the conflation of the divine with the human body. Fire provides a complex system of metaphors and symbolizes the union of God and man as their mutual essence is 'fire'. The Supreme Truth or Brahman is understood through the metaphor frame of fire and realized through the ritual fire of religious practice:

> That which is the sun who abides in the clear sky, is the Vasu (the air that moves) in the mid-region, is the fire that dwells in the sacrificial altar and in the domestic hearth as the guest, is the fire that shines in men and in the gods, as the Soul, is the fire that is consecrated in the sacrifice, is dwelling in the sky as air, is born in water as submarine heat, is born in the rays of the sun, is the fire that is directly seen as the luminary, and is born on the mountain as the rising sun – that is the Supreme Truth, the Reality underlying all.

Here the fire that is a 'guest' in the altar and the domestic hearth – the actual fire of ritual and functional fire of the home – symbolizes the Sacred Fire that is present in man, the Gods and the sun. When the human spirit becomes enlightened through meditation, it merges with the Brahman – the ultimate cosmic power, or Supreme Truth. Fire is employed both symbolically and metaphorically to express this merging of divine elements because its nature is to destroy boundaries between entities and, in so doing, unify them.

If we watch a fire, we see that, over time, those elements that appeared as at first separate – the coals, or the logs, or even the flames themselves – are no longer separate but combine. The theological position expressed by this fire metaphor is a non-dualistic one because it argues that God and the soul are of the same substance – in this case fire. This merging of multiple entities could also be expressed by other metaphors, such as water, since drops are separate but combine into a unitary whole when they enter a river which, in turn, flows into an ocean. For example, in the following we see a blend of both a fire metaphor ('melt') and a water metaphor: 'purified of the blemish of manifold thought, in the pristine and pure condition, he became one, with *all (worldly) tendencies* **melting away like water-drop in the ocean**.' The rejection of dualism is clearly expressed in the following:

> In reality I am the same infinite Brahman even when I am experiencing myself as a finite self owing to Ignorance. Now by the onset of knowledge I am really that Brahman which is my eternal nature. Therefore I realise this identity by *making myself, the finite self, an oblation into the fire of the infinite Brahman* which I am always.

It is significant here how Brahman is described as equivalent to a 'fire', though difficult, perhaps, to work out whether this is a metaphoric use of 'fire'.

Religion is largely a complex system of metaphors, but it is not always easy to distinguish between metaphoric and literal senses of 'fire' metaphors since religion also often involves different individuals perceiving different degrees of metaphoricity. When compared with the Avesta, we find that the Rig Veda and the Upanishads share a preponderance of natural fire lexis; however, the Upanishads have a wider range of word types and tokens for functional fire and organic fire, with words such as 'spark', 'kindle' and 'fuel', for which translation equivalents were found only to a very limited extent, in the Avesta. This may be because in the Avesta the symbolic meaning of Sacred Fire blocks the emergence of fire metaphors, whereas there is clear evidence of metaphor in the Upanishads. One of the characteristics of metaphors in religious discourse is that they are systematic and their meanings contribute to the coherence of religious texts. This is particularly the case with fire metaphors in Hinduism because – since their meaning is concerned with the unitary – they are typically *not* introduced individually but as part of a complex, poetic and mystical discourse characterized by repetition and by extended and elaborated metaphors. Before we examine this complex use of metaphor, it is first necessary to identify the main conceptual frames in the Upanishads.

SPIRITUAL DEVELOPMENT IS FIRE is a frame that models the understanding and explanation of mystery:

> The father said to him, 'Dear boy, just as when a single ember of the size of a firefly left over from a large burning fire, is made to blaze up by adding straw and it burns much more than before, **even so, dear boy, of your sixteen parts, only one part remained, and that being nourished by food, has been made to blaze up;** and by that you perceive the Vedas now. Hence, dear boy, the mind is **made up of food,** the Prana ('life force') is **made up of water,** and **speech is made up of fire.**

The generating power of spiritual knowledge that leads to an understanding of the Vedas is modelled on the stages of a fire, from ember to blaze. So, fire becomes the means of accessing the divine – whether symbolically through ritual practice, or metaphorically through the language of the Vedas; in the following there is direct reference to 'wisdom-fire' or the 'fire of wisdom':

> He whose engagements are all devoid of desires and purposes and whose actions have been burnt *by the fire of wisdom,* him the wise call a sage.
>     As *kindled fire reduces fuel to ashes,* O Arjuna, so does *wisdom-fire reduce all actions to ashes.*

The two concepts of 'fire' and 'wisdom' are blended in a single compound noun phrase. Just as in offering a sacrifice to a ritual fire, there is a merging of the offering with the flame itself so fire and wisdom become mutually interchangeable. This leads to the notion of the spirit as 'cosmic fire':

> The Vaisvanara wind overpowers the Antaryami wind and vice versa. In between these two warmth is exuded – the warmth is the spirit – **spirit is cosmic fire.** Also this has been stated elsewhere. **The fire within is the cosmic fire, the inner fire** by which food is digested.

There is indeed a strong sense of embodiment in Hinduism that rejects a body–mind dichotomy so that spiritual knowledge blends into the body, just as fire blends into the hearth:

> Just **as a razor might be hidden in a razor-case or as fire in the fireplace,** even so this self of intelligence has entered this bodily self up to the very hairs and nails.

Vyana moves in the ear, the eye, the loins, the ankles, the nose, the throat and the buttocks. Apana moves in the anus, the genitals, the thighs, the knees, the stomach, the seeds, the lions, the calves, the navel and **the seat of the anus of fire.**

The mind is at the tip of the neck, intellect at the face, egoism at the heart, self-conscious mind at the navel. Bone, skin, nerves, hair, flesh are parts of earth; urine, phlegm, blood, semen are of water; hunger, thirst, laziness, delusion and **sex of fire.**

Through the transforming practice of yoga the body becomes a manifestation of the spirit so that it merges with spiritual knowledge. The body contains spiritual knowledge but requires 'igniting' by consciousness. Taking this metaphor further, the body itself becomes the fuel that is a precondition for the 'fire' and becomes something that can be sacrificed in the pursuit of supreme knowledge.

Such metaphor elaborations are connected to each other through merging the frames: MAN IS FIRE, COMMUNICATION IS FIRE, LANGUAGE FOR SPIRITUAL KNOWLEDGE, SPIRITUAL DEVELOPMENT IS FIRE. If all these entities are understood in terms of fire, this entails that they are all equated with each other, so that man, communication and spiritual knowledge all become united under the single impersonal absolute known as the Brahman, and this impersonal absolute is framed as fire. We find such merging of metaphors with different topics but the same source domain of 'fire' in another passage reflecting a similar extended metaphor as the one above:

The institutor of the sacrifice, in the case of the sacrifice offered by a Sannyasin who has attained supreme knowledge in the manner already described, is his own Self. His faith is his wife; his body is his sacrificial fuel; his chest is his altar; his hairs are his holy grass; the Veda he has learnt is his tuft of hair; his heart is his sacrificial post; his desire is his clarified butter; his anger is his animal to be immolated; his austerity is his fire; his sense-control is his immolator; his gifts are his dakshina; his speech is his Hotir priest; his breath is his Udgatir priest; his sight is his Adhvaryu priest; his mind is his Brahman priest; his hearing is his Agnid priest; the span of his life is his preparatory rite; what he eats that is his oblation; what he drinks that is his drinking of soma juice; when he delights himself that is his Upasad rite; when he walks, sits and stands that is his Pravargya rite; that which is his mouth that is his Ahavaniya Fire; that which is his utterance that is his offering of oblation.

First the body parts are described in terms of sacrificial objects, then other qualities are described using fire metaphors culminating with the idea of the mouth as a Sacred Fire so that his words also become a form of sacrifice.

The complex interaction of fire metaphors to convey both physical and spiritual meanings can perhaps best be represented as a conceptual blend. Conceptual blends are comprised of a generic space, two input spaces and a space where a blending takes place as a result of the integration of the generic space with the two input spaces (Fauconnier and Turner 2002), as illustrated in Figure 6.1.

In the first input space there are entities relating to the human body and soul: their needs, their expression and their departure. I have incorporated both physical and spiritual elements in this same space so as to avoid imposing a body/soul Cartesian dualism between body and mind. However, a more detailed representation might treat

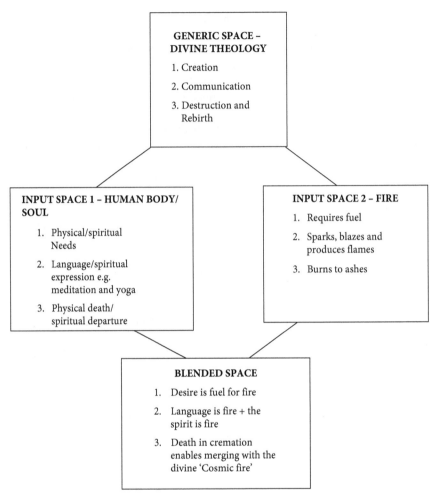

**Figure 6.1** Fire metaphors and blending in Hinduism

the physical and the spiritual as a blend within a blend. In the second input space, I have elements relating to fire, the need for fire, its manifestation and its termination. The generic space governs the elements from the input spaces that filter through to the blended space and here there are slots for creation, communication and destruction. In the blended space, the needs of the human body are described as the need of fire for fuel. Verbal expression is blended with the manifestation of fire, and physical death with cremation by fire.

As evidence of the first element in the blended space consider the following extract on sexual desire:

Having (attractive) tresses and putting on collyrium, women, difficult to touch but pleasing to the eyes are (verily) **the flames of the fire of sin and they burn men as though they were straw.** Women pleasing and cruel, **are the fuel for the**

**hell-fires, that inflame even at a distance and though juicy (loveable) are devoid of moisture (flavour).**

That person alone is entitled to renunciation who has undergone the forty purificatory rites (samskaras), has detachment from all (worldly) things, has acquired purity of mind, **has burnt out desires, envy, intolerance and egotism**, and is equipped with the four disciplines of spiritual life (sadhanas).

Here we have two contrary forces. The first element in the blend is overpowering sexual urges, such as lust, with men represented as passive 'straw' to bear burnt; there is evidence of the frames LUST IS FIRE and WOMEN ARE FIRE. The second element in the blend are spiritual practices such as meditation and yoga; spiritual practice is described as a purifying fire that burns away desires based on a frame PURIFICATION IS FIRE. So, in the conceptual blend the flames of the fire symbolize both creative and destructive forces: desires such as lust are countered by purifying forces such as the yearning of the soul for divine knowledge: the blended space therefore integrates physical and spiritual elements that are combined with reference to the shared frame of fire. These contrary forces could also be represented using the force dynamic model, as in Figure 6.2.

FORCE A

ANTAGONIST: EXTERNAL FORCE
lust for women: material fire

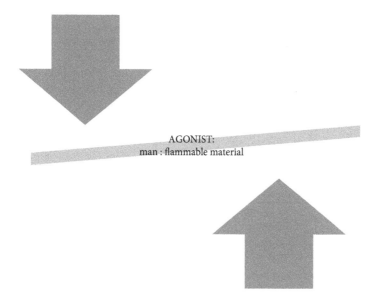

FORCE B

INERTIA: INTERNAL FORCE
renunciation & detachment by
meditation and yoga: spiritual fire

**Figure 6.2** Force dynamic analysis of desire in the Upanishads

When fire is conceptualized as desire, it is a material fire force that attacks or burns the agonist man, but there is resistance from a spiritual fire that is kept burning by renunciation and detachment.

## Summary

In the Avesta, fire was viewed as a sacred symbol for all valued entities – truth, justice, goodness and so on – and was the central element in rituals such as the elaborate preparation of the *Atash Bahram* ('Victory Fire'). The symbolic status of Sacred Fire therefore blocked the emergence of fire metaphors. In the Rig Veda we found a different situation where a range of complex metaphors constituted an elaborate discourse of poet-priests to pay homage to the fire God Agni. These frames for paying homage to the divine also legitimized their own status as animators of the ritual sacrifice. The Rig Veda represents a mid-point between the purely symbolic role for Sacred Fire in the Avesta and the emergence of complex religious beliefs that are expressed linguistically by fire metaphors in the Upanishads. The full emergence of complex metaphor frames in the Upanishads is indicative of a shift towards metaphors in which the source domain of fire frames an understanding of various aspects of the human condition: the nature of spiritual knowledge, the nature of man, women and their desires as well as a means of purification and release from the force of these desires by a counter, internal, spiritual force. I have suggested that this emergence of spiritual discourse characterized by complex metaphor frames can be understood by combining blending theory with the force dynamic model in which man's physical desires and spiritual resistance to them are conceptualized as opposing forces. These frames are summarized in Table 6.7.

When we considered the evidence of a shift from symbol to metaphor in the surviving theological texts of the Indo-Iranian tradition, we also found a pattern for which there was evidence in the Abrahamic religions. In the inception of both Judaism and Christianity we found evidence of a frame for Sacred Fire in which fire became

**Table 6.7** Fire frames in Indo-Iranian religious discourse

| Avesta | Rig Veda | Upanishads |
|---|---|---|
| FIRE FOR LIGHT | FIRE/AGNI IS A POWERFUL LEADER | SPIRITUAL DEVELOPMENT IS FIRE |
| FIRE FOR TRUTH | FIRE/AGNI IS A FORCEFUL TRAVELLER | MAN IS FIRE WOMAN IS FIRE |
| FIRE FOR JUSTICE | FIRE/AGNI IS AN HONOURED PERSON | SPIRITUAL COMMUNICATION IS FIRE |
| FIRE FOR GOODNESS | FIRE/AGNI IS A BRIGHT COLOURFUL LIGHT | LUST IS FIRE |
| FIRE FOR PURIFICATION | FIRE/AGNI STANDS FOR THE FIRE-PRIEST | PURIFICATION IS FIRE |
| FIRE FOR KNOWLEDGE | FIRE/AGNI IS A FRIEND | DESIRE IS A FORCE |

a force for divine punishment but also of divine display; this narrative was framed as DIVINE ANGER IS FIRE and DIVINE DISPLAY IS FIRE. The symbolic meaning of fire as the instrument of divine wrath was, and continues to be, central to understanding the Qu'ran. However, with the development of more complex emotional responses based on EMOTION IS FIRE and EMOTION IS A FORCE and the use of the simile forms such as 'emotion x burns like fire' we found the emergence of fire metaphors – initially in the Old Testament – to convey emotional responses associated with awe. Metaphors then became more systematically developed in the New Testament around the frame JESUS IS LIGHT and also in Pentecostalism with the development of frames for communication such as DIVINE LANGUAGE IS FIRE.

It is questionable whether the shift from symbol to metaphor over time, for which we have found evidence in Indo-Iranian religions, has diminished 'feelings of awe'. Was the raw power of the symbolism of Sacred Fire found in the Avesta more likely to evoke feelings of awe than the complex metaphors of the Upanishads? Or are both symbol and metaphor equally effective in evoking awe? The answers to these questions are likely to be strongly influenced by interpretations that arise as much from individual psychology as from social interaction. In either case it is difficult to explore such answers empirically since these are questions fundamental to the epistemologies and theologies that contribute to personal and social identity. What is perhaps more feasible is to trace how these concepts developed over time to become absorbed into the type of political language that I will refer to the 'discourses of authority' that are explored in Part Three of this book. Nothing accelerates the emergence of discourse as much as schism, and in the next chapter I examine fire metaphors in a seminal text that provides insight into the rift that developed in Europe between Catholicism and Protestantism in the sixteenth century: *Foxe's Book of Martyrs*.

Part Three

# Fire in Political Discourse

# 7

# Fire and Authority in Sixteenth-Century England: *Foxe's Book of Martyrs*

## Introduction

Throughout history, fire has been the most basic form of imposing power through the destruction of opponents' bodies, their weapons, their property, their land and – most importantly – their cultural symbols. This might take the form of burning their places of belief, their icons, statues or the burning of the books through which their beliefs are transmitted. Ideological uses of fire go back to the notion of the Sacred Fire. When fire was employed as a means for destroying rival emblems it became revered as a vehicle of divine action. Punishing opponents with Sacred Fire became a form of legitimizing action because it allied the forces of authority on this earth with divine forces. Fire thereby took on the role of imposing authority; but when embraced by its victims the force of this authority is undermined because it symbolized spiritual power overcoming material power. Voluntary participation by the victim in an act of conflagration became a means of self-empowerment because it entailed transforming the object into a subject and thereby created legitimacy through martyrdom.

At various times during the early modern period in Europe, Christian and Jewish martyrs were subjected to the terrible power of fire wielded by those in authority as an ideological test of their faith: recant or burn. The fire – known in catholic countries as the *auto de fe* – was intended not only to eliminate the physical body of a heretic but also to save his or her soul: a rejection of apostasy would avoid eternal hellfire. In this chapter, I focus on what is surely the most well-detailed and elaborate work of martyrology in the English Protestant tradition and is commonly known as 'Foxe's Book of Martyrs'. This is a lengthy and detailed sixteenth-century account of the courage of English Protestants, and their spiritual ancestors, who had been martyred – usually by fire – for refusing to recant their beliefs and thereby rejecting the doctrines of the Holy Roman Catholic Church.

By way of contextualizing the use of fire in this ideological struggle, in the first part of this chapter I consider some aspects of the relationship between fire and authority and more generally how fire would have been experienced as both familiar and threatening in the sixteenth century. I then consider the use of fire as a means of rebellion, for example, by Protestant iconoclasts who sought to eliminate symbols of authority. In the second part of the chapter, I examine the fire lexicon in *Foxe's Book of Martyrs* and explore some of the characteristics of 'fire' metaphors.

# Fire and authority

At the time when the *Book of Martyrs* was written, fire was, along with the plague and disease, the greatest single threat to human security as Keith Thomas describes:

> The towns were particularly vulnerable with their thatched roofs, wooden chimneys and crowded living conditions. Since there were no safety matches, people often chose to fetch a bucket of burning coals from a neighbour rather than waste time struggling with a tinder-box. At night they were dependent on candles, which when set down in a draughty place, could easily put a house on fire .... Once fire had broken out it seldom encountered much in the way of effective resistance. Fire-fighting techniques were virtually unchanged in England between the Normal Conquest and the death of Elizabeth I. Even the most advanced municipality possessed nothing more in the way of equipment than some leather buckets, a few ladders and iron hooks for pulling down thatch so as to stop the fire spreading .... There were no fire brigades, and the scene at a fire was usually one of unrelieved chaos. (Thomas 1971: 16–18)

Whole towns were devastated by fire, for example, Tiverton, Marlborough, Blandford Forum, Dorchester and Beauminster. Fires were so common in London that at the outbreak of the Great Fire in 1666 hardly anybody took much notice. There would have been an ambiguous relationship with fire because it was something about which people had much more direct experience in their daily life than they do today – relying on it for cooking, heating and lighting – but it was also something that, once out of control, became a force that could rapidly destroy them and their societies.

Prior to the sixteenth century, the practice of ordeal by fire was employed in judicial cases; this involved applying some form of heated object to a suspect as a way of testing their innocence or guilt. In some cases, this was a form of legal entrapment because burning indicated divine confirmation of guilt, while failure to burn was taken as a sign of alliance with the Devil because it overturned the laws of nature. One form of such ordeals that was practiced in the early medieval period involved walking on red-hot ploughshares. Edward the Confessor's mother Emma of Normandy proved her innocence from accusations of adultery by walking unscathed. Such ordeals were motivated by the notion of fire as an instrument of divine punishment. However, the use of ordeals decreased once the power of the state increased; it may have been that ordeals were a way of preventing feuds within small local communities by swiftly and transparently settling an issue. Once the power of the state had established a legal framework, there was less dependence on the supernatural aspects of the 'controlled miracle' that is implied by ordeals (Brown 1975).

But the fire ordeal could also be extended from the human body to objects so that if they survived a punishing fire, it implied some form of miraculous protection:

> Just as an individual might prove his or her innocence by emerging without ill-effect form the blaze or hot iron, so holy objects proved their sanctity in tests of fire. Many medieval miracles rested on the inexplicable survival, through an otherwise all-consuming fire, of some revered item, particularly the eucharistic host. (Aston 1993: 299–300)

Just as fire could be used as a legitimate method for gauging the truth of those suspected of a crime, or the authenticity of a holy object, so it offered a legitimate means of identifying those found guilty of a crime by the practice of branding. Originally developed as a simple technology for identification of livestock, it subsequently became a means of identifying criminals so that their status was indelibly marked on their body. Branding was also used as a means of identifying and marking an ostracized social group; for example, in 1547 the Statute of Vagabonds ordered that vagabonds and gypsies should be branded with a large 'V' on the breast. This law was repealed in England in 1550.

More broadly, fire was employed by the Roman Catholic Church to re-impose its authority within Christendom when threatened by the heretic or by the non-believer. From the late twelfth century many Cathars were burnt in France. Their main heresy was a belief in dualism: this held to a division between a materialist world that was inherently evil and a spiritual world that was inherently good. Paradise was guaranteed for those who rejected the material world through poverty, fasting and modesty. The first medieval Inquisition known as the Episcopal Inquisition was established in 1184. Gregory IX then established what has become known as the Papal Inquisition in the 1230s; as well as suppressing heresy, his aim was to formalize the procedures for the burning of heretics, who were otherwise being burnt at local initiative. The reason why many Cathars are reported to have embraced the fires in which they were burnt is because this entailed the elimination of their physical body but the eternal survival of their soul. The first mass burning of heretics took place during the Albigensian Crusade when 140 Cathar Perfects were burnt and according to a witness, Peter of Vaux de Cernay, many leaped joyfully into the flames.

The Inquisition later developed a renowned instrument of authority: the trial by faith or 'auto de fe'. It was equally well suited to deal with all forms of ideological opponent including pagans in the Spanish colonies in the New World. The trial integrated elements of theological ritual, display of political authority and high drama:

> It has been argued that the *auto de fe* was a ritual performance symbolically re-enacting the Last Judgement when all sinners stood before the throne of God. If physical punishment accompanied this theatrical rite of the Inquisition, it was essentially because punishment underlay the Christian notion of the Last Judgement Day. Thus, the Inquisition's methods of dealing with heretics and other transgressors of Catholic orthodoxy bore a notable resemblance to infernal punishment. At the same time, the *auto de fe* has also been characterized as a political ritual, an act of propaganda with a pedagogical aim: to teach the community to conform to the norms of Tridentine Catholicism and the interests of the absolute monarchy. The public display of punishment had to be as elaborate as possible, converting the auto into a theatrical pageant in which justice, as the instrument of power, descended upon the culprit and thus made its weightiness known to the spectators. (Cañeque 1996: 323)

Crucial to the *auto de fe* is that it was a form of theological contest in which the condemned was exhorted to recant his beliefs, allowing him to be garrotted rather than having to face the raw flames of punishment and retribution. But it was a contest and a spectacle with a clearly ideological purpose:

People generally viewed celebrations, punishments and executions as popular festivals, where the general public became witnesses to a criminal's punishment as well as participants in a sacrificial rite that purged society. For many, participation was both an act of the restoration of a world that had been damaged by a crime and a celebration of the religious sacrifice of a repentant sinner. In this sense, the garrotting and burning of the *autos de fe* can be considered ritual killings that were understood as edifying, sacred acts. They were public festivals centering on salvation and damnation. This accounts for the great effect of public executions – both religious and secular – which attracted large crowds eager to witness the last struggle of the sinner. (Cañeque 1996: 330)

The processes at work in the *auto de fe* can also be described using the force dynamic model as shown in Figure 7.1:

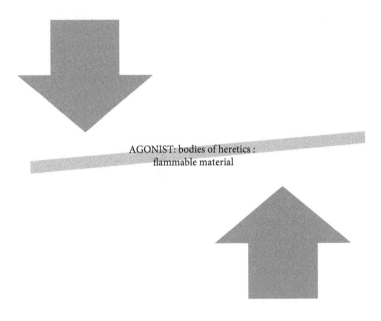

FORCE A

ANTAGONIST:
inquisitorial test to enforce recanting
of beliefs, with fire as a last resort

AGONIST: bodies of heretics :
flammable material

FORCE B

INERTIA:
continuing to hold heretical beliefs
by maintaining silence

**Figure 7.1** Force dynamic analysis of the *Auto de Fe*

The model illustrates the inquisitorial process as an antagonist acting upon the agonist, the material bodies of those accused of heresy; they are subject to a force of inertia because of their refusal to recant and resistance to any change in their beliefs. The drama of fire to impose religious authority contributed to social identities and the presence of the crowd symbolized their involvement in the ideological struggle. Should they intervene, they risked themselves becoming accused of heresy, but by failing to do so they became complicit with the authorities in an act of social purification:

> Fire was purgative in various contexts, personal and social, as well as spiritual. The use of burning to deal with physical infection (both of people and livestock) had long had its religious parallel in the burning of heretics and heretical texts. Fire eliminated the contaminating elements, freeing Christian society from pollution. In the words of Bernard Gui, the early fourteenth-century Dominican inquisitor: 'Heresy cannot be destroyed unless heretics are destroyed'. (Aston 1993: 299–300)

By analogy with cauterization as a way of restoring health to the physical body, metaphorically, the all-purging fire restored health to the body politic in a way that made is accessible to public cognition:

> In the case of spiritual infection publicity was part of the process; the cancer must be seen and known to be eliminated. Since this was part of the cure … the heretical books were burned, crowds were present to see the errors returned to ashes. Burning was the most effective method of cauterizing the poisoned limb, and society – the corporate body whose health was at risk – had to participate in the healing process. (Aston 1993)

Just as fire could materially destroy the cities that had little resistance against its power and in doing so destroyed the illnesses embedded within them, so, metaphorically and symbolically, it could restore spiritual health to the body politic.

## Fire and rebellion

I began this book by considering how the practice of self-immolation has become a medium through which an individual or group of individuals can undertake acts of political expression by inflicting on themselves unimaginable levels of pain. At the level of embodied meaning, this is effective as a form of political persuasion because it implies that their acts are motivated by deep inner spiritual conviction. The moral tables are turned when the victim embraces fire, either by self-immolation or by welcoming the pain inflicted by his oppressors. Fire lays claim to authority by destroying ideological opponents, since by burning them the perpetrators are delivering their opponents for divine judgement, so that the fires of punishment are just a preliminary of what is to come. But the force of such claims is rapidly overturned when these cruel actions are embraced by their victim, whose courage inspires awe among witnesses of their suffering. The willing acceptance of fire is therefore a way of inverting power relationships because it transforms the individual from the status of victim to that of martyr.

Given the vulnerability to fire in many historical periods, including sixteenth-century England, fire has always been a transformational agent – whether as an individual act of arson or as a co-ordinated politically motivated action. In the sixteenth century it was relatively easy for an individual to take revenge by acts of arson, the offender in many instances being unlikely to be caught. In other cases, outbreaks of fire were attributed to the actions of witches drawing on the supernatural. Given that people could almost instantly lose their home and their property, it is perhaps surprising how natural fire has always been as a means of retribution for the socially ostracized or those who experience feelings of rejection, exclusion, envy or hatred of those in power, or power itself. The rejection of authority has most typically involved the starting of fires and this has continued until the present day. As Canetti (1960: 90) has commented:

> The dangerous traits of the crowd are often pointed out and among these, the most striking is the propensity to incendiarism. This propensity has its roots in the burning of forests …. If the conflagration is large enough, a curious reversal of their old mass fear commands them to hurry to its site, and they feel there something of the glowing warmth which formerly united them. In periods of peace they have to go without this experience for a long time, but one of the strongest instincts of the crowd, as soon as it has formed at all, is to create such a fire for itself and to use its attraction to further its own growth.

In the London riots of August 2011, at least 100 homes were destroyed in the arson and looting,[1] and four London buses were burnt. The fires were symbolic of the social disorder that was triggered by news of the police shooting of Mark Duggan in an investigation of gun crime that spread rapidly through social media. A 68-year-old man Richard Bowes was attacked by a mob for attempting to stamp out fire in a waste-disposal bin, and he died three days later. It was the symbolic meaning of the poor man's actions that led to his death: the mob saw the fire as purifying because it was a fire of justice for the deceased Duggan.

The origins of the purifying fire of iconoclasm are deep-rooted and lie even in the Old Testament:
First, in the Second Commandment:

> You shall not make for yourself a carved image, or any likeness of anything that is in heaven above, or that is in the earth beneath, or that is in the water under the earth. (Exodus 20: 4)

And then later in the punishment for those who broke this commandment:

And you shall destroy their altars, break their sacred pillars, and *burn their wooden images with fire*; you shall cut down the carved images of their gods and destroy their names from that place. You shall not worship the Lord your God with such things. (Deuteronomy 12: 3–4)

The reason for burning the images was so that they could not be used again and for this reason anything that served as a symbol of a counter ideology should be put to the flames. This was particularly the case during the English Reformation. Thomas Cromwell, The Lord Privy Seal for King Henry VIII of England, personally supervised the burning of a wide range of highly symbolic pilgrimage statues: 'the images of the Virgin from Walsingham & Ipswich – along with other cult images – were publicly burnt at Chelsea in the presence of the Lord Privy Seal in July 1538' (Aston 1993: 304). In 1558, at the accession of Elizabeth, there were large bonfires of idols in London: statues; rood-lofts; sepulchres and censers; copes; vestments and altar cloths; banners; crosses and books were burnt (Aston 1993: 305). As the author goes on to point out:

It was not simply a question of eliminating a whole range of idolatrous objects from future use. People were to be welded to the new religious settlement by being personally involved in the ceremonial destruction of ritual objects of the old religion. (Aston 1993: 310)

The burning and destruction of symbols of Catholicism was both an expression of reinforcing the Second Commandment and an act of social rebellion against the imposition of an authority that was external to England. Just as the fires of the Inquisition could be employed to enforce the papal authority over heretics, so Protestants could invoke the legitimacy of fire and use fire to destroy their symbols of power. Fire therefore served a practical role for enforcing authority and symbolized a clash of ideologies: it was a contested element onto which competing belief systems could project sets of symbolic meanings in the creation of discourses of authority.

However, bonfires were also fun because they served as focal points of group action; the iconoclastic fires of Protestant England also fed their way into the national calendar:

Reforming bonfires were occasions of joy, much as the customary midsummer fires of St John's Day … St John's Day bonfires reflect some complicated interweaving between time-honoured habits and the upheaval inaugurated by the iconoclasts. Lighting fires in what Bossuet called an 'ecclesiastical manner' was an activity of Catholics as well as of reformed Protestants, and Lutherans too knew the propaganda value of flames. The old association of a purifying bonfire with the purifying season of Lent was given a new dimension by the image-burners. And in England some new days of bonfire lighting were added to the post-Reformation calendar. (Aston 1993: 312–313)

At the time of writing this chapter, the rotary clubs and round table organizations of England are busy preparing large bonfires to be lit alongside their fireworks display for what has become established as the national institution of Guy Fawkes Night. Many of these occasions will include the ceremonial burning of a 'guy' – a stuffed effigy of a man, the enemy, the other – who must be symbolically be burnt before the onset of winter.

## Foxe's 'Book of Martyrs'

The book known as the *Book of Martyrs* was the most important tribute to English Protestant Martyrs:

> Revered by many Protestants as a 'holy' book, it was frequently chained alongside the Bible for reading by ordinary people at many public places including cathedrals, churches, schools, libraries, guildhalls, and at least one inn .... Foxe's book serves as a window into sixteenth- and seventeenth-century English cultural history. (King 2006: 1–3)

The book, actually named *Actes and Monuments*, was originally published in 1563 and is a polemical testimony to the sufferings of Christians chronologically through history. It was fully illustrated, with over sixty woodcuts in the first edition, depicting the sufferings of early Christians. It was extremely successful, running to four editions during Foxe's lifetime, each increasing in length and in number of illustrations. It provides the most detailed and extensive account of the utilization of fire to impose authority in sixteenth- and seventeenth-century England. It was highly ideological as it sought to establish the Protestant martyrs as modern-day saints by providing a rigorous testimony to their sacrifice and therefore is a key text in understanding the role of fire in discourses of authority:

> Foxean martyrologies derive to a very considerable degree from manuscripts written by martyrs as they awaited execution or by copyists, to which the compiler added extracts concerning the prosecution of alleged heretics from documents including the episcopal registers that receive mention on the title page .... Foxe's goal is to preserve the speeches and deeds of 'true' martyrs in the form of documents that memorialize the faithful suffering of new-style saints. The book as a whole therefore functions in the manner of a symbolic reliquary that preserves for posterity the deeds and words that constitute the essence of saintly sacrifice. (Betteridge 1999 in King 2006: 8)

It is the courage shown by Protestants who are burnt as heretics that provides the predominant theme. Foxe offers an account of the martyrdom of Richard Atkins who was burnt by the Inquisition in Rome in 1581. Atkins had gone to Rome to make his views on Catholicism very clear; these included a personal diatribe against the Pope:

> I come likewise to let youre proude Antichrist vnderstand, that hee doth offend the heauenly maiestie, robbe God of his honour, and poysoneth the whole world with his abhominable blasphemies: making them homage stockes, and stones, and that filthy sacramēt which is nothing els but a foolish Idol.

He disrupted the Eucharist during a mass in St Peters by taking the chalice that contained the consecrated wine from the altar and threw it on the ground, and struggled with the priest to get hold of the ceremonial bread but was prevented from doing so by the intervention of the congregation. Foxe goes on to describe the rebel's fate:

> Within a while after, he was set vpō an Asse, without any saddle, he being from the middle vpward naked, hauing some englishe priestes with him to talke with him, but he regarded them not, but spake to the people in so good a language as he could, and told them they were in a wrong way, and therfore willed them for Christes sake, to haue regard to the sauing of theyr soules. All the way as he went, there were foure did nothing els but thrust at his body with burning torches, whereat he neuer moued, nor shronke one iote, but with a cherefull countenaunce, laboured to perswade the people often bending his body to meet the torches, as they were thrust at him, and woulde take them in hys owne hand, and hold them burning still vppon his body, whereat the people not a little wondered. (Book 12, p. 2174)

The key detail here is that Atkins faced his fire-wielding tormentors 'with a cherefull countenaunce': it is by reporting his embrace of his tormentors' fire that Foxe seeks to persuade the reader of Atkins' spiritual conviction. Between 1530 and 1546, during the reign of Henry VIII, sixty-one out of a total of sixty-three Protestant martyrs were burnt and during the reign of Mary I (1553–1558) at least a further 287 Protestants were persecuted – nearly all by being burnt (Morgan 2009: 259).

Throughout the *Actes and Monuments*, Foxe's rhetorical purpose is to emphasize the courage in adversity and spiritual strength with which the Protestants defy their ideological opponents. His lengthy accounts of their defiance (the twelve books of the 1583 edition exceed three million words in length) include descriptions of their humour and irony while in the very process of being burnt; for example, in the account of the martyrdom of Laurence:

> Kindle the fire of wood make no spare. Hath this vyllaine deluded the Emperour? Away with him, away with him. Whip him with scourges, jercke him with rods: buffet him with fistes, braine him with clubs, jesteth the traitour with the Emperour? Pinche him with fyrie tonges gyrde him with burning plates, bring out the strongest chaines, and the fireforkes, and the grated bedde of yron. On the fire with it, bind the rebell hande and foote, & when the bed is fire hot, on with him: rost him, broyle him, tosse him, turne him: on paine of our highe displeasure do euery man his office, O ye tormentors. The worde was no soner spoken, but all was done.

> After many cruell handlings, this *meeke lambe* was layd I will not say on his firye bed of yron, but on his *soft bed of downe*. So mightily God wrought with his Martyr Laurence, so miraculously God tempered his element the fire, not a bed of consuming paine, but *a pallet of nourishing rest* was it vnto Laurence. Not Laurence, but the Emperour might seeme to be tormented: the one broiling in the fleshe, the other **burning in the hart.** When this tryumphaut Martir had beene pressed downe with firepikes for a great space, in the mightie spirite of God he spake to the vanquished tyraunt:

> This side is now rosted inough, turne vp O tyraunt great.Assay, whether rosted
> or raw, thou thinkest the better meate.
>    O rare and vnaccustomed patience. O faith inuincible, that not onely burnest,
> but by meanes vnspeakable doest recreate, refresh, stablish & strengthen those that
> are burned, afflicted and troubled. (Book 1, p. 95)

The author spares no detail in describing the terrible physical torments that were
inflicted on Laurence. However, the more pain that is inflicted, the more his heroic
acceptance redirections its intention onto his tormentors. This is marked in the above
passage with the literal sense of fire terms in the first paragraph that may be contrasted
with the extended metaphors shown in italics and in bold in the second paragraph. His
religious conviction is such that the 'fire bed of iron' is transformed into a 'soft bed of
down' and a 'pallet of nourishing rest', and while the martyr's flesh is literally 'broiling',
it is the Emperor who is 'burning in the hart'. The martyr then offers his body as if
it were meat to be roasted – even cracking a joke in the process – thereby implying
that he no more values his body than he does dead meat. This demonstration of faith
illustrates how resistance to fire contributes its own voice of authority.

In Foxe's book, the inversion of the power and authority of fire became the means
through which a new ideology – that of the Protestant Church of England – is
established. It is based on the principle of repudiating the authority of foreign, Roman
influences and asserting the new ideology of an independent nation state. As Thomas
(1971: 87) summarizes:

> The individual stood in a direct relationship to God and was solely dependent
> upon his omnipotence. He could no longer rely upon the intercession of
> intermediaries, whether saints or clergy; neither could he trust in an imposing
> apparatus of ceremonial in the hope of prevailing upon God to grant his desires.
> The reformers set out to eliminate theatricality from church ritual and decorations,
> and to depreciate the status of the priesthood.

Language was central in this struggle for religious freedom in particular over the issue
of whether there was the freedom to read the Bible in English. William Tyndale, who
first translated the Bible from Latin into English, was executed in Antwerp in 1525; he
was strangled while tied at the stake, and then his dead body was burned. The English
Bible came to symbolize the rights of the English to access God directly rather than
through the intermediary of the Catholic Church. This inversion of power relations is
often linguistically conveyed through the transformational power of metaphor.

There is much dispute over the accuracy and objectivity of Foxe's account of
Protestant martyrdom; clearly he was writing from the perspective of a Protestant and
an Englishman who rejected the authority of the Pope; there is no attempt to conceal
this. What is beyond doubt is the importance of the text in preparing the way for the
development of an English Protestant identity and John Burrow refers to it as, after the
Bible, 'the greatest single influence on English Protestant thinking of the late Tudor and
early Stuart period' (Burrow 2008: 296). It provides insight into a discursive tension
between descriptions of the use of fire for executing Protestants, and the use of fire

metaphors to reflect Foxe's own ideological position; it therefore provides insight into deeply contested views on authority.

## Analysis of fire metaphors in *Foxe's Actes and Monuments*

For this study I have used the fourth edition published in 1583. This edition contains 2,035 pages and is comprised of twelve books. For the purposes of analysis, I have used a searchable online version available at:
http://www.johnfoxe.org/index.php

Table 7.1 shows the use of the core fire lexicon; the spelling of 'spark' and 'lamp' has been modified to reflect those used by Foxe as current at its time of publication:

**Table 7.1** FIRE in *Foxe's Actes and Monuments* (1983 edition)

| Fire frame | Fire term | Total uses | Uses as a metaphor |
|---|---|---|---|
| **Natural fire** | fire(s) | >500 | – |
| | burn | >500 | – |
| | flame(s) | 81 | 6 |
| | heat (n) | 27 | 21 |
| | smoke (n) | 33 | 11 |
| | fiery | 25 | 10 |
| | blaze/ablaze | 0 | 0 |
| | smoulder | 0 | 0 |
| | incandescent | 0 | 0 |
| | glow | 1 | 1 |
| | flare | 0 | 0 |
| | flicker | 1 | 1 |
| Total | (Excluding 'fire' and 'burn') | 168 | 50 |
| **Functional fire** | candle(s) | 64 | 11 |
| | illuminate | 10 | 10 |
| | lampe(s) | 13 | 6 |
| | torch(es) | 15 | 0 |
| | melt | 6 | 5 |
| | scorch | 8 | 1 |
| | stoke | 8 | 1 |
| | beacon(s) | 7 | 0 |
| | heat | 2 | 1 |
| | smoke (v) | 2 | 0 |
| | fan | 1 | 1 |
| Total | | 136 | 34 |

(continued)

| Fire frame | Fire term | Total uses | Uses as a metaphor |
|---|---|---|---|
| **Organic fire** | kindle | 100 | 75 |
| | inflame/inflammatory | 63 | 63 |
| | ashes | 93 | 4 |
| | extinguish | 42 | 42 |
| | sparke(s) | 26 | 25 |
| | embers | 1 | 0 |
| | cinders | 1 | 0 |
| Total | | 326 | 209 |

## Natural fire

As might be expected in accounts of martyrdom through burning at the stake, there are many references to the literal use of fire in the persecution and torture of Protestant martyrs but the occurrence of 'fire' and 'burn' were so frequent that it was not possible to analyse them all. Of the remaining natural fire terms, 30 per cent are classified as metaphors – a much lower proportion than organic fire terms – mainly because of the actual use of fire as a means for punishing and despatching heretics. The proportion of natural fire terms classed as metaphor would be much lower if 'fire' and 'burn' were included, as there were many uses of both words to refer to the literal burning heretics. A sample of the first 100 uses of 'fire' and 'burn' shows they were exclusively used with literal senses. According to Foxe, as many as 300 Protestants were burnt at the stake during the reign of Queen Mary, during which their persecution reached its height. We should recall that in an age where magical powers were attributed to embodied relics – such as Christ's blood, or a body part of one of the saints – the complete physical destruction of heretics was considered to be ideologically necessary.

However, Foxe's account is not restricted to heresy in England: because of the wider rhetorical purpose of establishing the English Protestants as equivalent to the Catholic saints, it was vital to provide a much broader account of the treatment of heretics by the Catholic Church through the ages. Therefore, he included a survey of earlier historical accounts of martyrdom from Biblical times until the present. The geographical range of the accounts covered the whole of Christendom and emphasized the contrast between the spiritual values of the martyrs and the cruelty of their oppressors. In the following account of the martyrdom of Eulalia in Portugal, Foxe emphasizes the fortitude of the accused heretic based on her inner conviction: 'it is an easie matter to breake a britle substance, but the inward mind shalt not thou hurt for any thing thou canst do.' Her inquisitors tempt her by the prospect of escaping a terrible fate if she shows some form of symbolic acceptance of the Catholic Church:

> Either shalt thou be beheaded with this sword, or else with these wild beastes shalt thou be pulled in peeces, or els by being cast into the fiery flames shalbe (although lamentably bewailed of thy friends and kinsfolks) consumed to ashes. What great matter is it for thee I pray thee, to escape al this? If thou wilt but take & put with

thy fingers a little salt & incense into the censers, thou shalt be deliuered from al these punishmēts.

The martyr spurns this offer, as it would jeopardize her beliefs:

> To this Eulalia made no aunswere, but being in a great furye shee spitteth in the tirauntes face, she throweth downe the Idoles, and spurneth abroad with her feete the heape of incense prepared to the censers ...

As a result, her executioners continue with their macabre persecution, while the martyr continues to display her faith:

> then without further delay, the hangmen with both their strengthes tooke her, & puld one ioynte from an other, and with the talantes of wilde beastes, scotched her sides to the hard bodes: she all this while singing and praysing God in this wise. Beholde, O Lord I will not forget thee: what a pleasure is it for them O Christ that remember thy triumphant victoryes, to at-tayne vnto these high dignities, and still calleth vpon that holy name, al stained and embrued with her owne bloude.

For rhetorical effect, Foxe stresses the contrast between her suffering body and her emotional response to what is happening to her:

> This sang she with a bold stomacke, neither lamentyngly nor yet wepingly, but being glad and mery, abandonyng from her mind all heauines and griefe, *when as out of a warme fountain* her mangled members with fresh bloud bathed her white and fayre skinne.

Fire is introduced as the last stage in her persecution – the one that will eliminate her body from the earth for eternity:

> Then proceede they to the last and final torment, which was not only the goring and wounding of her mangled body with the yron grat, & hurdle, and terrible harrowing of her flesh, but burned, on euery side with flaming torches her tormented brests, and sides: her heare hanging about her shoulders in two parts deuided (wherewith her shamefast chastitie and virginitie was couered) reached downe to the ground: but when the cracking flame fleeth about her face, kindled by her heare, and reacheth the crowne of her head: thē she desiring swift death, opened her mouth and swalowed the flame, and so rested shee in peace. (Book 1, p. 117)

This description works by contrasting her spiritual courage and modesty (she is referred to as a virgin), with the terrible physical punishments inflicted on her material body. The act of welcoming fire as she swallows the flame is central to Foxe's rhetorical purpose of reversing the power relationships between the authority of the Church and Protestants. Although the Church and its Inquisition have the power to inflict physical suffering, they lack spiritual legitimacy for their actions; by contrast, the physical vulnerability of the young female heretic is compensated for by her faith – from which she derives spiritual authority over her ideological opponents. In the contest of fire as a source of legitimacy she is clearly the winner! This is summarized using the force dynamic model in Figure 7.2.

The inquisitorial fire is the antagonist and acts upon the agonist – Eulalia – whose spiritual resistance to recantation is shown as force B, inertia: by not doing anything she is resisting the authority of her tormentors who demand that she recants her beliefs.

When Foxe uses fire as a metaphor, it is invariably negative and conveys the causes of emotions such as anger, pride, greed or lust:

> Vpon these words **a fire began to heat & kindle betweene them.** In so much that they began to rate and reuile one the other, that the whole multitude therewith disquieted, began to be set on a hurrey. (Book 5, p. 451)

FORCE A

ANTAGONIST:
persecution by fire

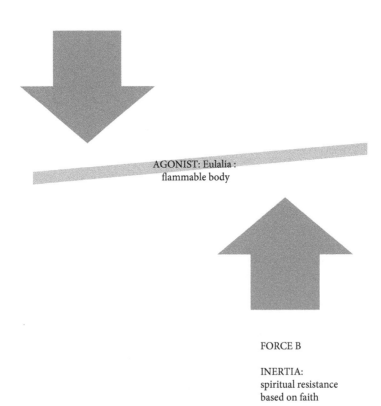

FORCE B

INERTIA:
spiritual resistance
based on faith

**Figure 7.2** Force dynamic analysis of Eulalia's Martyrdom

And thirdly, as for hipocrisy there be also some, whose intollerable pride & malice is so manifest and notorious, **kindled vp like fire**: that no cloake or shadow of hypocrisy can couer it, but are so past all shame. (Book 5, p. 440)

He also wrote his letters vnto the king of England, embulled with gold Declaring in the same, that the Bishop of Rome so **flamed with the fire of auarice and manifest concupiscence** ... (Book 4, p. 324)

These metaphors show the generic frame CAUSES ARE FORCES and, more specifically, THE CAUSE OF AN EMOTION IS THE CAUSE OF A FIRE. When examining the word following the phrase 'fire of' we find: persecution, wrath, fury, hell, purgatory, affliction and temptation. With very few exceptions, Foxe avoids any positive evaluation of fire since the rhetorical purpose of his work is to contrast the cruelty of the Catholic Church with the heroism of the Protestant martyrs. Fire becomes a metonym for tyrannical authority and its repressive actions are associated with hellfires and framed as UNCONTROLLED EMOTION IS EXTREME TEMPERATURE and THE LEVEL OF TEMPERATURE FOR THE INTENSITY OF EMOTION. A metonymic relationship also shows in 'burning zeale' and 'inflamed pen' in the following:

All these thinges well considered, tell me [M. Cope] I pray you, is treason suche a straunge and vnketh thyng in your popecatholike churche, that your **burning zeale of obedience** to kings and princes, can not read the story of the L. Cobham & sir Roger Acton, but your pen must needes be **inflamed to wryte** against them, and yet so many traytors in your owne Calenders neither seene, nor once spoken of?

The metaphors imply that Cope's inflexible adherence to Catholicism will lead to the burning of Protestants. The metaphors are integrated with a cause–effect frame EMOTION IS A FORCE in which the emotionally based zeal of Catholics causes their opponents to be punished by fire. This metonymic frame is similar to Kövecses (2002: 115) frame CAUSE OF A SITUATION IS CAUSE OF HEAT (FIRE) and captures the behaviour of those who were ideologically opposed to Protestants and sought to persecute them.

A similar cause–effect metonymy occurs in figurative uses of 'fiery' and 'heat'. Although generally 'fiery' is used literally, when figurative there is a blend of a metaphoric use of 'fiery' to refer to the anger of the oppressors with a metonymic frame for fire as an instrument of martyrdom. In the following account of the martyrdom of Robert Samuel, a woman who shows sympathy to the heretic, Rose Nattingham, is herself threatened by the 'fiery handes' of the perpetrators of his martyrdom:

As this godly martyr was going to þᵉ fire, there came a certaine maide to him, which tooke him aboute the necke and kissed him, who being marked by them that were present, was sought for the next day after, to be had to prisone and burned, as the very party her self informed me: Howbeit, as God of his goodnes wold haue it, she escaped **their fiery handes**, keeping her selfe secreate in the towne a good while after. (Book 11, p. 1728)

Since it is the hands that cause the fire in which heretics will be burnt, the EMOTION IS A FORCE frame is implied. 'Heat' can also be used metaphorically based on an integration of the frames ANGER IS FIRE and EMOTION IS A FORCE, as illustrated by the following account of Thomas Hitton:

> When persecution for the same word in the dayes of king Henry the 8. **grew to bee somewhat hote**, tooke his iourney toward Rochester in Kent, intendyng to haue gone to Douer, & so to haue crossed the seas into Fraunce and other countries for a tyme, where reposing himself a while, he might be free from **the heat of persecution**. (Book 12, p. 2159)

Metaphoric uses of 'heat' are invariably negative – as implied by the underlying metaphoric and metonymic frames. As with 'fiery' they imply a state of emotion that when applied in theological dispute leads to intolerance and its outcome: the persecution of heretics based on THE LEVEL OF TEMPERATURE FOR THE INTENSITY OF EMOTION. An interesting example of how metaphor supports this underlying negative script for fire – in which an uncontrolled emotion, caused by a difference of religious opinion, leads to the burning of theological opponents – is the association between 'haste' and 'heat' in the following:

> before any question of their crime was: following therein (as seemeth) more the **heat of hastynesse**, then the path of righteousnesse. (Book 4, p. 242)
> certayne that were about the king (to the number of foure) hearing him thus to cōplayne and lament: addrest thēselues in great **heat of hast**, to satisfye the agreeued minde and quarrell of their prince. (Book 4, p. 246)

The metaphoric collocation of 'heat' and 'hast' implies that the decisions to persecute people as heretics were not grounded in proper deliberation, but taken quickly and upon the basis of emotional reaction rather than reasoned judgement – the fire of the lynch mob rather than legitimate authority. It shows evidence of the frame THE LEVEL OF INTENSITY OF AN EMOTION IS THE LEVEL OF INTENSITY OF A FIRE.

'Smoke' metaphors are used in a similar way as 'heat'; they are exclusively negative as in the following:

> The factious discorde in Italy betweene the Guelphes, and Gibillines, which the part of a good bishop had bene to extinct: so little he helped **to quench the smoke**, that he of all other was **chiefest firebrande to encrease the flame**. (Book 4, p. 365)

The context here implies anger, or 'discorde', that is aroused by a 'firebrande' that causes the flames of persecution. Part of the framing of natural smoke is that it is something temporary and this aspect is profiled in the following analogies that emphasize the evanescent nature of both language and emotions:

> And therefore, this heauenly smel of Gods word, wil not **as a smoke passe away with the winde:** but it will descende and rest in some cleane soule, that thirsteth thereafter. (Book 5, p. 552)

Even the transitoriness of life itself can be profiled using the smoke frame:

> But my dearly beloued, open the eyes of your faith, & see how short a thing this life is, euen **a very shadow and smoke**. Againe, see how intollerable the punishment of hel fire is, and that endles. (Book 11, p. 1668)

Another aspect of the 'smoke' frame is its attribute of blocking light:

> But how, as Iudas among the Apostles, as Symon Magus among the disciples, as a candle new queinte that stincheth all the house in steede of a light lanterne, **as a smoke that blindeth** mens eyen, in place of cleane fire. (Book 5, p. 572)

The same sense of smoke as something that obscures followers from the truth occurs in the following, but alongside the idea that it is only temporary and will soon dissipate once the Lutherans are punished:

> The Cardinals and Byshops were euer in the kynges eare, tellyng hym that these Lutheranes were nothyng els, but such as **caryed vaine smoke in their mouthes**, which being put to the fire, would soone vanish. (Book 7, p. 927)

In metaphors, then, smoke is a component of the natural process of fire that is not to be valued either because of its cause – wrath – or because it typifies the transitory nature of life. Metaphorically, its effect is also to obscure vision and sometimes this is also the case with more literal uses of 'smoke':

> That done, there wasa cōpany of bookes which were cast into the fire, and by chaunce a Communion booke fell betwene his handes, who receyuing it ioyfully, opened it, & read so long as the force of the flame and smoke caused him that he could see no more:

Here it is the smoke that prevents the devout Protestant from reading his religious texts, and it is therefore easy to see the metonymic basis for many smoke metaphors.

In understanding metonymy it is also relevant to consider 'consume' because it is a verb that specifies the effect of wasting away on a body or other material entity. I have discussed earlier (see page 32) how 'consume' can refer to the action of either illness or fire – and for that reason is not classed as metaphor since these are quite concrete or embodied meanings. Foxe employs both senses:

> also what a pestiferous sicknes was in al the City, which not onely consumed young men and children: but also men of middle age, and old men in like maner, and that this plague came first by straungers vnto the poore of the Citty, and so infected the rich. (Book 6, p. 712)
>
> Under the raigne of the late Queene Mary, but in all thinges submitted themselues obediently to the lawes thē in force, and yet the cruelty of the said Deane and his accomplices in perpetrating such murther as aforesayd, raged so farre, that whereas, whilest the sayd persons did *consume with violent fire*,

the wombe of the sayd Perrotine being burned, there did issue frō her a goodly man childe, which by the Officers was taken vp & handled, and after in a most despightful maner, throwne into the fire, and there also with the sely mother most cruelly burnt. (Book 11, p. 1969)

Here the use of 'consume' implies a high level of force that could characterize either illness or fire. For example, the noun form 'consumption' refers most commonly to illness rather than fire:

His wyfe at length fell sicke of a *consumption* and dyed in his armes, no man had a more godly woman to his wyfe. (Book 12, p. 2113)

A metaphoric sense of 'consume' is in relation to time – since time is an abstract concept and therefore does not have the embodied sense implied by illness or fire, and could be paraphrased with the synonym 'wasted' as in the following that occur in a debate between West and Thomas Cranmer:

*West.* Because we will not **consume and spend the tyme in waste,** this your writyng which you exhibite. (Book 10, p. 1456)
*West.* Thus **you consume time,** which might be better bestowed on other matters. (Book 10, p. 1467)

'Consume' could also occur as part of extended metaphor – in the following advice against excessive indulgence an analogy is developed in which the effect of 'riches' and 'worldy honor' are understood in terms of the effect of fire:

Beware of riches and worldly honor: for without vnderstansting prayer, and fasting, it is a snare and also pouertie, all whiche are **like to consuming fire,** of whiche if a man take a little, it will warme hym, but if hee take too much, **it will consume him.** For it is hard for a man to cary fire in his bosome, and not be brent. (Book 11, p. 1725)

In this regard, like the action of fire itself – with its highly negative associations as a means for the destruction of the saintly Protestants – the force implied by 'consume' is that to which Foxe is opposed, so the original literal paraphrase of 'using' became gradually replaced by that of 'wasting' – this serves to reactivate the negative associations that are present in the earlier illness sense of 'consumption'.

## Functional fire

Before the age of electricity, the only source of illumination was provided by the light from naked flame – a candle, lamp, torch or – when outdoors, a beacon. The provision of light permitted the religiously minded to read, and in most cases the only text that they would be likely to read would have been the Bible. It is not, then, surprising that knowledge becomes associated with light generally because of the embodied experience of seeing and because of the primacy of sight as a source of information and also more specifically with spiritual knowledge. Building on Lakoff and Johnson's (1980: 48) UNDERSTANDING IS SEEING and Lakoff and Turner's (1989: 190) KNOWING IS SEEING Charteris-Black (2004: 189) proposed the conceptual representation SPIRITUAL KNOWLEDGE IS LIGHT.

My earlier study demonstrated that nearly 10 per cent of all metaphors in the Bible draw on the semantic field of light to describe some aspect of spiritual experience, and the preceding chapter also showed extensive support for the salience of light in expressing forms of spiritual knowledge in Hinduism. There appears to be an embodied potentially universal motivation of such metaphors in so far as human beings acquire knowledge from sight, and all plants require light in order to grow, but also cultural specific orientations that extend this knowledge to areas of spiritual experience.

Three of the core lexical items in the *Actes and Monuments* relating to the concept of 'functional fire' – illuminate, candle and lamp – all suggest the frames: FAITH IS LIGHT, GOODNESS IS LIGHT and SPRITUAL KNOWLEDGE IS LIGHT; they can also be traced back to their Biblical source, as clearly the ideological purpose of its author is to go back to the true source of spiritual knowledge – the Bible, for which the translator of its English version Tyndale had been burnt.

All ten uses of 'illuminate' are metaphors referring to spiritual knowledge; both 'hearts' and 'minds' are referred to as being the embodied location of spiritual knowledge:

> But as touching the sacrament he woulde as yet hold his peace, vntill such time as the Lorde shall otherwise **illuminate** *the hartes and mindes* of the clergye. (Book 5, p. 446)

This implies that religious knowledge arises from a combination of emotional and cognitive activity. The light frame can also be developed through extended metaphor:

> as though the Church (frō which Christ our sauiour promised himselfe neuer to depart) hath erred hitherto alwayes in darcke shadowes of ignorance and perdition, tyll now it should be **illuminate** with **newe resplendent beames** of Luther. (Book 7, p. 789)

There are sixty-four references to 'candle' the majority of which are literal; for example, in the following account of the martyrdom of Cuthbert Simson, his brother has a dream about him:

> Whereupon being sore troubled, hee awaked, and called hys wife, saying: Kate strike lighte, For I am much troubled with my brother Cutbert thys nyght. When she hadde so done, he gaue himselfe to reade in his booke a while, and there feeling sleepe to come vpon him, he put out the candle, & so gaue himselfe agayn to rest. (Book 12, p. 2056)

In the following a papal legate experiences a bad dream after spending the night writing letters to the Pope:

After his labour when night was come, thinking to refresh himselfe, he began to rise: and at his rising, beholde there appeared to hym a mighty blacke dogge, of a huge bignes, **his eyes flamyng with fire**, and his eares hanging low downe welneere to the ground, to enter in, and straite to come toward hym, & so to couch vnder the boord. The Cardinall not a little amased at the sight thereof, somewhat recouering himselfe, called to his seruauntes, which were in the outward chāber next by, to bring in a candle, and to seeke for the dog. (Book 12, p. 2131)

It is significant that the account of the dream itself involves fire and then a candle is illuminated to seek out the nightmarish dog. Eventually, the Cardinal dies – presumably as a form of divine punishment. The flaming eyes of the dog are doubtless an intimation of the hellfires that await him! But this literal use of 'candle' hints at a highly negative semantic prosody.

The plural form 'candles' is exclusively literal in meaning and typically occurs in listing the various Catholic ritual practices that were condemned by Protestants:

and not in fasting, keeping of holydayes, watching, singing, and long praiers daily and all day lōg, hearing of masses, setting vp of candles, running on pilgrimages and such other things, which as well the hypocrites, proud people, enuious and subiect to all wicked affections, do. (Book 8, p. 1280)

Foxe's rhetoric typically contrasts the practices he recommends for good Protestants with the corrupt ones of Catholics that he exhorts his readers against following:

exhort your hearers … not to repose their trust or affiance in other workes deuised by mens fantasies besides scripture: as in wandering to Pilgrimages, offering of money, candles, or tapers to fained Reliques or Images, or kissing, or licking the same, saieng ouer a number of beades not vnderstanded ne minded on, or such like superstition. (Book 8, p. 1120)

Even the singular 'candle' is typically negative when used literally because of its association with Catholic ritual; the phrase 'book, bell and candle' occurs quite frequently as in the following:

With them the said pope had ben so depely offended & angred a litle before, þᵗ the great charter of the liberties of England (wᵗ great indignation & countenance most terrible) he rent and destroyed, by sentence definitiue condemning it for euer. And by and by therupon cursed all the other rebels, *with booke, bel, and candle.* The greater captaines of them (with the citizens of London) for that assay were pronounced excōmunicate by name, & remained still interdicted.

The phrase 'book, bell and candle' refers to a highly dramatic ceremony known as the 'anathema' that was employed by Catholics to excommunicate those whose behaviour was deemed beyond forgiveness. The ceremony involved a bishop holding a book and a bell who would recite a ritual formula in the presence of twelve priests – each of whom would be holding a lit candle; at the end of the recitation, the priests would respond 'So be it, so be it, so be it', upon which the bishop would close the book and ring the bell, then the priests would snuff out their candles by dashing them to the ground and the offender would be formally excommunicated. The symbolic power of the candle was also attractive to those practising witchcraft:

> An other coniecture may be hereof, for that, if the Duches had entended any suche haynous treason against the kings life, as by burning of a waxe candle to consume him ... (Book 6, p. 727)

Whereas literal senses of 'candle' tend to be negative, metaphoric uses of 'candle' are exclusively positive because they evoke the positive frame FAITH IS LIGHT, as for example in the following account of the martyrdom of Latimer and Ridley:

> Then brought they a fagot kindled with fire, and layd the same downe at D. Ridleys feete. To whome Maister Latymer spake in this maner: be of good comfort maister Ridley, and play the man: wee shall this day *light such a candle by Gods grace in England, as (I trust) shall neuer be put out.*

Here the candle that cannot be extinguished is a metaphor for the enduring spiritual conviction of the Protestants. We saw in Chapter 2 how language and ideas typically 'spread', based on the behaviour of fire, and therefore fire provides a model for the adoption of a religious faith. In this Protestant text the image of the candle as a source of spiritual inspiration is based on the contrast between light and darkness and the concepts GOODNESS IS LIGHT and EVIL IS DARKNESS; in this frame that derives from the New Testament, the light from the candle spreads and therefore becomes an image of a faith that spreads through the language of the Bible:

> Let Christ be your scope and marke to pricke at: let hym be your patron to worke by: let him be your ensample to folow: geue him as your hart so your hand, as your minde so your toung, as your fayth so your feete, and let his word **be your candle** to go before you in all matters of Religion.

Once the religious frame of the New Testament is activated, the candle is no longer a symbol of corrupt papal ritual but a metaphor for true spiritual knowledge:

> You are **the light of the world**: a city builded on the hil cannot be hid: Neither do men *light a candle, & put it vnder a bushell,* but vppon *a candle sticke, that it may shyne, and geue light* to them in the house. (Book 7, p. 964)

Here Foxe is quoting directly from Matthew 5: 13–15. The imagery of the candle would be readily recognized by his readership, in so far as they gave emphasis to the framing of religious faith in the New Testament. The same allusions would be recognized in metaphors relating to 'lampes':

how many yeres a man shall lye in Purgatory for one sinne if he buy not plenty of *the oile that runneth ouer our lampes to slake the sinne withall*, and so forget hel whiche cannot be slaked, to prouide for Purgatory. (Book 11, p. 1773)

This clearly alludes to the Parable of the wise and foolish virgins in the Book of Matthew (25: 2–4):

Then the kingdom of heaven shall be likened to ten virgins who took their lamps and went out to meet the bridegroom. Now five of them were wise, and five were foolish. Those who were foolish took their lamps and took no oil with them, but the wise took oil in their vessels with their lamps.

The framing of religious behaviour within simple everyday experiential knowledge – that a lamp requires oil if it is to provide light – invites a comparison between actions on this earth and the eternal fate of the soul. From the perspective of Protestant ideology considerations of the after-life overrode those of the here and now, so that *any* form of physical suffering – including being burnt at the stake – could be justified if it influenced the fate of the soul in the after-life. It was therefore an appeal to divine authority that underlay the resistance of the martyrs to other forms of authority such as the Catholic Church, its Pope, its hierarchy of cardinals – or even its representatives on earth appointed by divine right.

A similar positive frame is provided by 'melt', which when used as a metaphor invariably collocates with 'heart', to convey an intensely positive emotional experience of empathy, compassion and joy as in the following:

Notwithstãding al these great threats Peter wrought miracles still amongst the people, doing thē to know that glory therfore ought to be geuē to Iesus, by whose power and name they were doue. Wherwith the harts of the people **melted for ioy**: so that they folowed after the Apostles, whyther soeuer they went. (Book 8, p. 1135)

In the examination of Richard Woodman, he claims: 'I seeing their blindnesse and blasphemie, **it made my heart melt**, and mine eies gush oute with teares' …. (Book 12, p. 2010)

As noted in Chapter 2, such uses of 'melt' draw on the metonymic frames WARMTH FOR AFFECTION and LEVEL OF TEMPERATURE FOR THE INTENSITY OF EMOTION and imply an emotion that is under control; these contrast with ANGER IS FIRE and UNCONTROLLED EMOTION IS EXTREME TEMPERATURE which are the dominant frames for persecution activated by natural fire terms such as 'fiery' and 'heat'.

## Organic fire

Fire was frequently framed as an organism by using metaphor: all of the instances of 'inflame'/'inflammatory' and 'extinguish' were metaphors, nearly all of the instances of 'sparke' and three quarters of the uses of 'kindle' were metaphors. The only exception to this pattern was 'ashes' – which in most cases retained its literal meaning. However, there were interesting contrasts in the prosody of 'kindle' and 'sparke' – 'kindle' is generally used as metaphor to describe the inception of a negative emotion such as anger or malice, whereas 'sparke' is more commonly used to profile a positive emotional or spiritual quality. 'Kindle' is more strongly associated with negative qualities derived from the frames ANGER IS FIRE, and EMOTION IS A FORCE, whereas 'sparke' is associated with positive qualities arising from the frame SPIRITUAL KNOWLEDGE IS LIGHT. The following examples illustrate this contrast:

> And so great malice **was their kindled in their brestes**, that when all things were in peaceable tranquilitie, they made and raysed most cruell and bloudy intestine or ciuill warres. (Book 1, p. 125)
>
> And further they were commaunded that they should shew not so much as **one sparke of mercy or compassion** vpon vs. (Book 1, p. 103)

The implication of 'kindle' is that – following the organic process of fire – the resentful feelings of those in authority will continue to grow and will eventually lead to the burning of Protestants:

> These seeking (for the furtheraunce of theyr vngodly purpose) to reuiue, stirre vp and **kindle** euil and pernicious humours in their Prince and soueraigne Lord (Book 8, p. 1266)

Typically, Foxe draws on the FIRE IS ANGER frame by combining a negative attribute – grudge, malice and so on – with the verb 'kindle' and a reference to the location of the emotion in the body such:

> In the tractation of this kings history, before was declared what grudge did **kindle in the harts** of the Barons agaynst the king. (Book 4, p. 396)

As we saw in the section on natural fire, with the pattern fire of + negative emotion, the frame ANGER IS FIRE is often integrated with the frames EMOTION IS A FORCE and CAUSE OF A SITUATION IS CAUSE OF FIRE:

> The next moneth folowing, whiche was Februarye, came out an other bloudy Commission from the king and Queene, **to kindle vp** the fire of persecution, as though it were not hoate enough already .... (Book 12, 1994)

A number of different types of torture were inflicted on the heretics, but it is their burning that comes to represent all of these; so 'the fire of persecution' becomes a synecdoche in which the final stage of the persecution frames all previous forms of bodily punishment. In some cases, 'sparke' is used in a similar way:

> In somuch, that there hath not chaunced betwene them these many yeares, so much as one **sparke of** discorde and dissention. (Book 4, p. 334)

However, another use of 'sparke' is to indicate the absence of a positive quality by the use of a negative form ('not', 'no', 'neither' etc.) as in the following:

> Besides this, the laitie are miserably robbed & spoiled of their goodes, by these light & vile officials. In whose conscience there is **no sparke of** christian pity and godlines, but only a wicked desire, & couetousnesse. (Book 7, p. 885)
>     to thinke euer more hereafter, that ye haue neyther **one sparke of** learning, nor yet of godlines in you. (Book 8, p. 1207)

In these metaphors, the aspects of the 'sparke' frame that are active are the knowledge that a sparke is both very small and does not necessarily cause a fire. This contrasts with 'kindling' as it implies a much higher level of certainty as regards the causation of a negative outcome following the frame CAUSE OF A SITUATION IS CAUSE OF FIRE. In such cases, 'sparke' is used to describe positive spiritual qualities that *do not flourish*. However, when used in the plural form, 'sparkes', there is a greater likelihood of these positive qualities coming to fruition:

> the righteous **shall shine as the sparkes** that runneth through the red bushe, they shall iudge the nations and haue dominion ouer the people, and their Lord shal raigne for euer. (Book 12, p. 2165)

Since many 'sparkes' are more likely to start a fire, Foxe implies that the righteous shall receive their due rewards on the day of judgement.

We have already seen how 'inflame' invariably conveys a negative evaluation, as it implies an emotion that caused the persecution of Protestants. 'Inflamed' blends the emotion state with its outcome in the form of the actions taken against Protestants, and their precursors such as the Lollards:

> Certayne it is and vndoubted, that the Prelates in those dayes being so mightely **inflamed** against these Lollards, were not altogether behind for their parts, nor vtterly idle in this matter, but practised against them what they could, first to bring them into hatred, and then to death. (Book 5, p. 595)

The use of 'inflamed' primes a connection between 'hatred' and 'death' and implies that the Prelates' actions of inflicting suffering on their opponents is based on cruel emotional forces rather than on faith. The only exception to the generally negative evaluation of anger is where zeal (religious passion) overrides this emotion, as when John Clarke in France smashes some idolatrous catholic images:

> he, the day before that the people of that city should go out to the suburbs to worship certaine blind idols neere by (after an old vse and custome amongst them receiued) **being inflamed with the zeale of God,** went out of the Citie to the place where the Images were, and brast them all downe in peeces. (Book 7, p. 902)

Here the author presumably approves of the smashing of images, since a religiously inspired emotion provides legitimacy for his actions. But when 'inflamed' occurs with emotions such as lust, it frames them as out of control:

> Also hee left no mischieuous nor lasciuious acte vnattempted, but was the vtter enemie of all womanly chastity, which vsed to send the honest wiues whome he had adulterated with shame and dishonestie vnto their husbandes (being worthy Senators) after that he had rauished them. He abstained from no adulterous acte, but was **inflamed with the inquencheable lust** of deflouring of women. (Book 1, p. 107)

Here, the embodied experience of increased bodily temperature is associated with lust. So, EMOTION IS A FORCE is not inherently positive or negative in its evaluation.

When employed as a metaphor 'extinguished' refers to the suppression of Protestants and their faith – based on the frame SPIRITUAL KNOWLEDGE IS LIGHT/ FIRE; it is therefore employed as a metaphor for an authoritarian act by the forces of repression and religious intolerance:

> Like as the Pope thinkeeh now that this Gospel wil ouerthrow his kingdom of maiestie. And therfore sought they all means possible, how by death and all kindes of torments vtterly **to extinguish** the name and memorie of the Christians. (Book 1, p. 60)

The entity in the object position is something that is valued and, by implication, the subject of 'extinguish' is something delegitimized, the Pope, a named individual, or Satan himself. 'Extinguish' implies efforts to eliminate completely any religious opposition.

'Ashes' is more commonly used with its literal sense, which occurs thirty-one times in variations of the phrase 'consumed/burnt/turned into/to ashes'. It is also sometimes used with a symbolic meaning referring to the ashes that form part of a religious ritual:

> Tenthly, that hee had affirmed, that if hee were out of prison, he would not come to Masse, Mattins, nor Euensong, nor beare Taper, Candle, or Palme, nor goe in procession, nor would receiue holy water, holy breade, ashes, or paxe, or any other ceremonie of the Churche then vsed within this Realme. (Book 12, p. 2040)

This sense originates in the ceremonial use of ashes on the first day of the Christian Lent that originated in the forty days spent by Christ in the desert during which he endured temptation by the Devil. This day is known as 'Ash Wednesday' because some Christians mark their foreheads with a visible cross of ash. The ritual is accompanied by the words: 'remember that you are dust, and to dust you shall return' (Genesis 3: 19). So, 'ashes' typically serve as a metonym for death:

> Oh wretched and vnhappy man, what art thou but **dust and ashes?** And wilt thou resist thy maker that fashioned thee and framed thee? (Book 10, p. 1444)

Ashes occur at the very final stage of an event – cremation – and stand for the whole experience of death and therefore are a form of synecdoche. Most uses of 'ashes', whether quite literal, as in 'burnt to ashes', or metonymic as in 'dust and ashes', were treated as literal. Metaphoric uses of 'ashes' occurred in instances where the frame for fire includes the knowledge that it can revive itself spontaneously. The following extended metaphor describes the instructions of a Papal Bull issued to King Richard of England to authorize and encourage the speedy and widespread suppression of the Lollards:

> Go to therefore my sweete sonne, and indeuour your self to worke so in this matter, as vndoubtedly we trust you will: that as this **firebrand (burning and flaming ouer sore)** beganne vnder your president or gouernment: so vnder your seuere iudgement and vertuous diligence, might, fauour, and ayde: **not one sparke remaine hid vnder the ashes, but that it be vtterlye extinguyshed and spedely put out.** (Book 5, p. 528)

Here, 'ashes' contributes to an extended metaphor that emphasizes the danger of a Lollard revival and argues for the complete eradication of heresy.

## Summary

In part one of this book, we saw how fire came to enact and symbolize the control of man over his environment. And we have also seen how control over the discourse of fire contributes to the status and position of a priestly class across many different cultures. In Chapter 4, we saw how the concepts of DIVINE DISPLAY IS FIRE and DIVINE ANGER IS FIRE constitute what I have described as a prophetic discourse that underlies the authority of the Abrahamic religions as they allied themselves with the powerful symbolic meanings of fire.

In this chapter, through an analysis of the lexical field for fire in a sixteenth-century ideological text, *Foxe's Book of Martyrs*, I have illustrated how those in authority sought to prevent ideas they viewed as heretical from spreading and displayed their control over fire by burning their opponents and their symbols thereby enforcing their authority. I have illustrated how fire metaphors based on 'natural fire' words and 'organic fire' words blend the frames ANGER IS FIRE with EMOTION IS A FORCE. They also blended CAUSE OF A SITUATION IS CAUSE OF FIRE with THE LEVEL OF INTENSITY OF AN EMOTION IS THE LEVEL OF INTENSITY OF A FIRE so that their metaphoric 'emotion' senses are grounded in the expectation that the force of a 'hot' emotion will lead to the actual burning of Protestant martyrs. By contrast, 'functional fire' metaphors are motivated by the frame FAITH IS LIGHT and frequently allude to the New Testament. There are interesting differences in terms of semantic prosody between metaphoric uses of 'kindle' that are exclusively negative, and those for 'sparke' that are usually positive and this is taken as further evidence of the tension between the contrasting frames: ANGER IS FIRE, EMOTION IS A FORCE and SPIRITUAL KNOWLEDGE IS LIGHT.

However, in terms of fulfilling his rhetorical and ideological purposes, Foxe's most significant themes are elaborate and detailed accounts of the heroic suffering endured by Protestants and their demonstration of faith by a willing embrace of their persecutors' fire: this has been analysed using the force dynamic approach. This testimony to spiritual strength is perhaps the most persuasive component of the work and metaphor contributes to a heroic narrative of suffering endured. The discourse of authority was therefore challenged by re-invoking a sense of awe, not for the fire itself but for the spiritual courage of those who endured its inflictions on their bodies.

# 8

# Fire Metaphors in British Political Rhetoric

## Introduction

So far we have seen how tracing the archaeology of fire terms has provided insight into various theological and ideological texts in which fire has been understood as somehow divine in origin – a magical and inexplicable phenomenon of nature that never loses its power to fascinate and attract. Fire is intrinsically a form for display of the unknown. Through the light if gives off, it offers a source of 'illumination' into the nature of religious experience and through the 'heat' it gives off it reminds us, through embodiment, the importance of physical and emotional proximity in the experience of being alive. Deprive a plant of life and it will soon die, deprive a human of emotional warmth and he or she will lose his or her ability to experience the intimate relationships that make life worth living. Fire glows and warms, it is our friend and neighbour – and our sexual partner too. But it has the capacity for excess when we burn our fingers or put our hand into the flames; in the previous chapter we saw how the emotions of the religiously intolerant are 'kindled' and become 'inflamed' – leading to the *actual* burning of their opponents. In this chapter, I examine how discourses of awe and authority were subsequently developed in British political rhetoric.

Given the fascination of fire and its salience in human consciousness, we might expect politicians to rely extensively on fire metaphors. Yet, an earlier study (Charteris-Black 2011) found that actually there were many other areas of human experience that were much more common in political metaphors, which include journeys, people (i.e. personifications), war and conflict, health and illness, creation and destruction. Only between 1 and 2 per cent of all metaphors drew on the literal senses of fire terms. However, it may be that their relative infrequency contributes to a higher rhetorical impact. Although they are likely to be more visible and therefore more closely allied to the speaker's overt intentions, their greater originality may sound more eloquent and convey emotional intensity.

Classical rhetoricians classified speeches into three distinct types: deliberative, forensic and epideictic (Charteris-Black 2014: 6). This classification was on the basis of the contexts and circumstances where the speeches were given. Deliberative speeches are given in decision-making bodies such as parliament; forensic speeches are typically given in law courts and epideictic speeches are made at ceremonial events such as post-election victory speeches. The speeches used in this chapter and the next one are either deliberative or epideictic. Originating in the Greek word for 'show' or 'display', epideictic speeches are addressed to an audience that is not required to make a decision but was assembled to honour or commemorate a particular individual. The speaker seeks to display eloquence in evaluating another by praise or criticism of past actions. Conversely, deliberative speeches have the purpose of establishing the benefit or harm that may be expected from a future course of action. The speaker constructs an argument drawing on a range of means of persuasion to consider a range of possible outcomes and wins support for one of these. According to Aristotle, deliberative speeches would typically consider one of the following subjects: whether to go to war or to make peace, defence, imports and exports. The general purpose (*skopos*) of a deliberative speech was to judge the course of action most likely to enhance human happiness; political speeches typically involve working out the advantages and disadvantages of different courses of action in terms of how far they might contribute to socially valued outcomes. I hope to demonstrate the role of fire metaphors in political rhetoric and the type of concepts in which they are grounded.

## Fire metaphors in British political rhetoric

To assist with the task of investigating discourses of awe and authority in British political speeches, I have assembled a research corpus of 167 speeches (505,324 words) made by sixteen politicians in the period 1960–2010 that I will refer to as the 'British sample' (see Appendix 1). I have supplemented this with searches of the Hansard Corpus of British Political Speeches that I refer to as 'Hansard'; this is a database of all the 7.6 million speeches given in parliament during the period 1805–2005.[1] Given that these 'speeches' are made in a debating context, they can be considered entirely deliberative rather than epideictic and the use of a large reference corpus allows me to identify whether, and in what way, a metaphor identified in the British sample is typical of British political rhetoric.

The British sample of half a million words is from a range of genres including party conference speeches and speeches given in parliament. The speeches were by experienced male and female politicians from both major parties. The number of speeches for each politician varied according to his or her status. So, for example, there are more speeches by those who were prime ministers. However, I also needed to include a measure of impact and influence; so although Enoch Powell was never prime minister I have included some of his speeches. Table 8.1 gives an overview of the frequency of the core fire lexicon and metaphoric uses of this lexicon by British politicians, using the framework introduced in Chapter 2.

Around 45 per cent of all the core fire terms used in the British sample are metaphors; sixteen core fire words do not occur at all – these include 'fiery', 'smoulder', 'incandescent', 'scorch' and 'incendiary'. This is partly because these words are less frequent in the language and also because of rhetorical considerations as regards their appropriateness in the genre of the political speech – for example, some of these are likely to arouse very intense emotions that may be associated with extremism. However, they do occur in the larger Hansard corpus, for example, the expression 'incandescent with rage' occurs seven times and 'smouldering resentment' occurs twelve times.

**Table 8.1** Fire metaphors in the British sample

| Fire frame | Fire term | Total uses | Uses as a metaphor |
|---|---|---|---|
| **NATURAL FIRE** | fire(s) | 60 | 12 |
| | burn | 16 | 3 |
| | glow | 4 | 4 |
| | flame | 2 | 2 |
| | blaze | 1 | 1 |
| | flicker | 2 | 2 |
| | flare | 1 | 1 |
| TOTAL | | 86 | 25 |
| **FUNCTIONAL FIRE** | heat | 13 | 4 |
| | beacon | 10 | 10 |
| | melt(down) | 5 | 3 |
| | torch | 5 | 3 |
| | smoke | 4 | 2 |
| | lamp | 3 | 1 |
| | brand | 3 | 3 |
| | illuminate | 1 | 1 |
| | stoke | 1 | 1 |
| TOTAL | | 45 | 28 |
| **ORGANIC FIRE** | fuel | 31 | 7 |
| | spark | 9 | 9 |
| | inflame/inflammatory | 4 | 4 |
| | ashes | 4 | 3 |
| | (re)kindle | 3 | 3 |
| | snuff out | 3 | 3 |
| | extinguish | 2 | 2 |
| | embers | 2 | 1 |
| TOTAL | | 58 | 32 |
| OVERALL TOTALS | | 189 | 85 |

Many fire words occur much more commonly with their literal senses; this is the case with 'fire', 'burn' and 'fuel' – for which I provide an example each:

This year saw some of the busiest nights in the *Fire* Brigade's recent history and I pay tribute to all of London's firefighters for managing the situation with their usual professionalism and incredible bravery. (Johnson, 2012)

What a contrast from a year ago when England's cities *burned* in a week of riots. (Clegg, 2012)

We will work to cut down the use of fossil *fuels*, a cause of both acid rain and the greenhouse effect. (Thatcher, October 1988)

Fire-related issues are of interest to politicians because they relate to the government's primary role of ensuring security; for example, there are a number of references in political speeches to the London riots of 2011 (as in the first two examples above). 'Fuel' has also come to refer to the provision of energy in general – whether for transportation, cooking or heating – rather than to the physical action of natural fire.

A group of other words are *only* used metaphorically in political speeches; these include 'flame', 'glow', 'flicker', 'flare', 'beacon', 'spark', 'kindle', 'inflame' and 'snuff out'. For example, in Hansard, the most frequent words (collocates) occurring after 'glowing' are 'terms', 'testimony', 'tribute' and so on, all implying some form of compliment. The 'flames of' are typically negative such as 'war', 'nationalism', 'inflation' and so on as in:

> Unfortunately, the mirror image of that narrow brand of Scottish nationalism seems to be creeping into the leadership of the Conservative party, which is **fanning the flames of** *English nationalism*'. (Reid, 27 July 1999)

Words following 'flicker of' include 'hope', 'doubt' and 'recognition'. Typically, entities that 'flare up' are 'troubles', 'disputes' or a named geographical region, such as the Balkans. This suggests that such metaphors are conventional and indicative of a mid-level, familiar rhetorical style that characterizes many speeches, for example:

> The purpose of terrorism lies not just in the violent act itself. It is in producing terror. **It sets out to inflame,** to divide, to produce consequences which they then use to justify further terror. (Blair, 18 March 2003)

Here the speaker is seeking to give a negative evaluation of acts of terror that will be used as a warrant to support his rhetorical purpose of winning a vote to declare war on Iraq. A set of fairly routinized metaphors is more likely to activate pre-existing knowledge frames – so that terrorism typically 'inflames' in a way that war may not – depending on its representation in ideology; so a war of 'liberation' would not be viewed as inflaming a situation in the way that a war of tribal conquest might be.

Where words occur with both metaphoric and literal senses they are more likely to be novel and more rhetorically expressive when used as metaphors. These more 'rhetorical' metaphors may also be repeated and extended, for example, consider the following:

> We did not know it at the time but the **torch we lit** in Britain, which transformed our country – **the torch of freedom** that is now the symbol of our Party – became the **beacon that has shed its light** *across the Iron Curtain into the East*. (Thatcher, 13 October 1989)

Here the allusion to the 'torch' is repeated and introduces a more elaborate metaphor frame as the image of torch is extended by reference to the act of lighting it (and the agents of this action – the 'we') and its effect of 'shedding its light' across those parts of the world assumed to be in darkness, such as the former Soviet Union. The metaphor of 'torch' is substituted by another metaphor 'beacon' so the development of the fire frame is closely related to the speaker's purpose in evoking a moral frame of reference based on notions such as UNDERSTANDING IS SEEING and GOODNESS IS LIGHT; they also echo those used by Churchill, for which I proposed the frame BRITAIN IS LIGHT (Charteris-Black 2011: 78).

There are also individual preferences by politicians in their use of fire metaphors; Table 8.2 shows which politicians most commonly used a particular fire metaphor and in selecting the speaker I have taken into account the number of times that they have used the metaphor that is shown in bold; I have only included those metaphors that were used at least three times by a speaker and the total number of their words recorded in Hansard.

**Table 8.2** British politicians' use of fire metaphors in Hansard

| Fire term + (frequency) | Name | Example |
|---|---|---|
| | | **Natural fire metaphors** |
| glow (20) | Benjamin Disraeli | Member for Louth has had an opportunity of addressing the House at considerable length, and in the vein of **glowing** rhetoric which we always listen to with pleasure … |
| flame (16) | Lord John Russell | It enabled them to preserve those great classical works which at the time of the revival of letters were found in the monasteries and convents, and which amid the din of arms, and amid a state of ignorance, might have led to barbarism, yet kept alive that sacred **flame** from which we have derived our civilisation … |
| fiery (10) | Benjamin Disraeli | I might add that I am here surrounded by many who have a personal recollection of that brilliant perception and that **fiery** eloquence which he certainly possesses more than most of the men I have been acquainted with … |
| flare (7) | Douglas Hurd | That is one possibility: if, even with the arms embargo, the fighting **flared** up because the generals on either side mistakenly thought that they could achieve military victory … |
| blaze (5) | Edward Kenealy | In his opinion the present **blaze** of glory in which the Judges of the Queen's Bench shone, was a **blaze** of fire that would consume them, as Semele was consumed by the glory of her lover … |
| flicker (4) | Roy Jenkins | The Government's financial stance begins to have just a **flicker** of sense only on the assumption that the road to health is through the intensification of the bleeding to which the economy has been subjected over the past six years … |
| smoulder (3) | Harold Wilson | The Chancellor should realize that the **smouldering**, burning resentment which he has kindled by his action will enflame and embitter educational policies for as long as a Conservative Government cling to office … |
| incandescent (3) | Tom Dalyell | I shall never forget the morning when it became clear that six picket breakers were operating: the late Superintendent Donald MacKinnon, an equable highlander, was **incandescent** with anger … |

(continued)

**Table 8.2** British politicians' use of fire metaphors in Hansard (*continued*)

| Fire term + (frequency) | Name | Example |
|---|---|---|
| **Functional fire metaphors** | | |
| candle (16) | Partrick Comrack | It was Kate Adie: I was in the Committee Room when she talked about the bravery and professionalism of our British soldiers and said quite unashamedly that no one could hold a **candle** to them … |
| illuminate (14) | Winston Churchill | This light would **illuminate** for them not only the past but the future: it would not be right to discuss in public, in time of war, these intimate matters of naval defence, and I ask the House with confidence to support the Admiralty in their decision … |
| beacon (8) | Nicholas Soames | Certainly, at the present time, the British and American economies are bright **beacons** burning in a pretty dismal picture … |
| melt (8) | Lewis Silkin | would have rendered unnecessary the throwing of the whole question of the planning of land into the **melting** pot … |
| branded (8) | Isaac Butt | to the illustrious name of patriots, to the elevated character of a religious people, lovers of your priests which transcends all; or you will sink and fall down to the lowest depths of infamy and degradation, to be for ever **branded** as renegades and recreants, with dishonour and disgrace … |
| scorch (4) | Sidney Shephard | he can now state the Government's policy with regard to compensation for losses incurred by commercial interests in Burma as a result of the **scorched** earth policy and the Japanese occupation … |
| torch (4) | Gordon Brown | Now even the deputy Prime Minister is semi-detached: who are left carrying the **torch** onwards? |
| fanned (4) | Jack Straw | It is clear, tragically, that there is a degree of insurgency – much of it **fanned** from outside Iraq … |
| searing (3) | Barney Heyhoe | Does he agree that it is a **searing** indictment of the Labour party that it seems to be more intent on encouraging such action in the interests of its own sordid politics than on being concerned with patient care? |
| **Organic fire metaphors** | | |
| extinguished (15) | Arthur Balfour | we took away all inducement to tenants to buy, that the desire to purchase would be **extinguished** … |
| inflame (11) | Robert Peel | instead of entering upon an indefinite inquiry into the state of Canada, at a time when the minds of men were **inflamed** … |
| ashes (10) | Austin Mitchell | The only logic of what was done by the Government during 1979–81 is that which is to be found in the belief that phoenix will rise from the **ashes** … |
| fuelled (8) | Jeremy Corbyn | Conflicts abound around the world, **fuelled** by inequality and the profiteering of arms manufacturers … |
| dampen (8) | Harry Barnes | known as the Tobin Tax after the name of the Nobel Laureate who originated the concept, could both help to **dampen** down the scale and scope of speculation and raise substantial revenues … |
| snuff out (4) | Edward Garnier | has mentioned to me a case involving a little girl in his constituency who unwittingly ate a biscuit containing peanut and died as she ran the few yards to the school sanatorium – a young life literally **snuffed out** in seconds … |

**Table 8.2** British politicians' use of fire metaphors in Hansard *(continued)*

| Fire term + (frequency) | Name | Example |
|---|---|---|
| embers (4) | Archibald Southby | from this country against the rulers of Germany and Italy we shall thereby advantage ourselves very much: I think it may have some effect on latent fires and cause smouldering **embers** to break into flame one day … |
| ignite (3) | Robert Sheldon | No one is against that, but Mrs: Thatcher **ignited** runaway house price inflation … |

## Natural fire metaphors

There were twenty-five natural fire metaphors in the British sample (see Table 8.1) and generally these had strongly positive discourse prosodies. Natural fire is associated with strongly positive traits such as motivation, enthusiasm and passion relying on the frame POLITICAL CONVICTION IS FIRE and contributing to a discourse of authority. This shows in Table 8.2 with collocations such as 'glowing rhetoric', 'fiery eloquence' and 'flicker of sense'. The fire itself is the passion, the heat from the fire is the intensity of the passion and the light from the fire is the hope that arises from this emotion. Political conviction implies a particular type of emotion associated with the politician's commitment to a set of beliefs that is evident from their style of delivery and is likely to contribute to the emotional response of audiences. But it is also hyperbolic, authoritative and forceful and hence contributes to a discourse of authority. POLITICAL CONVICTION IS FIRE is a domain-specific realization of the more generic EMOTION IS FIRE. Similarly, POLITICAL CONVICTION IS FORCE is a domain-specific realization of EMOTION IS A FORCE and THE LEVEL OF INTENSITY OF AN EMOTION IS THE LEVEL OF INTENSITY OF A FIRE. This is summarized in Figure 8.1.

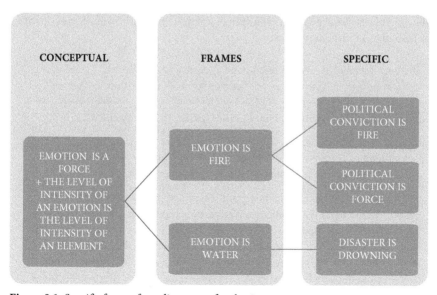

**Figure 8.1** Specific frames for a discourse of authority

Here we see an inheritance structure in which emotions can be viewed as different types of forces, such as fire, water and so on, and there are others such as a wild animal or an opponent that are not included; when these general frames from the natural world are taken up in specific domains they inherit the same implications, so that when a fire metaphor is used in a political speech it implies a degree of emotional force and a level of intensity that is authoritative. Please refer to Figure 3.5 to recall how this may be analysed in terms of force dynamics.

As well as appealing to pathos, such fire metaphors also appeal to ethos by drawing on the frame SPIRITUAL KNOWLEDGE IS LIGHT. The rhetorical purpose of invoking the positive associations of natural fire characterizes both the political left and the political right as they struggle to demonstrate their moral authority and to imply a sense of divine purpose. In post-Second World War rhetoric, many of these natural fire metaphors take their inspiration from Churchill:

> **If the light of freedom which still burns so brightly in the frozen North should be finally quenched**, it might well herald a return to the Dark Ages, when every vestige of human progress during two thousand years would be **engulfed**. (Churchill, 20 January 1940)

This is an elaborate metaphor that combines images from the world of nature – of light, fire, temperature and water – that activate a religious frame. In this frame, the victory of Nazi Germany is represented as a victory of the forces of darkness over the forces of light. Rhetorically, this is conveyed by images of an apocalyptic, unnatural future. The metaphors involve a powerful spiritual dimension to the struggle against Nazism – a discourse of awe –activating frames such as GOODNESS IS LIGHT. The rhetorical effect is to combine appeals to ethos and pathos: if a cause is truly right then it will necessarily arouse powerful emotions that will motivate followers to act. However, the merging of passion with justice has an on-going rhetorical appeal: consider the following extracts from post-war politicians seeking to emulate Churchillian style with similar blends of pathos and ethos:

> The hon: Member for Westmorland and Lonsdale (Mr: Collins), … said at the Conservative party conference: politics should be about passion, excitement … and above all about optimism: He also said: it's time for Conservatives to put some **fire in our bellies**, to get up off our knees. (Darling, 19 November 2002)

> And then into the hands of everyone of us as we knock on doors, visit the factories, tour the shops, get out and campaign with **some fire in our bellies**, with some pride in what we have done. (Blair, 28 September 2004)

> Of why you are there in the first place. Every one of us in this hall has strong political convictions: Civil liberties. Internationalism. Human rights. Political reform. Responsible capitalism. Fighting climate change. But every one of us has a political passion too. **The fire inside** that drew us to politics in the first place. Let me tell you what I care most about. My passion is ensuring a fair start for every child. I have a simple, **unquenchable belief**: that every child can do good things, great things if only we give them the opportunities they deserve. (Clegg, 21 September 2011)

In each case, the speaker is alluding to the grand style employed by Churchill in his wartime speeches but incorporating it for the more prosaic purpose of motivating a political party at its annual conference. In each case, a natural fire metaphor expresses passionate commitment to a political cause based on the frame POLITICAL CONVICTION IS FORCE. Notice how in each extract fire is located *within* the human body – something that, like emotions, are an integral part of our being. Notice how in the first two extracts the speaker employs the 'internal' fire metaphor to refer to himself *and* to his audience. Clegg develops the emotional appeal into an ethical one by elaborating the metaphor into 'unquenchable belief'; this is clearly an echo of Churchillian style – with the same metaphorical use of 'quench' that activates a water scheme, but water used to extinguish a fire. It is likely that Clegg's use of 'unquenchable' originates in Churchill's:

> Why, Sir, if we had been confronted at the beginning of May with such a prospect, it would have seemed incredible that at the end of a period of horror and disaster, or at this point in a period of horror and disaster, we should stand erect, sure of ourselves, masters of our fate and with the conviction of final victory **burning unquenchable in our hearts.** Few would have believed we could survive; none would have believed that we should today not only feel stronger but should actually be stronger than we have ever been before. (Churchill, 20 August 1940)

In Hansard the entities that are described as 'unquenchable' are 'spirit', 'optimism', 'faith', 'love', 'hope' and 'enthusiasm'. It is likely that the Liberal Democratic leader sought to emulate the motivational effect of fire metaphors by alluding to Churchill at the critical moment when a speech ends, and where it is most crucial to profile the idealism of their cause:

> We think we've got it tough now. But it was much, much tougher in their day. It was only their resolve, their resilience and their unwavering determination that kept **the flickering flame of Liberalism** alive through our party's **darkest days.** (Clegg, 26 September 2012)

Here he was alluding to:

> There is another scale of values. History **with its flickering lamp** *stumbles along the trail of the past,* trying to reconstruct its scenes, to revive its echoes, and **kindle with pale gleams** the passion of former days. What is the worth of all this? The only guide to a man is his conscience; the only shield to his memory is the rectitude and sincerity of his actions. (Churchill, 12 November 1944)

There were nine instances of each of the phrases 'flickering flame' and 'flickering light' in Hansard that seek to evoke a poetic style, as in the following in a debate on the West Indies Bill:

> They did not see beyond the immediate moment: contrary to our frequent assumption that people are rational in their judgment, often they are nothing

of the kind: they are impelled by emotions, fears, apprehensions and traditions: reason, although it plays a little part, is **a flickering flame** *that can easily be blown out.* (Sorensen, 3 March 1962)

From such uses there is evidence of the frame: POLITICAL CONVICTION IS FIRE/FORCE. While 'flickering' implies a low degree of force, 'fiery', 'blaze' and 'incandescent' imply a much a higher level of force. However, there are interesting and subtle variations in the type of evaluation conveyed that are revealed by analysis of context. For example, a phrase that occurs forty-nine times in Hansard is 'blaze of glory', which might be thought positive at first, however, in context it is nearly always ironic and therefore negative:

> or is this ('city price'), like all the other inner-city projects launched by the Government, a project launched in a **blaze of glory** and forgotten six months later? (Vaz, 29 June 1994)

> We have a distinct feeling that the Millennium Fund will bring with it a **blaze of glory** that will be centred on the capital: a large proportion of the moneys that are going to good causes will go to the Millennium Fund: therefore we on these Benches feel that any money that is going to projects for the Millennium Fund should be divided around the country. (Lloyd, 17 June 1993)

There is sometimes a difference in the evaluation of a fire metaphor depending on whether it occurs in a singular or plural form. In Hansard there are twenty-three instances of the collocation 'fiery speech' and twenty-six instances of 'fiery speeches'; when used in the singular the evaluation is generally positive or neutral, while in the plural it is invariably negative, for example:

> I see him now – his eyes blazing forth with indignation and his rusty tousled head of hair standing on end – leading forth on the miseries of the Gorbals district and the East End of Glasgow: I was quite moved: I thought everybody appreciated to the full the enthusiastic and **fiery speech**: the whole passion of the man called out for justice to be handed out to the working classes in the various parts of the city. (Nicholson, 18 June 1947)

> This is a simple matter of cause and effect; and no amount of rhetoric can alter it: Water does not flow uphill and no amount of talking, no **fiery speeches**, no; not even strikes – will ever make it. (Buchan, 2 April 1980)

The plural form invariably implies an excess of emotion and a futile expenditure of effort:

> The whole 1992 programme, which will bring so many benefits to everyone, was essentially a British campaign: while others have been willing to make **fiery speeches** and indulge in European rhetoric about the ideals of the internal market, they have at the same time been willing to impose restrictions and to indulge in chauvinism. (Marshall, 15 November 1989)

The differences between positive and negative evaluations can be explained by the different frames: the plural form draws on the frames UNCONTROLLED EMOTION IS EXTREME TEMPERATURE and ANGER IS FIRE, whereas the singular form is based on the frame POLITICAL CONVICTION IS FIRE. The negative sense of potentially damaging emotion – rather than political conviction – occurs with other collocations such as 'fiery orators', 'fiery oratory' and 'fiery rhetoric':

> I do not put much trust in what is normally called persuasion: In times of industrial crisis, when mass meetings are addressed by **fiery orators**, passions become inflamed, tempers roused, and I do not believe that men under those circumstances will calmly go away, sit down and talk over the merits or demerits of any particular situation: it is at those times that mobs will collect, and when mobs do collect very ugly incidents follow and sometimes even the rule of mob law gets under way (Balfour, 1 May 1946)
>
> The Chancellor of the Exchequer is skating on thin ice when he gives such a rosy view of the outlook for the British economy: He displays his usual **fiery rhetoric** in the House and exudes glowing optimism – both qualities that are not altogether suitable when one is skating on thin ice: (Byers, 18 November 2002)

These collocations imply that the speaker is aware of the authority and influence of politicians but is also prepared to challenge it. This contrasts with the phrase 'incandescent with rage' that emphasizes the conviction of their beliefs rather than the danger of their effect:

> My right hon: Friend deserves great credit for obtaining massive sums for the industry, but does he know that 4,200 Airbus workers in my constituency are **incandescent with rage** at the refusal of a regional grant? (Jones, 30 March 2002)
>
> I am glad that my good friend the late Lord Benson was not alive at the time the report was published because he would have been **incandescent with rage** at its contents: (Sedgemore, 21 July 1995)

Here the speakers believe that the anger of the airbus workers and of Lord Benson is justified because it is based on conviction: it is a warranted self-righteousness. So the frame EMOTIONS ARE FORCES does not in itself convey a positive or negative evaluation; if the anger is viewed as somehow justified by the context then there may be a positive evaluation of conviction, however, if it is purposeless and self-indulgent it becomes an unwarranted discourse of authority.

Both frames continue to be used by contemporary politicians consider how David Cameron activates the political conviction frame:

> But there are the things you do because it's your passion. The things that **fire you up** in the morning, that drive you, that you truely believe will make a real difference to the country you love. And my great passion is building the Big Society. (Cameron, 19 July 2010)

> Creating a bigger society. Creating a country which feels like a community
> .... where our relationships are better and the glue that binds people together
> is stronger. Where we actually think about people's well-being when we make
> decisions. These are the things I'm most passionate about in public life. This is
> what is in my heart. **It's what fires me up** in the morning. (Cameron, 23 May 2011)

As with the previous examples, there is explicit reference to passion and belief as located *within* the individual so as to convey a high level of speaker commitment to the proposition. Their effect is reinforced by the fact that in both cases they occur at the start of highly significant speeches in which Cameron espoused his philosophy of the 'Big Society'. The use of fire metaphors corresponds with other features in Cameron's rhetoric such as his use of intensifiers – such as 'incredibly' and 'absolutely' – that contribute to an emotionally expressive style that seeks to establish consensus by hyperbole and to avoid accusations of blandness or lack of commitment (see Charteris-Black 2014b).

Once we examine natural fire metaphors in context we find that they occur very commonly at *the beginning* of a speech; for example, of the twelve metaphoric uses of fire/fires, six occur near the start of the speech and this is precisely because it is at this stage where it is most necessary for the speaker to establish credibility with the audience through an appeal to ethos that will frame subsequent discourse. A similar influence of context on the position of fire metaphors is when they occur at the end of speeches – in the coda. The stage of a speech that is crucial for motivating an audience by inspiring them to action by arousing the emotions through an appeal based in conviction; here is how Peter Hain ended a speech:

> So, let's put our supporters on full alert. **Let's fire their enthusiasm** with a radical
> vision for the future. A future of big challenges. United as a party. In Wales and
> across Britain. Local parties and unions. Members and leadership. Working
> together. We can win and we must win. (Hain, 28 September 2004)

An emotional appeal using a fire metaphor is a very common way for left wing politicians to terminate a speech; however, these motivating metaphors in left wing rhetoric are more common with metaphoric use of 'flame' as in the following by Michael Foot, the left wing leader of the Labour Party in the 1970s.

> So I am not asking for any dull uniformity or anything of that sort. I am asking
> this Movement to exert itself as it has never done before. To show qualities that
> we have, the Socialist imagination that exists in our Movement. The readiness of
> re-forge the alliance, stronger than ever, between the Government and the trade
> unions, and above all to show the supreme quality in politics, **the red flame of
> Socialist courage.** That this is what we have got to do to save our country, and that
> is what can come from this Conference. (Foot, 29 September 1976)

At the time, the relationship between the Labour Party and the Trade Unions was central to the strength of the Labour movement and Foot refers to it as 're-forge the alliance' – a hint that the relationship has weakened. In fact the 'red flame' metaphor had been used by another politician, Barbara Castle, in a debate on the National Health Service in the House of Commons the preceding year:

> What the Minister of State can tell us clearly in his winding-up speech is that he and the Government renounce the policy of the Labour Party conference: Let them take the opportunity of this debate to tell the Labour Party that that policy option is closed, not only for now, but for the future, and to say clearly that they will not tolerate attempts to black private hospital building or political decision-making in planning applications: We shall wait to hear those assurances and we shall judge how brightly burns **the red flame of the Government's courage**: the proposals put forward by the Government are damaging to the interests of the patient and the Health Service …. If the legislation gets through, let no one inside or outside the House be under any doubt that following the next General Election we shall repeal it. (Castle, 21 November 1975)

The 'red flame' activates a frame that includes reference to industrial Britain where steel foundry workers would use flames to heat iron ore: the red flame was grounded in the physical force of the foundry. The metaphor occurs in the context of describing the emotion of courage – a relatively successful attempt to arouse, and unify an audience by 'welding' them together! This effect whereby a metaphor is triggered by an actual literal sense of a word is a widespread characteristic of metaphor – consider the following:

> I say it also because the fact that the British Empire stands invincible, and that Nazidom is still being resisted, **will kindle again the spark of hope** in the breasts of hundreds of millions of down-trodden or despairing men and women throughout Europe, and far beyond its bounds, and that **from these sparks there will presently come cleansing and devouring flame**. The great air battle which has been in progress over this Island for the last few weeks has recently attained a high intensity. (Churchill, 20 August 1940)

Here the 'devouring flame' is a metaphor motivated by the concept PURIFICATION IS FIRE – the fire that cleanses – and is then immediately followed with reference to a great air battle in which there will have been many instances of *actual* fire. So, the metaphor activates concepts for purification originating in discourses of awe and integrates these with the actual physical destruction of enemy aeroplanes. In fact, Churchill was not the first to use this metaphor, as it was first used in a debate on drunkenness in 1834:

> To meet the increased demand engendered by this increased dissipation, new houses of entertainment sprung up in every direction, in the shape of winevaults and gin-shops, in the large sea-ports and manufacturing districts, and taverns, and ale-houses, in the agricultural provinces: the Government, too, instead of checking the evil, added **only fresh fuel to the already too rapidly devouring flame**. (Buckingham, 3 June 1834)

Here the flame is one of impurity rather than purity. Conceptual metaphors such as POLITICAL CONVICTION IS FORCE/FIRE and PURIFICATION IS FIRE provide frames that integrate embodied experience with cultural knowledge.

Fire is used to burn debris and other unwanted things, and in social revolutions it symbolizes a rejection of the past order – as when rioters and revolutionaries set fire to buildings that symbolize power. It has a historic link to ideas originating in alchemy that are associated with efforts to purify base metals into gold through applying heat. As we will see in the next chapter, the expression 'the Sacred Fire of human liberty' is used extensively in American political rhetoric (see also Charteris-Black 2004: 100ff.). As well as drawing on the artistic proofs of ethos and pathos, Castle and Foot's 'red' fire, brings in another far-left symbol – red as the colour of Communism. The 'red flame' metaphor activates a conceptual representation that has a rich network of associations for 'fire' metaphors, actual fires and the symbolism of the colour red. This network of associations draws on underlying schemas that contribute to long-term mental models for a better society – even if it requires actual fire to destroy oppressors. Whether or not it is effective is another matter – the idea of being burnt in a fire may make Socialism appear dangerous (as well as courageous) and activate an alternative frame DANGER IS FIRE.

In some cases, a mental model for destruction – driven by conceptual knowledge of actual fire – provides the basis for its use as a symbol; in the following speech Nic Clegg blends reference to the actual fires that occurred during the London riots of August 2011, with the symbolism of the Olympic torch – the Sacred Fire:

> What a contrast from a year ago when England's cities burned in a week of riots. When the images beamed to the world were not of athletes running for the finishing line, but the mob, running at police lines. When the flames climbed, not from the Olympic torch in east London, but a furniture shop in south London. A 140 year-old family-run business, which had survived two world wars and countless recessions, razed to the ground. (26 September 2012)

There is, then, in discourses of authority, often a conceptual proximity of actual natural fire with metaphoric fire – fires of anger and destruction are associated with fires of hope and purification. They are also based on the conceptual metonym LEVEL OF TEMPERATURE FOR THE INTENSITY OF EMOTION. Skilful rhetoricians are able to draw on these frames to create powerful images that may have an unconscious appeal since knowledge of fire's dual capacity to maintain and to threaten life is embedded in millennia of human experience and hence deep-rooted in the human brain. It is perhaps this hard-wired appeal of 'fire' metaphors that accounts for the powerful appeal of a metaphor that was used by the left wing politician Tony Benn in an Interview on the David Frost show on BBC One on 12 December 2008:

> You see **there are two flames burning in the human heart** all the time. The **flame of anger** against injustice, and **the flame of hope** you can build a better world. And my job at 83 is going round and **fanning both flames** … because people need encouragement. Everyone needs encouragement if you're going to do the best you can.

The quotation was taken up by social media probably because it reflects these two powerful, and at times conflicting, emotions that are rooted in the mental models that we have for fire. As we have seen from the frames, ANGER IS FIRE in Chapter 2, and POLITICAL CONVICTION IS FORCE/FIRE, fire activates idealistic passions for a better world, as implied by Foot's 'red flame of Socialist courage', and appeal to discourses of awe. There is a strong correlation in experience between positive human emotions and our experience of a warming body, so that intense emotional response activated by feelings of anger and hope can be expressed hyperbolically as a 'flame' drawing on the frame THE LEVEL OF INTENSITY OF AN EMOTION IS THE LEVEL OF INTENSITY OF A FIRE. Appeals to ethos and pathos are integrated in such a way as to overcome other alternative frames for fire – such as lust, danger or destructive emotion. It is these positive frames that typify the use of natural fire metaphors in political speeches from all shades of the political spectrum.

## Functional fire metaphors

Functional fire differs from natural fire because it activates a frame for the controlled use of fire for a particular human purpose – typically keeping warm or cooking through the application of heat, giving light, or the use of smoke to describe cause and effect relationships. Functional fire is indicated by words from the semantic fields of heat, light and smoke since these are the properties of fire that relate to acts of human agency. For example, torches and beacons were the only means of providing light prior to electricity and the application of heat is crucial in industrial production; fire produces smoke and this causal relationship is embedded in mental frames through sayings such as 'there is no smoke without fire' and smoke can also be used to conceal from vision and this agentive use of fire occurs in the expression: 'to create a smokescreen'.

There were only twenty-eight functional fire metaphors in the British sample these comprised 31 per cent of all the metaphors, and 64 per cent of all the functional fire terms, so when a functional fire word is used it is more likely than not to be metaphoric. In Table 8.1 we saw expressions such as 'melting pot' and 'scorched earth' were often used. The most frequent fire term was 'heat' but this was more commonly used with a literal sense; the second most common metaphor (after 'fire') was 'beacon' with ten instances followed by 'torch' and 'heat'; other potential metaphors such as 'sear', 'scorch' and 'fan' did not occur in the British sample (although they did in Hansard, e.g. 'scorched earth policy' is used ninety-four times in the period 1803–2005). In Hansard the expression 'beacon of hope' occurs forty times, 'beacon of excellence' seventeen times and 'beacon of democracy' ten times supporting the claim that it is the most frequent functional fire metaphor. Hansard shows that Nicolas Soames has used the 'beacon' metaphor eight times. It is closely challenged by 'torch' metaphors with 'torch of freedom' occurring twenty-nine times and 'torch of liberty' seven times in Hansard.

Charteris-Black (2014: 155ff.) illustrates and analyses how 'beacon' works as a symbol in a way that I will briefly summarize here, though from the additional perspective that it is a metaphor that originates in discourses of awe. Conceptual knowledge of the function of a beacon is that it provides a warning light from a high location so that it can be seen from afar. Therefore, the use of 'beacon' as a metaphor activates ideas of political success by activating and integrating frames based on conceptual knowledge relating to LIGHT, FIRE and UPWARDS location. The frame for 'beacon' activates a rich range of associations, or 'entailments', that explain how it works as a metaphor for hope and emotional enthusiasm. The image of light is widespread in religious imagery – it is associated with seeing, and 'conceptually' seeing is linked to knowing and understanding of things that are hidden, like the divine. As we have seen previously, because of its mysterious and equally divine origins fire activates powerful emotions such as hope and enthusiasm (e.g. 'to be fired up'), desire ('to burn with passion'), moral cleansing (e.g. 'the red flame of courage') as well as everyday purposes such as keeping us warm and cooking. The beacon image therefore symbolizes hope and aspiration by evoking the following concepts arising from the frames activated by these source domains:

CONTROL IS UP
GOOD IS UP
GOD IS LIGHT
KNOWLEDGE IS LIGHT
HOPE IS FIRE
PURIFICATION IS FIRE

We saw in the section on natural fire how Churchill drew on nature for persuasive images of light and darkness. Many of these conceptual frames are equally present in the beacon frame in the following text:

How would the race of men have risen above the apes? How otherwise would they have conquered and extirpated dragons and monsters? How would they have ever evolved the moral theme; how would they have marched forward across the centuries to broad conceptions of compassion, of freedom, and of right? How would they ever have discerned those **beacon lights** which summon and guide us across the rough dark waters, and presently will guide us across **the flaming lines of battle** towards better days which lie beyond? (Churchill, 20 January 1940)

Coming at the concluding stage of the 'the House of Many Mansions' speech Churchill needed to arouse his audience, who were facing defeat, with the motivation necessary to continue the struggle. He did this by drawing on a discourse of awe – a religious framework of spiritual truth – by representing the struggle against Nazism as a mythical combat with the forces of darkness. The beacon metaphor is framed within journey and time frames that assume the view of history as progress. The phrases 'moral theme' and 'of right' provide an ethical warrant that is then reinforced with 'light' metaphors drawing on the frames GOD IS LIGHT and KNOWLEDGE IS LIGHT. There is also a morale-raising prediction of a better future.

One of the rhetorical advantages of functional fire is that it blends the frames for space (upwards) and for light thereby creating a complex network of positive meanings. It is likely that given the strategic importance of drawing the United States into the war, Churchill was using a metaphor that would also appeal to an American audience, which as we have seen would well be aware of the rhetorical force of the 'Sacred Fire of human liberty'. This may well account for his reliance on a discourse of awe.

We should bear in mind that the literal basis for the beacon metaphor is the lighthouse, where the source of light was referred to as the 'lamp'. Originally, the lamp was an open fire and later a candle; in 1781 the Argand hollow wick lamp and parabolic reflector was developed. In the early part of the nineteenth century, lard or whale oil was used to fuel the lamp and this was later replaced by kerosene. It was not until the twentieth century that electricity and carbide (acetylene gas) were used to replace kerosene – so for much of history it is fire rather than electricity that was used to power the lighthouse so that it could serve its role as a beacon; however, with the declining awareness of the use of actual fire in warning signals, the metaphoric potential of the 'beacon' increased. By using a traditional metaphor for safety, Churchill was evoking thousands of years in which Britain had protected its shores from nautical invasion. Beacons had warned of the invasions of the Romans, the Saxons, the Danes and the Normans and therefore evoke discourses of authority as well as discourses of awe depending on the audience's cognitive frames.

In more recent political contexts, the frame HOPE IS FIRE has gradually become more salient as the historic sense of 'beacon' erodes; in more contemporary political rhetoric the 'beacon' metaphor is used to motivate people to action, and to reject the despondency that entails inaction. For example, between 1998 and 2005, outstanding primary or secondary schools were officially awarded the title 'Beacon School'. The following are both from Party conference speeches by Margaret Thatcher, who is clearly alluding to Churchill; the first implies some parallels between the Soviet Union and Nazi Germany:

> Mr. President, a strong and united Western alliance is a guarantee of our peace and security. It is also a **beacon of hope** to the oppressed people of the Soviet bloc. (Thatcher, 8 October 1982)

The second implies that the European Community presents the same threat at Nazism and the Soviet Union:

> Mr President, we are careful about money and rightly so. We're the second biggest net contributor to Europe, paying over £2 billion a year.
>
> But – and it is a crucial but – we shall never accept the approach of those who want to use the European Community as a means of removing our ability to govern ourselves as an independent nation. *[applause]*
>
> Our Parliament has endured for seven hundred years and has been a **beacon of hope** to the peoples of Europe **in their darkest days.** Our aim is to see Europe become the greatest practical expression of political and economic liberty the world over. And we will accept nothing less. *[applause]* (Thatcher, 12 October 1990)

In this important speech in which she positions herself as a leader who will claw back from 'Europe' the economic concessions too generously granted by her predecessors, she reminds her European audience that it was Britain who saved them initially from Nazism and then from Soviet Marxism. The 'beacon' becomes a metaphor for safety, the safety that was originally offered by the lighthouse. In terms of rhetorical arrangement and timing, Thatcher emulates Churchill by employing the 'beacon' metaphor at the start of the concluding phase of the speech and the speech finishes with the rousing and patriotic commitment: 'we pledge in this Party to uphold these principles of freedom and to fight for them. We pledge it to our allies overseas. And we pledge it to this country which we are proud to serve'. Here we have a discourse of awe transmuted into one of authority.

Clearly, the beacon frame held a strong appeal for Margaret Thatcher as it was under her leadership that a beacon or torch became the symbol or logo of the Conservative Party. This provides convincing evidence of the frame FREEDOM IS A FIRE. A search of the Hansard shows that the expression 'flame of freedom' occurs twenty-seven times and 'torch of freedom' twenty-nine times as in the following:

> He is so full of reverence for the great leaders of English literature and statesmanship that he can not make a speech in this House without doffing his hat metaphorically and paying homage to them: We admire his consistency, because we believe that he has observed in them the **flame of freedom burning brightly** and is attracted and drawn by the vision of that freedom. (Hobhouse, 11 March 1932)

> It is absolutely essential that young people not only formally remember but recognise those who fell for this country – first because many of those who fell gave up their youth for succeeding generations, and secondly because, unless **the torch of freedom** and the sacrifices made are passed from generation to generation, we shall not retain the will power to stand up for democracy and freedom: that is what the people who died in the second world war died for. (Reid, 11 March 1997)

Once Thatcher had revived this metaphor, it was exploited as a theme in Conservative Party rhetoric, by representing any opponent as an opponent of freedom:

> For we Conservatives were the pathfinders. We did not know it at the time but the **torch we lit** in Britain, which transformed our country – **the torch of freedom** that is now the symbol of our Party – became **the beacon that has shed its light** across the Iron Curtain into the East. Today **that beacon shines more strongly** than at any time this century. (Thatcher, 13 October 1989)

Although in a bid for the now fashionable green vote, Cameron changed the Conservative Party logo to a scribbled oak tree in 2006, he continued to echo the beacon metaphor:

> And But if you care about our country, you've got to care about the health of our institutions. And today one of them, more than any other, is in a serious state of decline. Our parliament used to be **a beacon to the world**. But the expenses scandal made it a laughing stock. (Cameron, 8 October 2009)

It is also significant that Cameron positions the 'beacon' metaphor strategically at the most salient point in the speech as a way or introducing the final part of the speech:

> They called our economy the sick man of Europe. But we came back and turned this country into **a beacon of enterprise**. (5 October 2011)

We cannot always measure rhetorical effect through frequency alone, and it is evident that 'beacon' metaphors are typically positioned towards the final stage of a speech, or at very early at points where it is necessary to construct interpretative frames. Cameron's use of the 'beacon' metaphor may have been partly in response to Blair's use of the beacon frame in the speech containing the highest number of 'beacon' metaphors – his first Party Conference Address as leader entitled 'A beacon to the world' that he gave on 30 September 1997. Blair uses the 'beacon' metaphor eight times, introducing it early on and reiterating it again in the epilogue so that it contributes to the coherence of the speech. He commenced his speech: 'today I want to set an ambitious course for this country. To be nothing less than the model 21st century nation, a beacon to the world.' And he commenced the speech coda:

> Today, I issue a challenge to you. Help us **make Britain that beacon shining throughout the world.** Unite behind our mission to modernise our country. (30 September 1997)

These framed the main argument of his speech; but it was then sustained by 'beacon' metaphors relating to claims about different areas of government policy:

> Our education system – **a beacon to the world** ....
> The NHS was **a beacon to the world** in 1948. I want it to be so again.
> We cannot be **a beacon to the world** unless the talents of all the people shine through.

In gauging the rhetorical impact of fire metaphors, it is crucial to examine at what points in the speech they are introduced, and we find their distribution is not random but designed to introduce a strong ethical and empathetic appeal. Usually this is by placing them towards the beginning and the end of speeches as their effect would be diluted if they were distributed regularly throughout a speech; but in this speech he uses the metaphor to introduce new arguments that support the general claims about Britain's status. It is also significant that Blair understood the discourse of awe as it was exploited by Churchill and now sought to reclaim it is a symbol for the left; this makes the beacon a contested symbol over which political parties compete to take ownership in competing discourses of authority.

In this section we have found that functional fire is employed rhetorically for creating a strongly positive frame of interpretation by activating concepts related to freedom and hope. Natural fire metaphors are reliant on arousing embodied emotional responses through POLITICAL CONVICTION IS FIRE, and THE LEVEL OF INTENSITY OF

AN EMOTION IS THE LEVEL OF INTENSITY OF A FIRE. Functional fire metaphors rely on motivating an audience by appealing to a discourse of awe – and this is implied by the conceptual frames HOPE IS FIRE and FREEDOM IS FIRE.

## Organic fire metaphors

The psychological basis for viewing organic fire is that many metaphoric senses of words from the semantic field of fire refer in other contexts to the attributes of living things. Because, metaphorically speaking, fire is 'alive', these metaphors can evoke the same sort of emotional responses that we have to living things; so, for example, we are happy when babies are born (usually), and when nature is budding; conversely, we feel despondent at the prospect of death – whether in animate organisms or in nature itself, when autumn is typically a time of wistful reflection, signalling as it does the coming of a winter. Metaphors originating in organic fire therefore offer an influential way of thinking about political issues so that entities and events that are positively evaluated are framed as alive by using words such as 'spark' or 'kindle'. Conversely, those that are negatively evaluated are framed in terms of entities that were once alive and are now dying – with metaphoric uses of words such as 'snuff out' and 'extinguish' – or in terms of entities that are dead with metaphoric uses of words such as 'embers' and 'ashes'. Potentially, therefore, fire activates pre-existing knowledge frames for fire that are well described by Stephen Pyne:

> First, fire does biologically what human ceremonies have unfailingly declared it to do: it promotes and it purges. It shakes and bakes. Around its flames revolves an ecological triangle, a circulation of biochemicals, species, and communalities. It stirs molecules, organisms, landscapes ... Fire upsets, shreds, reorganizes, revives, and quickens. (Pyne 2001: 15)

Between the extreme points of the life cycle are other metaphors representing fire as in a state of flux that can be increased – 'fuelled', 'inflamed' or decreased – 'dampened' or 'extinguished'. Evaluation using metaphors that frame entities in terms of organic fire therefore depends on the stage in the organic cycle and the entity that is being evaluated. A political action that contributes, metaphorically, to a good thing is positively viewed as 'giving birth to' it, and a political action that, metaphorically, 'extinguishes' a bad thing is also positively viewed. The converse is also true so that it would be a good thing to 'extinguish' poverty, and a bad one to 'fuel' tensions. Generally, those metaphors that contribute to an increase in fire – such as 'inflame' – are negatively viewed as they activate a schema for danger through the excess or the intensity of the fire. They are based on a combination of the frames THE LEVEL OF INTENSITY OF AN EMOTION IS THE LEVEL OF INTENSITY OF A FIRE and UNCONTROLLED EMOTION IS EXTREME TEMPERATURE.

There were thirty-two 'fire as an organism' metaphors in the British sample (see Table 8.1) representing over half of the total uses of organic fire terms. Around 38 per cent of all metaphors were organic fire metaphors – particularly 'spark', 'fuel' and 'inflame'. In Hansard metaphoric phrases included 'spark of enthusiasm' ($n=19$); 'spark of imagination'

($n = 18$); 'inflammatory speeches' ($n = 277$); 'inflame passions' ($n = 229$); 'inflammatory language' ($n = 206$).

'Spark of humanity' occurs thirty-seven times in Hansard, 'spark of hope' occurs twenty-nine times and 'spark of liberty' occurs thirteen times. For example:

> The Minister could have stood up against the vile, xenophobic and racist nonsense spoken by the hon: Gentleman, and show **a spark of humanity** in respect of unaccompanied child refugees. (Corbyn, 6 July 1993)
>
> I think that many of the things which he has said and done since he has been elected have given some of us at least **a spark of hope** that he may succeed in moving the European community, which alone he represents, in the direction which Sir Edgar Whitehead may have tried to lead them but certainly failed. (Healey, 28 February 1963)

As with beacon metaphors, 'spark' metaphors are most effective when they are employed systematically to construct an argument as for example by Thatcher:

> We want to renew **the spark of incentive** in our economy because without that new jobs cannot and will not be created. (Thatcher, 14 October 1977)
>
> Oh! the schemes won a number of architectural awards. But they were a nightmare for the people. **They snuffed out any spark** of local enterprise. And they made people entirely dependent on the local authorities and the services they chose to provide. (Thatcher, 9 October 1987)
>
> But the philosophy of enterprise and opportunity, which has **put the spark back** into our national economy — that is the way – and the only way – to rejuvenate our cities and restore their confidence and pride. (Thatcher, 14 October 1977)

Effectively, the use of 'spark' by Thatcher in this speech conceptualizes fire as a life force – as is implied by the choice of 'rejuvenate' in the last example. As I suggested in a discussion of political myth, in these two party conference speeches – ten years apart – Thatcher frames the policies of each political party as: CONSERVATIVE POLICY IS A LIFE FORCE and LABOUR POLICY IS A DEATH FORCE (Charteris-Black 2011: 41ff.). In addition to *snuff out,* a frame for death is also activated by other metaphors such as *cut the heart, dying, sapping, decay.* The death frame contrasts with a frame for life that is activated by, as well as '*spark*', *give heart back to, growing, recovery, take root, sprang.* The one chain associates Labour policy with death while the other associates Conservative policies with life based on the frame LIFE IS FIRE. These two interacting metaphor chains are employed to create contrastive frames that structure the whole speech: death metaphors occur in the first three paragraphs of the 1987 speech, while life metaphors occur only in the last paragraph. Thatcher also evokes the death frame in her use of 'ashes':

> So it's ironic that as enterprise and liberty rises **from the dead ashes** of State Control, the Labour Party here is still trying to blow life into those old embers. (Thatcher, 13 October 1989)

This metaphor occurs early in the speech towards the end of the prologue as a way of framing the whole of the remainder of her argument, which is broadly an attack on Socialism.

This use of organic fire appeals at the subconscious level to earlier evolutionary feelings about fire as necessary for protection from danger; by using them at critical moments in her speeches Thatcher was inviting a mythic way of thinking. In this respect, she was adopting something like the earlier voice of the Oracle at Delphi where females with mysterious powers could predict the future. At some unconscious level then Thatcher realized that:

> Fire was a god, or at least theophany; fire was myth, fire was science, fire was power, we could call it forth as we could not call forth floods or hurricanes or earthquakes or droughts .... Certainly fire's possession altered social relationships, groups defined themselves by their shared fire. Domestication itself most likely began with the tending of flame. Like a being, it had to be conceived, fed, protected, put to bed, awakened, trained, controlled, exercises, bred – in effect, socialized into human life. It required constant attention, it needed a protective shelter ... Someone had to gather the endless fuel, someone had to fuss over the flames and nurture the coals, and someone had to oversee its proper use. For it to expire was a calamity. (Pyne 2001: pp. 24–25)

But like other unstable entities, fire can go out of control and become threatening and dangerous, and it is this aspect of the fire frame that is activated by metaphors such as 'fuel', 'stoke' and 'inflame'. In Hansard metaphoric phrases included 'fuel the flames of' ($n = 24$); 'fuel conflicts' ($n = 21$)' and 'fuel suspicions' ($n = 13$). They were generally used to refer to the actions of an inanimate, abstract entity and are typically used to evaluate negatively some aspect of economic policy:

> Government destroyed jobs **by fuelling** inflation; trades unions destroyed jobs by restrictive practices; militants destroyed jobs by driving customers away. But that is the past and whatever the problems, we have got to tackle them, not with words, not with rhetoric, but with action. (Thatcher, 8 October 1982)
>
> We had a housing system that failed to meet demand, so prices shot up and **fuelled** an unsustainable boom. (Cameron, 5 October 2011)
>
> So let us take the lead in building a new economy for the new century. An open, outward looking economy in the world's biggest single market. A strong, balanced economy built on productive investment, not **debt-fuelled** consumption. (Clegg, 26 September 2012)

In every case except one, the evaluation of 'fuel' metaphors was negative by activating a frame for danger; 'fuel' here implies supplying more fuel than is necessary and the resulting increase in force will cause loss of control over a social or economic situation and so are motivated by the frame AN UNCONTROLLED SITUATION IS AN EXCESS OF FUEL. This is modelled using force dynamics in the next chapter (see Figure 9.1, p.196).

The most common economic metaphor in Hansard for 'fuelled' is 'fuelled inflation' that occurs twenty times. The earliest use of the expression was in 1974:

> The introduction of threshold agreements by the Tory Government was just one more example of the way in which their policies have **fuelled** inflation and have created the situation with which we now have to deal and with which we shall deal'. (Dell, 23 July 1974)

This suggests that it may be a situation triggered metaphor as 1974 was the time of the Middle East oil crisis which may have created a negative association between 'fuel' and the economy, the metaphor then became extended to any type of economic problem:

> we have all got to face up to the unpalatable fact that the Social Contract has failed: indeed, it has not only failed; it is positively **fuelling** *the very unemployment* which it was designed to alleviate. (Earl of Gowrie, 25 November 1976)

It could then be extended further to any type of problem:

> This is not the time for **fuelling the flames** of political controversy: the economic blizzard is too severe for that: People are too worried and fearful about their jobs, about taxes, about rates, or whatever it may be, and we ought to be concentrating on areas where we can agree very broadly … (Pym, 30 November 1976)

The symbolic meaning of metaphors motivated by organic fire is partly metonymic since we know that fire can actually cause death or is in some ways associated with the practice of cremation. It is not therefore surprising that some uses of fire metaphors activate a frame for death; in the following the speaker is describing the BSE crisis when a large number of cattle had to be slaughtered and burned in order to prevent the spread of the disease:

> And then on an early August morning in Surrey, a farmer went out to tend to his livestock and what he saw terrified him, made him remember back to 2001 when all across our countryside clouds of smoke scarred the sky and for many in farms and villages, family dreams **were turned to ash**. (Brown, 24 September 2007)

Here the cattle are literally turned to ash as they are burned but they also symbolized the death of a farming family's hopes. The symbolic use of organic fire metaphors can also draw on a discourse of awe as in the speeches of Enoch Powell who occasionally refers to funeral pyres:

> Hundreds of men and women, professional or voluntary, have given years, even lifetimes, to the service of a mental hospital or a group of mental hospitals. They have laboured devotedly, through years of scarcity and neglect, to render the conditions in them more tolerable, and of late they have seized with delight upon

the new possibilities opening up, and the new resources available, for these old but somehow cherished institutions. From such bodies it demands no mean moral effort to recognise that the institutions themselves are doomed. It would be more than flesh and blood to expect them to take the initiative in planning their own abolition, to be the first **to set the torch to the funeral pyre**. (Powell, March 1961)

In this context, fire is viewed as the means to end a social ill – the removal of mental hospitals because they are inadequate. Here, rather than danger, it is the cleansing effect of fire that is activated by the frame PURIFICATION IS FIRE. Metaphoric uses of 'funeral pyre' occur forty-five times in Hansard, some alluding to Powell's speech:

> Enoch Powell may have **lit a funeral pyre** beneath mental asylums when his Mental Health Act 1959 began the process of shutting them, but today some 70 per cent: of the prison population have a mental health or substance abuse problem, or both. (Fox, 25 June 2002)

However, in other instances, and most famously in his so-called 'Rivers of Blood' speech the reference to a funeral pyre is designed to activate a frame for self-destruction rather than purification:

> It almost passes belief that at this moment 20 or 30 additional immigrant children are arriving from overseas in Wolverhampton alone every week – and that means 15 or 20 additional families a decade or two hence. Those whom the gods wish to destroy, they first make mad. We must be mad, literally mad, as a nation to be permitting the annual inflow of some 50,000 dependents, who are for the most part the material of the future growth of the immigrant-descended population. It is like watching a nation busily engaged in **heaping up its own funeral pyre**. (28 April 1968)

Powell implies that by allowing immigration on this scale the nation is engaged in an act of self-destruction of its national identity. Ideas of self-inflicted destruction are readily activated by the funeral pyre image:

> Either interest rates will have to rise, in which case there will be no investment and no growth in revenue, or the Government will start to print money, and cause inflation: I believe that that is the course the Government will take: the Government are carefully **erecting a funeral pyre** for the economy. (Hordern, 9 March 1976)

A frame for intentional self-destruction is triggered in the hyperbole of the 'funeral pyre' image to represent a policy as damaging. In mythic thinking life and death are closely related, and metaphors based on organic fire have the same potential for evoking a mythic framework, a discourse of awe, as we have witnessed with functional and natural fire metaphors.

# Summary

In the discourses of authority outlined in this chapter, we have found that politicians have a wide range of fire frames on which to draw depending on the type of speech they are giving, the audience to whom it is addressed, the type of evaluation that they need to convey and on the position within the speech. Where necessary, as when audiences require a sense of vision, politicians are eager to evoke discourses of awe based on the frames SPIRITUAL KNOWLEDGE IS LIGHT and HOPE IS FIRE. Fire metaphors have much potential for politicians who seek authority by drawing on discourses of awe, and constructing politics as a struggle between good and evil thereby encouraging mythic thinking. Fire metaphors create vivid contrasts between forces of life and death and therefore serve as prototypes for representations as heroes and villains. But speakers also develop discourses of authority based on the frames EMOTION IS A FORCE and POLITICAL CONVICTION IS FORCE/FIRE; these can be analysed using the force dynamic model. The speaker's own policies are based on frames such as PURIFICATION IS FIRE and FREEDOM IS FIRE. But where speakers are attacking their opponents' policies, they activate discourses of authority based on danger and death frames – these include AN UNCONTROLLED SITUATION IS AN EXCESS OF FUEL and DANGER IS FIRE. As with all semantics, politics is about creating meanings that are distinctive because of their place within a system; fire metaphors provide such a catalyst to achieve rhetorical ends by melding discourses of awe with discourses of authority.

# 9

# Fire Metaphors in American Political Rhetoric

## Introduction

In this chapter I undertake an analysis of fire metaphors in American political rhetoric; I am interested in the type of fire metaphors that occur, the frames they activate, and the relationship between discourses of awe and discourses of authority. I propose that in American political speeches discourses of authority are at least partly dependent on pre-existing discourses of awe. I am interested in the semantic prosodies of fire metaphors and how these compare with those for British political rhetoric. There are frames that overlap because of the interconnections between Britain and the United States – their shared language and common democratic values. One of the outcomes of sharing aspects of political culture is that there is evidence of metaphor borrowing between the two languages. But there are other frames that diverge because of differing historical influences. I hope to offer cultural, historical and environmental explanations of these divergences; for example, there is greater experience of *actual* fire in the American as compared with the British countryside.

As with British fire metaphors, an earlier study (Charteris-Black 2011) showed that there were many semantic fields *other than* fire that were more likely to be lexicalized in American political metaphors; these include journeys, personifications, creation and destruction, conflict and war, light and darkness, and life and death. Fire metaphors only comprised 1–2 per cent of all political metaphors, however, for the reasons discussed above, this does not undermine their rhetorical importance – especially given the significance of 'Sacred Fire' in American political rhetoric.

After presenting the findings on fire metaphors, I begin by analysing natural fire, discussing how it shows evidence of a discourse of awe; the largely positive association of fire metaphors continues with functional fire metaphors such as 'the beacon' and organic fire metaphors such as 'spark'. This contrasts with negative prosodies of fire metaphors arising from the frame AN UNCONTROLLED SITUATION IS AN EXCESS OF FUEL; I suggest that these negative senses constitute a discourse of authority and take their origin in metonymy, where fire can threaten and endanger life.

## Fire metaphors in American political rhetoric

To explore the use of fire metaphors in American political rhetoric, I compiled a corpus of 123 speeches given during the period 1933–2010 and was approximately the same length as the British sample – that is approximately 500,000 words. I will refer to this as the 'American sample'. The sample was selected according to similar criteria as for the British sample. While the absence of a female president made it difficult to attain an adequate gender balance, I have tried to compensate for this by including Condoleezza Rice. There is an approximately equal representation of Democrats and Republicans. As with the British sample, the number of words varies according to the status of the politician, their influence and their length of time in leadership roles. The American sample is given in Appendix 2. There are issues of authorship of speeches; however, since the aim of this study is to explore fire metaphors, I do not discuss these here (see Charteris-Black 2011: 6). Given the absence of an equivalent control corpus for political speeches such as Hansard for the British sample, findings were supplemented by analysis of a smaller searchable database containing all the American inaugural speeches.[1]

Table 9.1 gives an overview of the frequency and type of 'fire' metaphors found in the American sample with a comparison with the frequency of the same words when used as metaphors in the British sample. Given that the American and British samples are the same size, it is possible to make comparisons using a raw count of metaphors.

**Table 9.1** Fire metaphors, concepts and frames in the American sample

| Fire frame | Fire concept | Fire term | Uses as a metaphor (British in brackets) |
|---|---|---|---|
| **NATURAL FIRE** | FORM AND ACTION | fire(s) | 30 (12) |
| | | flame | 10  (2) |
| | | burn | 1  (3) |
| | | fiery | 1  (0) |
| | INTENSITY | blaze/ablaze | 1  (1) |
| | | smoulder | 0  (0) |
| | | incandescent | 1  (0) |
| | APPEARANCE | glow/afterglow | 7  (4) |
| | | flare | 1  (1) |
| | MOTION | flicker | 1  (2) |
| TOTAL | | | 53 (25) |
| **FUNCTIONAL FIRE** | EFFECT OF FIRE: HEAT | heat | 5  (4) |
| | | scorch/scorching | 2  (0) |
| | | sear/searing | 1  (0) |
| | | melt | 2  (3) |
| | | fan | 6  (0) |
| | | stoke | 1  (1) |
| | | brand | 0  (3) |

**Table 9.1** Fire metaphors, concepts and frames in the American sample (*continued*)

| Fire frame | Fire concept | Fire term | Uses as a metaphor (British in brackets) |
|---|---|---|---|
| | EFFECT OF FIRE: LIGHT | beacon | 13 (10) |
| | | torch | 4 (3) |
| | | lamp | 1 (1) |
| | | illuminate | 0 (1) |
| | EFFECT OF FIRE: SMOKE | smoke | 4 (2) |
| TOTAL | | | 39 (28) |
| **ORGANIC FIRE** | STARTING A FIRE | spark | 15 (9) |
| | | fuel | 12 (7) |
| | | ignite | 5 (0) |
| | CAUSING A FIRE TO GROW | extinguish | 5 (2) |
| | | inflame/ inflammatory | 2 (4) |
| | | ashes | 2 (3) |
| | | kindle | 1 (3) |
| | | incendiary | 1 (0) |
| | CAUSING A FIRE TO END | snuff out | 1 (3) |
| | | embers | 0 (1) |
| TOTAL | | | 44 (32) |
| OVERALL TOTALS | | | 136 (85) |

There are many more fire metaphors in the American sample as compared with the British sample (136 metaphors compared with 85) and the log likelihood statistical test shows that these findings are significant ($p < 0.001$). Each of the fire concepts occurred with a higher frequency in the American sample, and I suggest that this is because of a greater reliance in American political rhetoric on a discourse of awe. American fire metaphors are historically rooted in cultural frames that place emphasis on freedom and liberty so that fire metaphors are closer to the discourses of awe identified in the analysis of religious discourse – rather than to the discourses of authority in *Foxe's Book of Martyrs*.

There are also cultural differences in the extent to which expression of the emotions is valued, so the frame THE LEVEL OF INTENSITY OF AN EMOTION IS THE LEVEL OF INTENSITY OF A FIRE is more active in the American speeches. As a result, the symbolism of fire as a valued cultural artefact is closely allied with American national identity. By contrast, British 'natural' and 'organic' fire metaphors are more restricted to the frames for political conviction and danger – to discourses of authority. At times, British 'natural fire' metaphors emulate the idealism associated with fire metaphors in the American rhetorical tradition.

## Natural fire metaphors: A discourse of awe

There is a greater incidence of natural fires in the United States and fire is sometimes used as a metonym for the destructive power of nature in general. When destructive and threatening, fire is overcome and the act of fire fighting becomes a metonym for unified social action to resolve social problems, as in the following:

> When the earth shook and fires raged in California; when I saw the Mississippi deluge the farmlands of the Midwest in a 500 year flood; when the century's bitterest cold swept from North Dakota to Newport News it seemed as though the world itself was coming apart at the seams. But the American people, they just came together. They rose to the occasion, neighbor helping neighbor, strangers risking life and limb to stay total strangers, showing the better angels of our nature. You can ask the farmers in the Middle West who fought the flood there or the people in California who've dealt with floods and earthquakes and fires and they'll tell you that. (Clinton, 24 January 1995)

With its relatively low population density, the United States is liable to extensive natural fire, to the extent that the national parks have at times been used experimentally in fire management techniques to establish whether naturally occurring fire should be simply left to burn itself out, or whether forest managers should intervene to control it. This would not be possible within European countries where limited land areas and high-density populations require intervention. As the force of nature fire is neither intrinsically good nor bad, the overriding consideration is how far it threatens clusters of human habitations.

The impact of cultural and historical factors on American political metaphors can be seen with the frequent intertextual reference to 'fire' that alludes to George Washington's 'Sacred Fire of human liberty'. We saw from the analysis of Sacred Fire (Chapter 3, Section 'Summary') that this concept contributes actively to a discourse of awe. For example, in Roosevelt's third inaugural speech:

> The destiny of America was proclaimed in words of prophecy spoken by our first President in his first inaugural in 1789 – words almost directed, it would seem, to this year of 1941: '**The preservation of the Sacred Fire of liberty** and the destiny of the republican model of government are justly considered, perhaps, as deeply, as finally, staked on the experiment entrusted to the hands of the American people' .... If **we lose that Sacred Fire** – if we let it be smothered with doubt and fear – then we shall reject the destiny which Washington strove so valiantly and so triumphantly to establish. (Roosevelt, 20 January 1941)

These fire metaphors occur just at the commencement of the coda of the speech – a stage that I have argued is of maximum rhetorical significance. In this framing, the 'fire' represents the ultimate source of the values by which Americans define themselves as a nation: a nation born in the fires of a war of independence with a set of values held as permanent, available to all – wherever they lived in the world – and to be sustained for eternity: a discourse of awe. When Thomas Jefferson departed the Presidency in 1809 he described America as 'the solitary republic of the world, the only monument of human rights, and the sole depository of the Sacred Fire of freedom and self-government, from hence it is to be lighted up in other regions of the earth, if other regions of the earth shall ever become susceptible of its benign influence'. In epideictic speeches, such as inaugural speeches, or other commemorative celebrations of national identity, it is therefore a convention to allude at some point to the master metaphor of the founding fathers of the nation; by displaying familiarity with a rhetorical tradition, a speaker lays claim to legitimacy. It is for this reason that Roosevelt alludes to Washington's first inaugural.

The origins of the 'Sacred Fire' are in classical civilization:

> The Church of Rome gradually set up a tight organization by means of which it brought some uniformity in religious life over a wide area. In all temples (or churches as they were commonly called) priests observed basically the same liturgy. In this liturgy fire played a modest but essential part. Like the ancient Roman temples, all Christian houses of worship contained a perpetually burning altar fire – as a tacit reminder of the times when fire was precious group possession. The first in the church did not need to be more than a simple small lamp that would function during the services as a symbol of light, not of warmth or scourging heat. (Goudsblom 1994: 132)

So, the 'Sacred' Fire of American liberty is different from the more embodied British metaphors such as 'fire in our bellies' that are framed in POLITICAL CONVICTION IS FIRE because the concept of Sacred Fire originates in the frame PURIFICATION IS FIRE. Consider, for example, its use by Wilson:

> We are being forged into a new unity **amidst the fires that now blaze throughout the world**. In **their ardent heat** we shall, in God's Providence, let us hope, *be purged of faction and division, purified of the errant humors of party and of private interest*, and shall stand forth in the days to come with a new dignity of national pride and spirit. Let each man see to it that the dedication is in his own heart, the high purpose of the nation in his own mind, ruler of his own will and desire. (Wilson, 5 March 1917)

Here the situation triggered metonym of 'the fires that now blaze' – referring to the destruction of the First World War – triggers the frame of purification with notions of 'cleansing' and 'purging': American idealism is construed as the solution to global strife. 'Pure' occurs three times more frequently in the American as compared with the British sample. Table 9.2 illustrates more generally how the concept of PURITY occurs more frequently in American political lexis by comparing the lexical field for purity in the two samples.

I have only searched the actual forms shown in the table and only included those words that occurred at least 10 times in one of the samples. A statistical test (known as log likelihood) shows that these are significant findings that indicate a strong

**Table 9.2** Comparison of PURITY in British and American samples

| Word | British sample (505,324 words) | American sample (502,280 words) |
|------|-------------------------------|--------------------------------|
| clean | 75 | 97 |
| fair | 83 | 116 |
| honest | 19 | 42 |
| innocence | 30 | 58 |
| integrity | 9 | 27 |
| justice | 166 | 217 |
| legitimate | 11 | 25 |
| moral | 48 | 131 |
| principle/s | 135 | 169 |
| pure | 3 | 10 |
| sincere | 4 | 10 |
| virtue | 15 | 10 |
| TOTAL | 598 | 912 |

preference for words from the lexical field of PURITY in American political rhetoric. Consider, for example, the following:

> Over the past few years I have consistently preached that nonviolence demands that the means *we use must be as pure as the ends we seek.* I have tried to make clear that it is wrong to use immoral means to attain moral ends. (King, 16 April 1963)
>
> *We are a purely idealistic Nation,* but let no one confuse our idealism with weakness. Because we are free we can never be indifferent to the fate of freedom elsewhere. Our moral sense dictates a clearcut preference for these societies which share with us an abiding respect for individual human rights. We do not seek to intimidate, but it is clear that a world which others can dominate with impunity would be inhospitable to decency and a threat to the well-being of all people. (Carter, 20 January 1977)

Discourses of awe place greater emphasis on notions such as purity, innocence and the sacred. Although the idealistic frame of FREEDOM IS FIRE was imitated by the British Conservative party references to the 'torch of freedom' and Blair's metaphors for Britain as 'a beacon to the world', there is a greater concern with purity as a cultural construct in American political rhetoric. American 'natural fire' metaphors appeal primarily to a shared value system based on natural justice. This is particularly the case in epideictic speeches where American presidents are communicating the national ideals for which they stand. The dominance of light over heat in the framing of American 'fire' metaphors also shows when fire (in bold) is represented as contrasting with darkness (italicized):

> May the light of freedom, coming to all *darkened lands,* **flame brightl**y – until at last *the darkness* is no more. (Eisenhower, 20 January 1957)

And as hope kindles hope, millions more will find it. By our efforts, we have **lit a fire** as well – **a fire in the minds of men.** It warms those who feel its power, **it burns those** who fight its progress, and one day **this untamed fire of freedom** will reach *the darkest corners of our world.* (George W. Bush, 3 February 2005)

In the last excerpt, there is an extended metaphor that commences by locating a fire inside the mind, but then the fire moves outwards to become one that reaches the 'darkest corners of the earth'; this fire is not 'in the bellies' (as in Blair's metaphor) but in the centre of intelligence – 'the minds of men' – so it is more conceptual than fully embodied. The spreading of the metaphor over a whole section of the speech corresponds with the literal spreading of an actual fire. It is a fire whose defining property is that it expresses continuity of belief in a set of values that – as well as spreading in geographical range – also connect the speaker with his auspicious predecessors. References to ancestors often occur in American discourses of awe, as in the following:

Today, because each succeeding generation of Americans has **kept the fire of freedom burning brightly, lighting those frontiers of possibility,** we all still bask in the glow and the warmth of **Mr. Franklin's rising sun.** (Clinton, 27 January 2000)

As well as spreading in time, this contagious fire can also – like a real fire – spread in space, both within the country, but also beyond the shores of the United States:

The energy, the faith, the devotion which we bring to this endeavor will *light our country* and all who serve it – and **the glow from that fire can truly light the world.** (Kennedy, 20 January 1961)

So, American fire metaphors – originating from the Sacred Fire of George Washington, continuing with Wilson's purifying fires – are employed to frame *all* aspirations to freedom anywhere in the world. The spreading action of fire is rhetorically employed to frame the spread and growth of American ideals and beliefs, and, by drawing on a discourse of awe, frame them in universal terms. And because this set of ideals, that I am describing as a discourse of awe, is inspired by religious conviction, like prophetic discourse, it connects American political policies with the certainty of a satisfactory outcome:

We must as a united people **keep ablaze on this continent the flames** of human liberty, of reason, of democracy and of fair play as living things to be preserved for the better world that is to come. (Roosevelt, 3 January 1940)

Within this more explicitly religious framework, it is evident how the semantic field of religion features more prominently in the American sample. This is illustrated in Table 9.3 that compares this closely related semantic field in the American and British samples.

**Table 9.3** Comparison of RELIGION in American and British samples

| Word | British sample (505,324 words) | American sample (502,280 words) |
|------|:---:|:---:|
| church | 28 | 134 |
| divine | 3 | 12 |
| doctrine | 18 | 24 |
| god | 7 | 309 |
| miracle | 8 | 26 |
| pray | 17 | 88 |
| religion | 73 | 138 |
| sacred | 8 | 31 |
| sacrifice | 19 | 116 |
| soul | 13 | 47 |
| spirit | 71 | 249 |
| worship | 5 | 29 |
| TOTAL | 270 | 1,203 |

The words are sequenced alphabetically and, as with the PURITY sample, I have only included words that occurred at least ten times in one of the samples. The results are striking; Alistair Campbell, Tony Blair's communication advisor once told him 'We don't do religion' – and there is no clearer illustration of how far this comment is true than in Table 9.3. 'God' is the most frequent word in this field in the American sample and yet only occurs seven times in the British sample. 'Church' occurs around five times more frequently in the American sample; 'divine' occurs four times more often; 'pray' five times more frequently and 'worship' six times more frequently. Evidently, as a field of human activity, religion is embraced in American political discourse just as it is avoided in British political discourse.

In metaphorical terms, the American 'Sacred Fire' is one that burns, illuminates and purifies at home and abroad, in this time and for all time. Just as the burning altars that citizens kept in their home in Ancient Rome symbolized permanence, so those who sustain this spiritual fire are guaranteed a place in eternity. It is also the Sacred Fire that brings with it responsibilities:

> Sacrifices that we and our allies are making impose upon us all *a sacred obligation* to see to it that out of this war we and our children will gain something better than mere survival. (Roosevelt, 11 January 1944)
>
> This I propose to offer, pledging that the larger purposes will bind upon us all as *a sacred obligation* with a unity of duty hitherto evoked only in time of armed strife. (Roosevelt, 4 March 1933)

This interpretation of politics as an arena where the relationships between nation states arose from sacred obligations was a hallmark of Roosevelt's rhetoric. However, it is sustained by his successors; at times this more explicit invocation of a discourse of awe is part of a political identity that relies on religious status; for example, in the case of Martin Luther King:

> And I have watched many churches commit themselves to a completely other worldly religion which makes a strange, on Biblical distinction between body and soul, between the sacred and the secular. (King, 16 April 1963)
>
> I know you are asking today, 'How long will it take?' (Speak, sir) Somebody's asking, 'How long will prejudice blind the visions of men, darken their understanding, and *drive bright-eyed wisdom from her sacred throne?*' (King, 25 March 1965)

However, it has also continued in the language of politicians whose appeal is less explicitly based on religion:

> Posterity is the world to come, the world for whom we hold our ideals, from whom we have borrowed our planet, and to whom we bear sacred responsibilities. (Clinton, 20 January 1993)

Because of the lineage of natural fire as a source of light and therefore of spiritual inspiration, 'Sacred Fire' metaphors are always positive in their discourse prosody, and fire is a source of psychologically positive states such as hope, creativity and inspiration based in commitment to a cause:

> Tonight I ask everyone in this Chamber – and every American – to look into their hearts, **spark** their hopes, **and fire** their imaginations. There is so much good, so much possibility, so much excitement in our nation. (Clinton, 17 February 1993)

Here the creative firing of the imagination is a source of national motivation and an exhortation to act for the betterment of mankind. Though more secular in tone, this is still the rhetoric of the Pilgrim Fathers and of those versions of Christianity that take their inspiration from 'light' metaphors in the Book of John. It was this sort of 'fire' – the unquenchable fire of the human spirit – that was also invoked by Martin Luther King:

> He knew a kind of physics that somehow didn't relate to the transphysics that we knew about. And that was the fact that there was **a certain kind of fire that no water could put out**. And we went before the fire hoses; we had known water. (King, 3 April 1968)

King is referring to that fire that was first mentioned in 2 Maccabees:

> When the matter (restoring the fire) became known and the king of the Persians heard that in the place where the exiled priests had hidden the fire a liquid had appeared, with which Nehemiah and his people had purified the materials of the

sacrifice, the king, after verifying the facts, had the place enclosed and pronounced sacred. (2 Maccabees 1: 33–34)

The idea of an eternal fire that motivated Washington's Sacred Fire gives legitimacy to all those who sustained the fire and condemns those who seek to extinguish it. The knowledge of natural fire activated by these metaphors is of primitive natural fire that if left uncontrolled would destroy crops, buildings, towns and cities; it is the sort of fire that is caused by war and the use of fire-forging weaponry. Natural fire metaphors are therefore highly salient in American political rhetoric; when positive they refer to the ancient religious status of fire as a mystery, as something that is sacred and borrowed from the Gods.

## Functional fire metaphors: The beacon metaphor

In Chapter 8, I examined the origin of the 'beacon' metaphor in relation to the tradition of using a fire as a source of light to protect ships from danger, and analysed it as both a symbol of safety but also as a symbol of ideals motivated by concepts such as FREEDOM IS FIRE and HOPE IS FIRE/LIGHT. Rhetorically, there is extensive use of the metaphor in both the British and Americans samples – just as the Olympic torch is passed from hand to hand, rhetorically, the beacon metaphor has been passed backwards and forwards between American and British political rhetoric. Table 9.4 shows some American uses of the metaphor.

**Table 9.4** The 'Beacon' metaphor in American rhetoric

| Speaker | Date | Example |
| --- | --- | --- |
| King | 17 May 1957 | For all men of goodwill, this May seventeenth decision came as a joyous daybreak to end the long night of human captivity. It came as **a great beacon light of hope** to millions of disinherited people throughout the world who had dared only to dream of freedom. |
| King | 28 August 1963 | Five score years ago, a great American, in whose symbolic shadow we stand signed the Emancipation Proclamation. This momentous decree came as **a great beacon light of hope** to millions of Negro slaves who had been seared in the flames of withering injustice. |
| Nixon | 20 January 1969 | Let us pledge together to make these next four years the best four years in America's history, so that on its 200th birthday America will be as young and as vital as when it began, and as bright **a beacon of hope** for all the world. |
| Reagan | 20 January 1981 | We will again be the exemplar of freedom and a **beacon of hope** for those who do not now have freedom. |
| Reagan | 11 January 1989 | **And she's still a beacon**, still a magnet for all who must have freedom, for all the pilgrims from all the lost places who are hurtling through the darkness, toward home. |

**Table 9.4** The 'Beacon' metaphor in American rhetoric (*continued*)

| Speaker | Date | Example |
|---------|------|---------|
| Clinton | 4 February 1997 | a celebration of our common culture in the century that is past and in the new one to come in a new millennium so that we can remain the world's **beacon not only of liberty but of creativity** long after the fireworks have faded. |
| Obama | 27 July 2004 | America, which stood as **a beacon of freedom and opportunity** to so many who had come before. |
| Rice | 19 March 2005 | I am honored to be here at Sophia University, this great **beacon of learning,** this living example of the strong partnership between America and Japan. |
| Obama | 28 April 2007 | **We are the beacon** that has led generations of weary travelers to find opportunity, and liberty, and hope on our doorstep. |
| Obama | 16 November 2005 | That if we are to shine as **a beacon of hope** to the rest of the world, we must be respected not just for the might of our military, but for the reach of our ideals. |
| Obama | 22 April 2008 | America the same way my father saw it from across the ocean – as **a beacon of all that is good** and all that is possible for all mankind. |
| Obama | 15 June 2008 | And to all those who have wondered if **America's beacon still burns** as bright … |

The beacon metaphor did not first appear in American political rhetoric until Martin Luther King introduced it and only first appeared in an inaugural speech when Nixon used it in 1969; this relatively late use of the metaphor suggests that it may have been borrowed from Churchill who seems to have used it earliest with a metonymic motivation in the purpose of a beacon which is to guide shipping:

> …. how would the race of men have risen above the apes; how otherwise would they have conquered and extirpated dragons and monsters; how would they have ever evolved the moral theme; how would they have marched forward across the centuries to broad conceptions of compassion, of freedom, and of right? *How would they ever have discerned those* **beacon lights** *which summon and guide us across the rough dark waters, and presently will guide us across the* **flaming lines of battle** *towards better days which lie beyond?* (Churchill, 20 January 1940)

At this time it was critical to the British strategy to bring America into the war and Churchill does this by activating the metaphor of the beacon, and of Sacred Fire imagery to achieve this political goal. He does this by employing a symbol – the beacon (with its origins in discourses of awe) that subsequently in American rhetoric became synonymous with 'the American dream' – and with freedom from oppression. American uses are intertextual because they originate in John Withrop's rousing words to his fellow Pilgrims to inspire them to freedom from oppression:

> For we must consider that we shall be as a *city upon a hill*, the eyes of all people are upon us; so that if we shall deal falsely with our God in this work we have

undertaken, and so cause Him to withdraw His present help from us, we shall shame the faces of many of God's worthy servants, and cause their prayers to be turned into curses ... (John Winthrop, 1630)

The symbol of America as a shining city was then transferred to the symbolism of the Statue of Liberty – a female holding a beacon beckoning those seeking freedom to America – and it is this beacon of freedom that America sometimes offers to those suffering oppression in other parts of the world. By contrast, Churchill's use of the beacon metaphor was strategic: to appeal to American idealism so that they would enter the war. Subsequent uses by British politicians were driven by political pragmatism – making a general appeal to freedom whenever politically necessary – whether in relation to free enterprise (Cameron), education (Blair) or the Conservative Party in general (Thatcher) – rather than to a national set of ideals. The British use is strategic and heavily influenced by the symbolism of the Sacred Fire in American political discourse – where discourses of awe are more evident and explicit. Ronald Reagan provides the clearest explanation of the 'beacon' metaphor in American political discourse in his farewell speech:

> The past few days when I've been at that window upstairs, I've thought a bit of the 'shining city upon a hill.' The phrase comes from John Winthrop, who wrote it to describe the America he imagined. What he imagined was important because he was an early Pilgrim, an early freedom man. He journeyed here on what today we'd call a little wooden boat; and like the other Pilgrims, he was looking for a home that would be free. I've spoken of the shining city all my political life, but I don't know if I ever quite communicated what I saw when I said it. But in my mind it was a tall, proud city built on rocks stronger than oceans, windswept, God-blessed, and teeming with people of all kinds living in harmony and peace; a city with free ports that hummed with commerce and creativity. And if there had to be city walls, the walls had doors and the doors were open to anyone with the will and the heart to get here. That's how I saw it, and see it still. And how stands the city on this winter night? More prosperous, more secure, and happier than it was 8 years ago. But more than that: after 200 years, two centuries, she still stands strong and true on the granite ridge, and her glow has held steady no matter what storm. **And she's still a beacon**, still a magnet for all who must have freedom, for all the pilgrims from all the lost places who are **hurtling through the darkness**, toward home. (Reagan, 11 January 1989)

It is this national myth of America as the embodiment of high social ideals that have made the beacon a symbol that is used by both Democrats (King, Clinton and Obama) and Republicans (Reagan and Rice) as each party seeks to define the American dream in its own terms and position themselves as the true protectors of American patriotic idealism. However, it is noticeable that the 'beacon metaphor' has been used more by Democrats than by Republicans, who, generally, take a less favourable stance towards immigration.

Evidence of a similar discourse of aspiration related to the discourse of awe can be found in the use of 'stars' in American political rhetoric; there are only four references to 'stars' in the British sample but seventeen in the American sample;

> Together *let us explore the stars*, conquer the deserts, eradicate disease, tap the ocean depths, and encourage the arts and commerce. (Kennedy, 20 January 1961)
>    But I know, somehow, that only when it is dark enough, *can you see the stars*. And I see God working in this period of the twentieth century in a way that men, in some strange way, are responding–something is happening in our world. (King, 3 April 1968)

Initially, references to 'the stars' alluded to space exploration had a metonymic motivation, but reference to the stars seems to have come to symbolize a more general and unspecified search for a perfect truth that can be more directly linked to the discourses of awe found in part two of this book. In the following quote, there is a deliberate ambiguity as to whether Reagan is directly referring to the space programme or to American aspiration in general – or more likely to both, as the one came to serve as a metonym for the other:

> Go forward, America, and *reach for the stars*. We will never forget those brave seven, but we shall go forward. (Reagan, 4 February 1986)
>    We can reach for greatness again. *We can follow our dreams to distant stars.* (Reagan, 25 January 25 1984)
>    We believe faith and freedom *must be our guiding stars*, for they show us truth, they make us brave, give us hope, and leave us wiser than we were. (Reagan, 6 February 6 1985)

The rhetorical appeal of discourses of awe in American political speeches originates in an awareness of having a unique role in world history – a people specially appointed by God to provide the ideal nation to which other nations should aspire; this belief has sometimes been referred to an 'American exceptionalism' – the view that Americans are a special people with a sort of divine mission, or manifest destiny. It was a belief that originated with the Pilgrim Fathers who thought they were setting up a community that would be a model for the rest of the world to follow and who were escaping the oppressive use of fire that Foxe describe in his *Book of Martyrs*. The view that America was essentially a new nation, characterized by the values of freedom and equality rooted in democracy is symbolized by the beacon metaphor and draws on the traditions of the Sacred Fire – the fire that should be kept pure and uncontaminated. Functional fire metaphors therefore appeal to idealism based on conceptual frames such as HOPE IS FIRE and FREEDOM IS FIRE.

However, it seems that for rhetoricians the beacon is also a symbol for American power, so that America views itself as the beacon: the divine agent whose historical destiny is both to protect and, at times, to extend the reach of its fundamentally sacred values – through firepower if necessary.

## Organic fire metaphors

Around one-third of the fire metaphors in the American sample were organic fire metaphors. I will focus on the two most frequent metaphors 'spark' and 'fuel' because they provide an excellent contrast in their semantic prosodies. Essential to the ideal of freedom in American rhetoric is the idealization of 'free enterprise' and around half of the instances of 'spark' in American political speeches is directly to some form of economic activity related to free enterprise:

> For the past five years, we have worked to bring **the spark of** private enterprise to inner city and poor rural areas with community development banks, more commercial loans into poor neighborhoods, cleanup of polluted sites for development. (Clinton, 27 January 1998)
>      Preserving the individual and business tax deductions that will stimulate saving and investment, removing unnecessary Federal regulations **to spark** productivity and maintaining a healthy dollar and a stable monetary policy, the latter a responsibility of the Federal Reserve System. (Ronald Reagan, 26 January 1982)
>      The spirit of enterprise **is sparked by the sunrise** industries of high-tech and by small business people with big ideas-people like Barbara Proctor (Reagan, 25 January 1984)
>      Those awful tax cuts **haven't sparked** business investment; private borrowers are being crowded out of the capital markets. (Reagan, 2 March 1984)
>      **A sparkling** economy spurs initiatives, sunrise industries, and makes older ones more competitive. Nowhere is this more important than our next frontier: space. Your former colleague, my first Secretary of the Treasury, led that effort and **sparked** our long boom. (Clinton, 27 January 2000)

Quite frequently these are one-off metaphors; however, the metaphor itself is contested between the political left and right. For example, in the following an extended metaphor explains the positive outcomes of government-initiated social reform programmes:

> It is time – this may be the most radical thing I've said in seven years in this office – it's time for Washington to show a little humility. There are **a thousand sparks of** genius in 50 states and a thousand communities around the nation. It is time to nurture them and see which ones can **catch fire and become guiding lights.** States have begun to show us the way. They have demonstrated that successful welfare programs can be built around more effective child support enforcement practices and innovative programs requiring welfare recipients to work or prepare for work. (Reagan, 25 January 1988)

The use of this organic fire metaphor likens the processes of social progress to those of an organism, so that just as it is in the nature of an organism to grow, a 'fire' ignited by a 'spark' will be one that spreads through the society. The idea here is of the productive fire of swidden farming where fire was connected with productive use of the land. But the 'spark' metaphor also corresponds with the discourse of awe that I have identified in the analysis of natural and functional fire.

Metaphoric uses of 'fuel' were nearly twice as common in the American sample and there were similarly negative evaluations of 'fuel' to those found in the British speeches as in the following:

> And to those who would try to use the current crisis as an opportunity to widen the conflict, stay out. Iran's arms shipments and support for terror **fuel the fire** of conflict in the Middle East. And it must stop. All over the world people are being torn asunder by racial, ethnic and religious conflicts **that fuel** fanaticism and terror. (George W. Bush, 4 April 2002)
>
> The divide of race has been America's constant curse. And each new wave of immigrants gives new targets to old prejudices. Prejudice and contempt, cloaked in the pretense of religious or political conviction are no different. These forces have nearly destroyed our nation in the past. They plague us still. **They fuel** the fanaticism of terror. And they torment the lives of millions in fractured nations all around the world. (Clinton, 20 January 1997)
>
> So let us be very clear about exactly who they and we are fighting. Some of the insurgency is **fueled by** the same thugs and henchman who enforced Saddam Hussein's tyranny for decades. (Rice, 30 September 2005)
>
> Instead, what they've seen is inaction and tinkering around the edges of our education system – a paralysis that is **fueled by** ideological battles that are as outdated as they are predictable. (Obama, 25 October 2005)

The 'fuel' metaphor profiles notions of causality so that when a particular 'ideology' is represented as threatening, and also likely to lead to actions that are opposed to the interests of the United States, it is described as 'fuelling' and can be framed as AN UNCONTROLLED SITUATION IS AN EXCESS OF FUEL. The implication is, perhaps, that such anti-American attitudes and beliefs may eventually lead to actual conflict and acts of aggression against the United States so the frame also integrates DANGER IS FIRE. Typically, these metaphors profile fire as out of control. Figure 9.1 shows how this metaphor can be analysed in terms of force dynamics.

AN UNCONTROLLED SITUATION IS AN EXCESS OF FUEL implies that force A, a human agent, exerts a greater strength than force B, a social situation, and that therefore the social situation will become unbalanced. If we imagine an entity positioned on the horizontal bar, it would be likely to fall off. From a cognitive point of view, the FIRE IS DANGER frame is quite broad and is partly reliant on metonymy: the knowledge that fires often occur in actual situations of unrest. The effect of 'fuel' to imply deliberate human agency to influence a social situation depends on our knowledge of the effect of human actions in adding fuel to a fire. It is perhaps strange that 'fuel' as a metaphor should take on such negative evaluations – given the importance of fuel to the American economy, but it is a verb rather than a noun, and so creates the image of a deliberate action of providing a source of fuel for a destructive type of fire – however, there are occasions when it is used with a positive sense:

FORCE A

ANTAGONIST:
human agent
add fuel

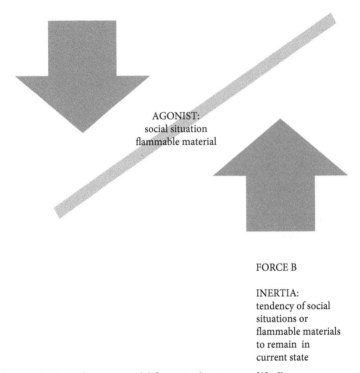

AGONIST:
social situation
flammable material

FORCE B

INERTIA:
tendency of social
situations or
flammable materials
to remain in
current state

**Figure 9.1** Force dynamic model for metaphoric uses of 'fuel'

This strategy **is fueled with** new thinking and new resources, but it rests upon a shared aspiration that is as old as the Americas themselves. It is the hope of the new world, a place where all human beings would have the opportunity to live and flourish in freedom, according to their God-given talents and that by the power of their example, they would be like a light that inspires all humankind to rise above injustice and poverty that has defined too much of our past. (Rice, 3 May 2006)

But somewhere, there have also always been people who believe that this isn't the way it was supposed to be – that things should be different in America. People who believe that while evil and suffering will always exist, this is a country that **has been fueled by** small miracles and boundless dreams – a place where we're not afraid to face down the greatest challenges in pursuit of the greater good; a place where, against all odds, we overcome. (Obama, 16 November 2005)

Here the social situations that are 'fueled' are inherently positive 'new thinking', 'miracles' and so on, and the activities that create change still imply human agency.

Once there are well-established positive frames for fire, there is the potential for them to be used creatively to re-evaluate their conventional semantic prosody; it is likely that this is what Rice and Obama were doing when they chose the verb 'fueled' with a fresh 'spin' to it.

## Metonymic fire and destruction

There were a few examples of another type of natural fire – one that destroys and was also caused by human agency; in the following quote a metaphorical firestorm is caused by words that were spoken by a politician:

> But the remarks that have caused **this recent firestorm** weren't simply controversial. They weren't simply a religious leader's effort to speak out against perceived injustice. (Obama, 18 March 2008)

The effect of the words spoken by the religious leader – and friend of Obama's – was to arouse fires of hatred, a destructive rhetoric that could itself be the cause of further destructive actions. This is the inversion of the spiritual fire appealed to by Martin Luther King, and one deliberately aroused by corrupt leaders:

> Doctrines that set group against group, faith against faith, race against race, class against class, **fanning the fires** of hatred in men too despondent, too desperate to think for themselves, were used as rabble-rousing slogans on which dictators could ride to power. (Roosevelt, 3 January 1940)

The aspect of fire profiled is still an inner fire that motivates individuals, but it is a corruption of spiritual fire and motivated by FIRE FOR INJUSTICE that is alluded to by Martin Luther King:

> I have a dream that one day even the state of Mississippi, a desert state, sweltering with the **heat of** injustice and oppression, will be transformed into an oasis of freedom and justice. (King, 28 August 1963)

This fire is the complete antithesis of FREEDOM IS FIRE, and the two are visually contrasted in his rhetoric. Such fires of injustice hark back to the Biblical fires of damnation as a punishment for those who practiced evil, and about which a Baptist preacher could terrorize his congregation with the notion that these fires of anger and punishment were actual fire that many believed would await those who had acted sinfully. These fires caused by negative emotions such as wrath, fear and strong sentiments of loyalty to the interests of one group that defined itself by hatred of another group could eventually lead to actual conflict:

> It is a crime against mankind that so much courage, and so much will, and so many dreams, must be flung on **the fires of war and death.** (Johnson, 12 January 1966)

It is significant that Roosevelt, King and Johnson were speaking at times of conflict when the reality of *actual* fire predominating is ever present so that 'fire' becomes a metonym, or more precisely, a synecdoche for conflict in general. As we found in *Foxe's Book of Martyrs*, these figures work through a chain of causation from ideas and emotions related to hatred and anger that then lead to aggressive actions involving weapons and causing actual fires. In this chain of development, there is also a shift from the metaphors that characterize 'inner' fire, to metonyms that describe the literal fire arising from a destructive inner fire. These metonyms can be framed as FIRE FOR POWER.

It is in the transition from metaphor to metonymy that we find a very different type of evaluation by the speaker – a switch from the use of fire as a symbol of spirituality and as a metaphor for all that is sacred (a discourse of awe) to fire as a synecdoche for military power: a discourse of authority. This figurative use of fire as a symbol for acts of destruction creates a different set of prosodies but is one that contributes to the higher frequency, and the higher level of salience, of 'fire' figurative language in American political speeches. Historically significant events in American history have often been associated with fire, precisely because fire has always been associated with war. This takes its origins in so-called Greek fire, a weapon attributed by legend to the Byzantine navy:

> Their ships were fitted with fire-throwing muzzles from which burning liquid could be shot at the enemy. The first was not extinguished by water, but continued burning. Any ship what was engulfed by it went up in flames. (Goudsblom 1994: 137)

With the development of gunpowder and its subsequent application in the production of firearms, fire became associated with military domination and power by force. We find this sense in the phrase 'baptism of fire'. For this reason, fire as a symbol of power could be used positively to refer to events in American history where fire had been necessary for the dominance over rival states, for example, during the Civil War:

> One hundred years ago, in 1865, following a terrible *test of blood and fire,* the compact of union was finally sealed. (Johnson, 4 January 1965)

The sealing of the Union is described as if it were the outcome of the application of heat. So, American 'firepower' can be necessary:

> That's what change is. Change is realizing that meeting today's threats requires not just our *firepower*, but the power of our diplomacy. (Obama, 3 June 2008)

Fire as a necessary source of legitimate political authority also shows in the expression 'hold one's feet to the fire':

> So I'd like to congratulate you all on the thoughtful presentations you've given so far about poverty and justice in America, and **for putting fire under the feet of the political leadership** here in Washington. But I am persuaded that the real credit

belongs to the people who sent us here, who pay our salaries, **who hold our feet to the fire**. (Obama, 28 June 2006)

Although literally holding someone's feet to a fire would be a form of torture, the metaphor refers to fire as a source of authority: it implies that it may be necessary at times to use fire to force people to do what is legitimate. This is fire as contributing to a discourse of authority. However, there was also the use of fire as source of military force by America's opponents, so that metonymic use of 'fire' can refer to the destructive fire of those who resist the 'Sacred Fire' of liberty:

Yet as long as others will challenge America's security and *test the clearness of our beliefs with fire and steel,* then we must stand or see the promise of two centuries tremble. (Johnson, 12 January 1966)

Metonymic fire is then an entity that can be used for self-protection, in which case it is a good fire, or it can be the bad fire of opponents. In the following quote, 11 September 2001, the day of the attack on the World Trade Centre is referred to as a 'day of fire':

September 11, 2001, made us see more clearly than ever how our values and our interests are linked and joined across the globe. **That day of fire** made us see that the best way to secure a world of peace and hope is to build a world of freedom. (Rice, 28 January 2005)

After the shipwreck of communism came years of relative quiet, years of repose, years of sabbatical – and then **there came a day of fire**. (George W. Bush, 20 January 2005)

We will remember every family that lives in grief. We will remember **the fire and ash**, the last phone calls, the funerals of the children. (George W. Bush, 11 November 2001)

Here there is reversion to primitive fire, the simple destructive fire whereby the emotion of the inner fires of hatred causes fire to be used as a weapon of war: from early human history fire has been used to destroy the material assets of an enemy and, more importantly, to destroy their morale. To invoke fire on an opponent is not only to burn up their food stocks but also to extinguish their hope and confidence in civilizing values. To fight the fire of opponents is heroic:

It is *the firefighter's courage* to storm a stairway filled with smoke, but also a parent's willingness to nurture a child, that finally decides our fate. (Obama, 20 January 2009)

The perspective on metonymic fire, fire as a symbol of power that forms a discourse of authority, depends on the identity of those who hold the fire and their intentions. While those who extinguish the fires of America's opponents are heroes, their firefighting tools can be wielded unjustly by the State, as when they are directed against America's own citizens:

I am mindful that only yesterday in Birmingham, Alabama, our children, crying out for brotherhood, *were answered with fire hoses*, snarling dogs and even death. (King, 10 December 1964)

It was a march of ordinary Americans – maids and cooks, preachers and Pullman porters who faced down *fire hoses and* dogs, tear gas and billy clubs when they tried to get to the other side. (Obama, 28 April 2007)

Hope is what led a band of colonists to rise up against an empire; what led the greatest of generations to free a continent and heal a nation; what led young women and young men to sit at lunch counters and *brave fire hoses* and march through Selma and Montgomery for freedom's cause. (Obama, 3 January 2008)

Notice how the metonym 'fire hoses' avoids reference to the individuals who are directing them: their anonymity is preserved by the metonym – even when they are extinguishing the fire of liberty. So, fire is contested as a source of legitimate power – American firepower – or as a source of oppression, when the weapons of the state – its fire hoses – are directed against those who are inspired by an inner fire, the fire 'that no water could put out'.

## Summary

In this chapter, I have identified a contrast in the semantic prosodies of American political rhetoric between the largely positive evaluation implied by metaphors drawing on a discourse of awe and a largely negative evaluation implied by those drawing on a discourse of authority. When American political rhetoric expounds a discourse of awe based on the frames PURIFICATION IS FIRE and FREEDOM IS FIRE – references to 'Sacred Fire', the 'beacon' and 'star' metaphors – it applies the positive associations of 'Sacred Fire' to the topic of the metaphors; this is reinforced by other lexical choices based on the concept of PURITY. However, discourses of authority based on metonymic conceptualizations of fire, originating in the dangers imposed by actual fires – whether from nature or from human agency when associated with social and political conflict – convey a strongly negative semantic prosody based conceptually on FIRE FOR POWER. This negative intention also shows in metaphors related to 'fuel' based on the frame AN UNCONTROLLED SITUATION IS AN EXCESS OF FUEL. Part of the appeal of Churchillian rhetoric to American audiences is because he employed strategic use of the symbolism of the Sacred Fire – the discourses of awe – to influence American policy.

# 10

# Fire Metaphors in Visual Media: British Political Cartoons

## Introduction: Political cartoons

This concluding chapter examines the evidence from metaphors in British political cartoons for cognitive models for fire. I will argue that, as well as understanding humour and satire, deciphering political cartoons also requires the ability to interpret visual and verbal metaphors. A common cause for satire is when public figures are represented as losing their temper: the idea of a public figure losing his or her temper is inherently newsworthy, and I will argue that visual representations of this seek to undermine discourses of authority. Since heat is part of the embodied experience of anger, and fire is a primary source of heat, many satirical cartoons include visual or verbal 'fire' metaphors. Therefore, understanding such 'fire' metaphors and interpreting their critical stance towards authority relies on, and contributes to, a range of cognitive abilities broadly known as visual literacy. In the first part of the chapter I consider some of the characteristics of political cartoons, with a particular focus on the type of knowledge that readers need to understand and interpret this genre. I then explore how fire is used in political cartoons that represent anger in public life. I suggest in particular the relevance of the frames EMOTION IS FIRE and EMOTION IS A FORCE. Since fire metaphors are used to describe topics other than anger, I follow this with a discussion of other narrative themes that predominate in cartoons depicting fire and that share the same purpose of developing an anti-authoritarian discourse.

Political cartoons are a humorous satirical genre whose purpose is to entertain and amuse while passing some form of comment, critical observation or parody on current political affairs:

> Cartoons use familiar political and cultural symbols in humorous, usually satirical and emotive ways designed to provoke an immediate positive or negative reaction on the part of the reader. Now most often appearing as a regular feature of daily newspapers, typically in the editorial section, political cartoons are a creative, provocative form of communication and a vital element of world popular culture. (Seip 2003)

They depict politicians, or other pre-eminent figures in public life such as royalty or celebrities, humorously by exaggerating their recognizable features. Such caricatures are drawn in a style that is distinctive of the cartoonist, so that the image instantly reveals the identity of its author to those familiar with his work (a list of editorial cartoonists shows that all twenty-five are men[1]). The political cartoon flourishes in democracies where the principle of freedom of speech protects cartoonists from action on the grounds of libel – except in the case of defamatory images that could be deemed as incitements to hatred. However, cartoonists have become targets of unlawful ideologically motivated violence, and cartoonists who satirized the Prophet Mohammed have been attacked and killed by Islamic fundamentalists[2]; it is unlikely that perpetrators of such attacks make any distinction between discourses of awe and of authority, between the secular and the sacred.

Fundamental to the interpretation of political cartoons is recognition of their authors' rhetorical purposes; these include explaining and offering humorous comment on current political events:

> The purpose of a political cartoon is to represent an aspect of social, cultural, or political life in a way that condenses reality and transforms it in a striking, original, and/or humorous way. The field of politics is often complex and bewildering, and cartoons offer a way of explaining the significance of real life events and characters through the means of an imaginary scenario. (El Refaie 2009a: 3)

Cartoons do a number of different things simultaneously: they serve to entertain, explain, comment and simplify. Metaphor offers the most effective way of combining these diverse objectives by creating imaginary worlds that reveal some aspects of reality that might be concealed by a literal rendering. Since cartoons intend to influence public opinion, politicians are typically represented by metaphors implying that they are immoral, greedy or dangerous – although occasionally they may be represented as benevolent.

Humour is a defining feature of successful political cartoons. It can arise from word play, caricature or by an interaction between words and image. Although harsh, critical comment will often be more humorous when subtle. Commentary on character commonly relies on visual metaphor because a real person is being satirized using a style and a medium that rejects the literal representations offered by photographs. The conventions of the genre give a free reign to the cartoonist's imagination, since within democratic systems of government the cartoonist is allocated the privileged status of Court Fool, as well as of artist.

Metaphors can be used in different modes of satirical communication: they can be entirely visually, or rely on an interaction between image and verbal cues. I will use the term 'visual metaphor' for purely image-based metaphors (although 'pictorial metaphor' was originally proposed (Forceville 1996)), I will use 'multimodal metaphor' (Forceville 2008) where metaphor arises from the interaction between words and images. This is because while ostensibly only two modes are used: the visual and the verbal, there are also representations of motion. The verbal elements can appear either in the image, for example, superimposed on an entity represented in the cartoon, or in a caption in a separate frame below the image.

The creation of political cartoons can best be understood by analogy with devising a crossword puzzle. In writing a crossword puzzle, the author necessarily works backwards beginning with the answer; similarly, the cartoonist must first decide the topic of his cartoon: the topical news event it refers to and the politicians to be depicted. But these events and identities will then be encrypted in an illustrative style involving visual distortion: just as the writer of the crossword puzzle encodes his answers in obscure verbal clues, so the cartoonist encodes his meaning by distortion, hyperbole and oblique reference. And just as the crossword puzzle solver interprets clues, so the cartoon reader deciphers visual clues – sometimes assisted by verbal clues. If the puzzle or cartoon is too easy, then the viewer will be unsatisfied, as El Refaie (2009a: 10) notes: 'in fact, if cartoons were too easy to understand, they would probably not provide the same sense of pride and achievement to those viewers who manage to solve these intriguing mental puzzles.' But, like the crossword, if the viewer cannot work out the clues and abandons the search for an answer, the cartoon will not satisfy either. A crossword only uses language, whereas a political cartoon relies primarily on the visual mode. For this reason, deciphering the political cartoon requires visual literacy; this has been described as 'an adequate capacity to identify images and to parse them according to the ways they refer to the world' (Elkins, in El Refaie 2009b: 3).

What is the nature of the 'visual literacy' required in the mental process of deciphering and decoding that I have likened to doing a crossword puzzle? Interpreting political cartoons initially requires the viewer to recognize who or what is/are visually represented (the noun element) and what the represented participant(s) are doing (the verb element). This requires the viewer to engage in a process of hypothesis formation in which visual representations, aided sometimes by words, are matched with possible political actors and current events to try to establish a frame of reference. Some of these hypotheses will be accepted and others rejected; cracking the code relies partially on establishing the contextual relevance of what is depicted. For example, to decipher a visual metaphor in which a politician is depicted as a boy (see Figure 10.5, p.214) we need to know *which* politician is depicted – for only then can a schema of immature behaviour be activated. Then we need to know *which* aspects of his current behaviour are represented as lacking maturity. Working out such mappings is a metaphoric process because it involves working out correspondences between the actual behaviour of a real politician and the fantasy-based representation of the 'politician as boy'. It may be assisted by clues – either in the caption or superimposed on the image; these may be verbal, for example, the name of a country may be shown as a label on a map, or visual, as when the flag of a country is used metonymically to refer to that country.

The use of labels containing words is known as 'anchorage' (Barthes 1977, in El Refaie 2009b) because it fixes the more ambient range of possible meanings that emanate from image components. The clues may be explicit, as when the name of a country or person is given in a label, or hinted at by a symbol; for example, the image of a fire-breathing dragon may be used to refer to China. Such symbols are also interpreted using metonymic frames, for example: DRAGON FOR CHINA. Informing this interpretation of metaphor is knowledge of the genre: it is because we know that political cartoons are a satirical genre that we are stimulated to search for some form of critical comment and evaluation. Understanding political cartoons therefore requires cognitive activation of a set of correspondence that are set up by visual metaphors *and* knowing that their purpose is to offer social and political comment on current events.

Something shown by empirical studies into political cartoons is that not all viewers understand them in the same way: people vary in their background knowledge of current affairs and in their levels of visual literacy (El Rafaie 2009b). One component of visual literacy is visual grammar (Kress and van Leeuwan 2006). A narrative theme may be developed by spatial positioning of elements and through the use of 'vectors' – strong lines created by the cartoonist that guide the eye movements of the viewer and indicate the direction of the action. Vectors can be reinforced by motion lines; these indicate such things as the speed of the action and whether movement is straight, or meandering, direct or indirect and therefore contribute to the narrative theme. For example, in cartoons depicting the Olympic torch there is often an image of several runners positioned in left to right sequence with motion lines to show speed (see figure 10.8, p.220). The narrative theme could be influenced by who is leading and who is following, how fast they are both running and whether the following runner is one of the same team (as in a relay) or one of an opposing team, as in an individual race. This could be indicated by the vectors arising from the runner's direction of gaze: is he looking forwards towards the finishing line, but with one arm held backwards to receive a baton from a member of the same team, or is he looking backwards towards a competitor? Individuals will vary in their ability to 'read' spatial relations, motion lines and vectors.

As well as varying in levels of visual literacy, viewers may also vary in the extent to which their understanding of metaphor is based on words, images or motion lines, and in the sequence in which they engage with these components of a cartoon: some will immediately read linguistic elements and then look at visual components and others will do the reverse. A more common approach may be alternating between modes, so examining some of the visual elements allows the reader to form a hypothesis about the relevant identities, referents and narrative; this hypothesis is then either confirmed or rejected by verbal information and further exploration of the visual components. Anger metaphors provide an excellent example of how viewers are able to draw on their visual literacy to interpret cartoons and so in the next section I show how understanding satirical political cartoons about anger often involves working out multimodal metaphors.

## Anger metaphors

The question I address in this section is: how is anger represented in political cartoons? The answer requires attention to the entities that are represented – for example, fire, animals and so on – and the style of drawing – for example, the techniques used to represent heat, motion or force. A typical example of a multimodal metaphor for anger is found in a cartoon published on the 7 March 2013 by the *Sun's* cartoonist Andy Davey that depicts the head of Alex Ferguson as an erupting volcano to convey the manager of Manchester United reputation for irascibility. There is fire coming from the top of the volcano-head, and motion lines surrounding it; there is thick black smoke coming out of the 'ears' of the volcano. The fire-filled eyes are looking straight out and make a 'demand' of the viewer. The visual integration of the source domain – a volcano, and a target domain – Alex Ferguson's irascibility – is known as 'fusion' because the same space in the cartoon shows both a human head and a volcano. The image is anchored by a sign alongside the volcano reading 'Mount Ferguson – Danger!' and two white-coated scientists are depicted as undertaking seismic texts in the foreground, for one there is a speech bubble which reads: 'the pressure's too high – it's gonna blow'. There is no separate caption in a frame below the cartoon.

The cartoon refers to the sending off of the Manchester player Nani in a Champion League's match against Real Madrid, after which Ferguson became engaged in an altercation with the manager of Real Madrid, Jose Mourinho. The metaphor here creates a close similarity, or 'fused', relationship between Ferguson and a volcano. The visual metaphor has a narrative theme in which a build up of pressure in Ferguson and the volcano leads to a metaphorical explosion. The multimodal metaphor is reinforced by the vectors formed by the smoke rising from the volcano-head and by verbal anchoring – the 'Ferguson' sign and the seismologists' prediction in the speech bubble: 'it's gonna blow'. These verbal elements support the reader in recognizing that Ferguson is represented satirically as angry and trigger contextual knowledge of what might have made him angry: Nani's sending off. The message is not particularly subtle or ironic and comments on this manager's proclivity for angry outbursts. Readers will vary in how far they know that Alex Ferguson boycotted the BBC for a period of seven years (2004–2011) as a result of a documentary called 'Fergie and Son' and once received a five-match touchline ban after comments he made regarding the referee. But the cartoon can be taken both to rely on knowledge of, and to reinforce, a stereotype about the emotional personality of this manager.

Understanding the cartoon requires accessing a general frame EMOTION IS A FORCE and a more specific one: THE LEVEL OF INTENSITY OF AN EMOTION IS THE PROXIMITY OF A VOLCANO TO ERUPTING; there is evidence of this in the familiar expression 'to erupt'. The *Daily Telegraph* reported that 'When a supporter unfavourably compared Juan Sebastian Veron to one of Ferguson's racehorses, the manager erupted' (Jim White, 8 May 2013). It is not only Ferguson who 'erupts': in another report: 'Ferguson felt there was nothing wrong with the facility and says that Keane "erupted" when they discussed the subject.' (Jeremy Wilson, *Daily Telegraph*, 23 October 2013). Another expression that shows evidence of this frame is 'to blow one's top'; the *Daily Mirror* reported the event that formed the topic of the cartoon discussed above:

Sir Alex Ferguson *blew his top* at the Turkish referee over a game-changing red card for Nani when United were leading 1–0. (*Daily Mirror*, 6 March 2013)

There are forty-eight British newspaper stories over the past five years containing both 'Ferguson' and the phrase 'blew his top', a further example is:

And yesterday he (Ferguson) *blew his top* at a press conference, directing a brutal tongue-lashing at Alan Pardew over comments made by the Newcastle boss the previous day. (*Daily Mirror*, 29 December, 2012)

**Figure 10.1** Cognitive script for anger

Lakoff and Kövecses (1987) proposed that metaphors for anger are based in underlying metonymies, so that the actual physiological experiences of anger – such as increases in heart rate and blood pressure, redness in the face and so on – provide the basis for metaphors such as to 'erupt' or to 'blow one's top'. Figure 10.1 shows a cognitive script for how anger is expressed in English (see also Figure 3.2).

Gibbs (1990) found empirical support for this script. In this cartoon the image represents the second and third stages: the event causing the anger is not depicted as the cartoonist assumes that readers will search for relevant information in the current news context. Together the scientist's comment 'the pressure is too high' and the vectors formed by steam coming out of the sides of the Ferguson-Volcano Head activate the second stage of the cognitive script for anger. There is also some evidence in circular motion lines next to the Ferguson-volcano of the third stage: the attempt to control the anger; these short circular lines are reinforced by the labels 'rumble, rumble' and 'fzzxxx' that are at various angles around the head; together these visual and verbal features imply that the explosive stage has not yet been reached. The time element and the knowledge of causes is reminiscent of the time bomb frame analysed in summary of Chapter 3 in the expression 'short fuse' based on the frame ANGER IS A TIME BOMB, which could be reformulated as AN ANGRY PERSON IS A VOLCANO. Indeed a search on the Nexis database of the press produces forty-six articles containing the phrases 'short fuse' and 'Ferguson' anywhere in the text – a similar number to 'blow his top'. In both cases, the humour also arises from hyperbole, since in reality the amount of damage caused by a volcano erupting or a bomb exploding is likely to be much greater than a football manager getting angry, and it is this satirical comment on the high intensity of Ferguson's anger that provides the topic of satire in these cartoons. We can analyse EMOTION IS A FORCE in such cartoons using the force dynamic approach, as shown in Figure 10.2.

If force A, the emotional force of Ferguson's anger, exceeds force B, his tendency to control his anger, there will be a change in Ferguson's emotional state; given the visual clues of force A – the vectors and motion lines – this is more than likely to be the case.

What is interesting about news stories on Ferguson is that although many describe his anger, others refer to other football celebrities who get angry, for example, Roy Keane; this suggests that once a cognitive script for anger is triggered by a particular celebrity it can be readily drawn on in developing news themes about other celebrities. Consider the following report with verbal equivalents of the visual representation in the cartoon, though this time in relation to the footballer Roy Keane and Ferguson's assistant Carlos Queiroz:

> Keane said that apart from goalkeeper Edwin Van Der Sar, none of the players raised any issues with his scathing remarks but claims Ferguson and Queiroz had

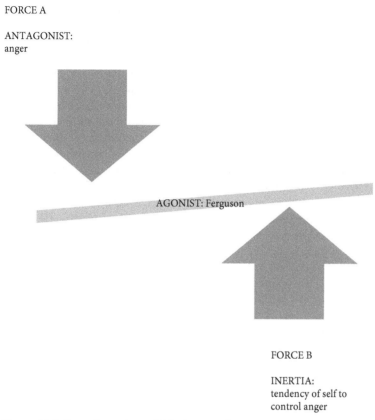

FORCE A

ANTAGONIST:
anger

AGONIST: Ferguson

FORCE B

INERTIA:
tendency of self to
control anger

**Figure 10.2** Force dynamic model for Ferguson's anger

'**steam coming out of their ears.**' And Keane, then United's captain, **flipped into his infamous red mist zone** when Queiroz said to him 'You have not shown any loyalty to your team-mates.' (*Express*, 6 October 2014)

Here there is a progression from stages 3 to 4, as the steam coming out of the ears implies attempts to control the anger – as implied by force B – whereas 'flipped' implies a loss of control; anger is attributed to a range of individuals in a narrative that continues with direct speech containing numerous asterisked swear words. It is interesting to note that verbal reports of these football celebrities rely on creating the same type of visual images in the mind of the reader as are depicted in cartoons.

There were other cartoons that also include a volcano as a symbol for anger and this may be because volcanoes demonstrate three separate characteristics of the EMOTION IS A FORCE model: first we know that in stages 2 and 3 (see Figure 10.1), there is a build up of pressure; second, there is an increase in heat in these stages, we know that a volcano becomes very hot when it erupts. In stage 4 there is failure to control a force and we know that a volcano may erupt; finally, at stage 5 – the retribution against the offender may take the form of the lava from the volcano affecting those in proximity to it. In force dynamic terms this implies that force B is overwhelmed by force A.

In some of the cartoons the drawing of the volcano makes reference to pressure, heat and eruption – this was the case with the Ferguson-volcano discussed above. However, in others the focus can be on a different stage in the anger script. For example, a cartoon by Steve Bell for the *Guardian* newspaper on the 19 November 2014 shows the head of Gordon Brown in the shape of a volcano looming over a town where a Scottish flag is flying; this refers to his role in the campaign for a 'No' vote in the referendum as to whether Scotland should leave the UK. Here there is no sign of heat or eruption but only pressure, for example, by the use of motion lines or labels with sound; these imply that although Gordon Brown is impassioned about the idea of Scotland leaving the UK, he is still in control; in Figure 10.2 force B is exceeding force A. The cartoon is an entirely visual metaphor with no words at all and is effective in conveying the impact that Brown's speech on this topic had on the vote in the Scottish referendum. His head as a volcano is much larger than the town implying that his status is larger than that of Scotland alone and the representation as 'in control' implies that the cartoonist is not taking a satirical standpoint towards the represented politician. The fact that in these fused volcano-head cartoons, the volcanoes are usually represented as the size of a human head supports research by Gibbs and O'Brian (1990) who found that when people heard anger metaphors such as 'flip your lid' they visualized a container that was the size of a human head – even though here the size of the head is exaggerated to being the size of a volcano. Clearly, hyperbole is a key component of humour in such images.

In other cartoons, figures are shown standing on the top of the volcano; this suggests the final stage in the anger script, when those who have caused the anger are in danger of retribution – as in stage 5 of the script for anger – because they will be destroyed when the volcano erupts. For example, a cartoon by Illingworth for the *Daily Mail* in 1963 (see Figure 10.3) depicts a volcano in the shape of a muscular ape that is just at the point of erupting; there are three figures standing on top of a lid; the motion lines from the side of the lid convey that it is under pressure from the volcano.

The figure on the top is labelled 'Bristol Bus Company', the figure in the middle is a policeman labelled 'Alabama' and the lower figure depicts George Wallace, the Governor of Alabama. The cartoon refers both to the Bristol Bus Company's refusal to employ a black man and Governor Wallace's opposition to the American government's attempts to enforce the desegregation laws. The depiction of the black man as an ape implies equivalent racist values to those who had motivated the ban on employment of Afro-Carribeans by the Bristol Bus Company and so shows support for their position. However, because the volcano is on the verge of eruption, the visual metaphor implies that the bus company is taking a contentious position as the figure on the top is balanced precariously in a dangerous location. In 1978, social disruption did occur in Bristol when there were race-related riots in the St Pauls district of the city.

In some cases, cartoons exploit less stereotypical aspects of our knowledge of volcanoes; for example, a cartoon by Nicolas Garland of the *Daily Telegraph* in 1993 shows Edward Heath and Anthony Barber pointing at a volcano in the shape of Wilson's head; the caption reads 'I thought he was extinct'. As predicted by conceptual

**Figure 10.3** Bristol Bus company

metaphor theory, there can be mappings from any aspects of the source domain, so while 'being extinct' is a less prototypical attribute of a volcano than 'capacity to erupt', a cartoonist can nevertheless bring it to our attention.

Volcanoes can also be used to represent situations as dangerous usually by placing labels on the volcano. For example, a cartoon by Nicholas Garland from 1973 depicts James Callaghan and Denis Healey as Romans looking at an erupting volcano; the words 'Government spending row' are on the volcano, implying that there will be a heated dispute over spending. Other situations that are represented as 'explosive' are: 'Central Europe' (W. K. Haselden, *Daily Mirror*, November 1918); 'International Hate' with a building labelled 'French Power' on the summit of the volcano (David Low, *The Star*, June 1923); 'Italian discontent' (David Low, *Evening Standard*, January 1941) and 'Central African volcano' (Victor Weisz, March 1959). We will recall that Figure 3.5 shows how force dynamics can be applied to fire metaphors that refer to social situations just as well as to people. But generally, there has been a shift from representing *situations* as volcanoes towards representing *people* as volcanoes and a reduction in the use of *verbal* anchoring. Post-1960, volcanoes tend to represent people rather than situations as volcanoes – as in the Alex Ferguson and Gordon Brown volcanoes – and are predominantly *visual* in mode. This may indicate an assumption by cartoonists of growing visual literacy arising from familiarity with conventions of the cartoon genre. There is perhaps less difficulty in blending together a person and a volcano in fused images through the concept of anger: with the angry person taking on the qualities of a volcano that is about to erupt, and the volcano taking on some of the characteristics of an angry person such as having moods that might lead it to erupt. Such interaction between two domains is a characteristic of creative use of metaphor and removes the distinction between the metaphor 'source' and 'target' as it is no longer clear whether a person is being thought of as a volcano or a volcano as a person: the ambiguity arising from such cognitive interaction evokes a more complex response.

## Fire in political cartoons

To assist with understanding fire metaphors in this genre, I use the British Cartoon Archive – an online archive of political cartoons from the time when they became widespread in the British mass press (the first decade of the twentieth century) until the present day.[3] The archive contains a range of cartoon sub-genres, but for this study only the 'newspaper' section of the archive was used, which contains 93,654 cartoons. The archive offers a 'subject' option that allows users to search for any words that occur in the cartoon, in its caption, or for entities that are represented visually; together these identify the cartoon's topic; the archive also provides relevant background information. For example, a cartoon by David Low published in the *Star* on 16 November 1920 shows a human looking monkey wearing a businessman's hat scratching his head and looking puzzled; the words 'European Imperialism' appear in a label on his chest. The monkey is surrounded by small stacks of burning nuts labelled with the names of Russian anti-Bolshevist leaders and the monkey is reaching towards one of these and appears to be burning his fingers. The smoke rising from smouldering nuts forms letters that spell 'Russia'. The caption below the cartoon reads: 'any other little pussy like to help me pull the nuts out of the fire?' The subject field shows the following subjects: 'Civil war'; 'Crimean Peninsula'; 'Russia'; 'victory', 'Bolshevism'; 'cats'; 'fires' and 'monkeys' so any of these terms would access the cartoon. The notes read: 'News: 16 Nov. Russia's long, bloody and chaotic civil war ended and Bolshevism triumphed. The final battle between the Red Army and the Whites ended in the Crimea with a resounding defeat for Baron Wrangel'. The more subjects that are used the more likely this particular cartoon will be accessed and readers may like to experiment with the archive.

Particular words that occur more frequently in the British Cartoon Archive than in the general language include 'fire', 'flare', 'heat', 'torch', 'illuminate', 'smoke', 'fuel' and 'ashes'. One reason is because these concepts lend themselves more readily to illustration as it is an easy subject for cartoonists to draw quickly; this is particularly important as cartoonists are typically working under tight time pressures to produce several topical cartoons a week. We might expect that in an essentially satirical genre such as the political cartoon, 'fire' words and 'fire' images would tend to be used more than in the general language. Anger is a common topic for political satirists and fire and associated concepts such as heat are common ways of representing anger. This is especially the case when the display of emotion contributes to humour; for example, 347 cartoons have 'anger' as a subject term and eighty-seven have 'happiness'. The fire lexicon can readily be used metaphorically to express intense emotions that are appealing to cartoonists since their main purpose is to undermine discourses of authority. For example, among cartoons identified by the search term 'smoulder', one has a caption 'None of your hot smouldering kisses this week Mr Ogilthorpe': the female speaker is shown surrounded by a fire that is extinguishing materials. Another shows an image of the Chelsea stadium with a large plaque on the wall reading 'Jose Mourinho smouldered here 2004-2007' – a reference to the manager's renowned performance of suppressed emotionality.

Sometimes the powerful emotions depicted in cartoons are more those of a social group than an individual. For example, a cartoon on the topic of the Ulster Orange Order marches depicts Orangemen parading, with one holding a banner reading 'Ulster says No to Inflammatory policing', while in front of him an Ulsterman is shown beating a barrel of gunpowder as if it were a drum. Another word that was often related to a dramatic increase in emotional expressiveness of a social group is 'flare', for example, a cartoon in the *Daily Mirror* from June 1966 has a caption 'Trawler rammed as Irish fish battle flares' another from the *Evening News* in September 1972 has a speech caption 'Y'know Dick these Peace talks could flare up into something more ugly than the war itself'.

Fire is intrinsically newsworthy in the sense that its association with danger, and responses to danger, naturally contributes to narrative themes. Since cartoons are responses to current affairs, and these often concern areas of conflict, wars, strikes and civil unrest, fire often serves as a metonym for cartoonists who are commenting on some aspect of social conflict. For example, 'ablaze' occurs as a subject term for cartoons that depict buildings or tanks that have been 'set ablaze', similarly 'incendiary' identifies a range of conflict situations and images of bombs and incendiary devices. In these images, fire serves as a synecdoche for a crisis situation. However, topics other than conflict can also be highly newsworthy, for example, fuel prices are another source of popular concern and public policy and so cartoons frequently make some reference to fuel prices. 'Smoking' is a controversial topic because of the effect on health, although in earlier cartoons smoking is a habit that helps to develop character and so is very frequently depicted in cartoons (the *Daily Mail* cartoon character Andy Capp, who stereotypes the British working-class man, is always depicted smoking).

These representations of social groups blend ideas of danger, associated with fire, with ideas of emotionality aroused by inter-group rivalries, so that an increase in the level of emotion represents some type of social danger or challenge to authority as predicted by the frame EMOTION IS A FIRE. Because anger is the most common emotion depicted in fire cartoons, it may lead to the use of fire in some form of political action. In this respect, the cognitive process when interpreting 'fire' cartoons is metonymic as much as metaphoric, so that a fire metaphor indicating anger also stands metonymically for the actions that typically arise from anger. We find this combination of metaphor and metonymy linguistically in words such as 'firebrand', that typically refer to a speaker who will inflame the emotions of audiences to such an extent that they will actually start fires, as in 'the **firebrand** Muslim cleric Abu Hamza'.

Because of its newsworthiness and potential for evoking emotional responses, and challenging discourses of authority, fire readily contributes to narrative themes, whether of heroism or as satirical comment on incompetent leadership. Evidence of the value of fire in creating narrative themes through visual and verbal-visual metaphor is that there are a number of narrative themes relating to fire and discourses of authority, and I will describe some of these dominant themes in the following sections. The first four themes relate to culturally familiar phrases; the next three to familiar cultural events – Guy Fawkes, the Olympic Games and the Ashes – and the last two to mythical animals: the phoenix and the dragon.

## Narrative themes

### Nero fiddled while Rome burned

The first group of cartoons ($n$ = 25) made some reference to the saying 'Nero fiddled while Rome burned' and represent the reaction of politicians during a political crisis as irresponsible because of their failure to act. They tend to occur in the mid-market press – the *Daily Mail*, the *Daily Express* and the *Daily Telegraph* – and originate from the apparent historical incident when the Roman Emperor Nero is claimed to have played the fiddle while Rome was burning; this action has come to provide a script for any leader who is responding ineffectively to a crisis. It is a synecdoche because a single action (playing a fiddle) implies a whole range of irrelevant or incompetent behaviours in the face of crisis. The politicians represented in this way include: Lord Stevenson, George Osborne; Silvio Berlusconi (where 'fiddle' had a sexual innuendo with reference to his sexual proximity in relation to very young women); Arthur Scargill; Geoffrey Howe; James Callaghan and Dennis Healey. In all cases, the represented politicians are wearing togas while playing violins, and are surrounded by a fire of which they are unaware. In some cases, the crisis situation represented by the fire is verbally anchored by labels such as: 'economic crisis'; 'coal industry: £875m losses' and 'winter power cuts'. In some cases the nature of the crisis is indicated by the caption; for example, 'Nero fiddles while Britain freezes'; 'Don't exaggerate, gentlemen! That burning smell is only Michael Foot heating tea and the toast for the T.U.C.!' and 'Nero's going too far! Not only no bread, but soon no circuses either!' However, there were no captions for post-1980 cartoons – suggesting that increasingly cartoonists assume sufficient visual literacy.

The cartoon shown in Figure 10.4 by Nicolas Garland for the Sunday Telegraph in 1994 depicts six Conservative Party ministers dressed as Romans playing the fiddle while surrounded by flames. The fire stands for the economic problems arising from the miners'

**Figure 10.4** Nero fiddled while Rome burned

strike that lead to a three-day week. The visual grammar depicts the politicians as framed by fire implying the extent of the crisis. It also works through the direction of their gaze – away from the viewer, away from the fire and away from each other – implying that they are so absorbed in playing the fiddle that they are not aware of anything else. Interpreting this aspect of visual meaning does not rely on context, although contextual knowledge would be needed to know that the fire referred to economic problems (as we saw in political speeches in expressions such as 'the fires of inflation'). The cartoon partially relies on 'reading' the cultural allusion 'Nero fiddled while Rome burned' as representing a general category of situations. Interpreting the cartoon relies on identifying that the fire is a synecdoche for a crisis and the socio-cultural knowledge that it is irresponsible to ignore a crisis. Even without full contextual knowledge, it is still possible to interpret some of the meaning by accessing the FIRE FOR CRISIS synecdoche and the visual grammar.

### The boy stood on the burning deck

The second group of cartoons ($n = 22$) made some reference to a once well-known poem by Felicia Hemans entitled 'Casabianca' that commences:

> The boy stood on the burning deck
> Whence all but he had fled;
> The flame that lit the battle's wreck
> Shone round him o'er the dead.

It was inspired by an original incident from 1798 during the Battle of the Nile when the son of the commander of the French ship Orient remained at his post and died in an explosion of the ship's magazine. The poem formed part of primary school education for at least 100 years until around 1950, although now only the first line is used as an allusion. Interpretation of this group relies on mapping the 'boy' onto a political identity. The 'boy' role has been variously ascribed by cartoonists to: James Callaghan, Harold Wilson, Gordon Brown and Tony Blair. It is significant that these were all Labour Party leaders and the only Conservative leaders to be depicted as 'boys' were John Major and Edward Heath. This suggests that the narrative theme is used by the right wing press when satirizing the political left, as immature or 'naïve'. The leader is represented as alone, usually with his back to a fire and with an emotionless expression. In all cases, there is an image of a boat on fire, and in some cases there is verbal content indicating the nature of the crisis – usually in a frame where the ship's name would be written; these 'names' include 'Iraqi spark' to refer to the Iraq war; 'Support for Sin Fein' (1987); 'Watergate' (1973); 'Arms for South Africa' (1971) and 'Free trade' (1931). When we consider the visual grammar, the boy is viewed from a long shot with a downward angle of viewing which puts the viewer in a position of authority over the 'politician-boy', and from an oblique angle that implies emotional detachment from him. It is significant that the boy in the original incident was a French boy on an enemy ship, therefore beyond the demands of normal sympathy towards a child faced by danger. Nearly all the cartoons contain the line 'The boy stood on the burning deck', usually as a caption but in some cases framed within the cartoon.

The cartoons could be interpreted without cultural knowledge, because a leader is represented as a boy, and our knowledge of the world informs us that boys may not be competent in dealing with dangerous situations, though recognizing the allusion to a powerful adult adds humour through irony. Interpretation of the cartoons relies on accessing from the visual grammar the frames YOUTH FOR NAIVITY and FIRE FOR CRISIS. As with the 'Nero fiddles' group, these cartoons make the satirical comment that the politician (typically left wing) is incompetent in dealing with the current crisis. For example, the cartoon by Dave Brown for The Independent in 2007 (see Figure 10.5) depicts an angry Gordon Brown as the 'boy' and the ship has Tony Blair as its figurehead; the fire represent the problems arising from the Iraq war that has been 'sparked' off. Although from an oblique angle there is an upwards angle of viewing that implies an audience who would like to be supporting ('looking up to') these leaders.

Here there is visual–verbal metaphor as the ship's name is 'Iraq spark' which triggers these frames and is then reinforced by the humorous parody of the poem in the corner of the cartoon. The poem makes a double satirical comment: both on Gordon Brown's well-known leadership aspirations and Tony Blair's leading the nation into a war that went out of control. The main difference between this group of cartoons and the 'Nero fiddles' group is that in this group the leader is represented as lacking sufficient experience to deal with the crisis whereas in the previous group the leader is represented as lacking in the desire to do so.

**Figure 10.5** The boy stood on the burning deck

## 'Liar, liar pants on fire'

There is a further large group of cartoons (*n* = 23) that make some reference to an established saying 'Liar, liar pants on fire', which is the first part of a playground rhyme: 'Liar, liar, pants on fire, hanging by a telephone wire!' The first attested use was in 1941 (though there is also a false trail to a poem called the *Liar* – inaccurately attributed to William Blake). These cartoons occur more commonly in the upmarket press (six in the *Guardian*, six in the *Independent* and three in the *Observer*) though both left and right wing politicians are shown as liars. They usually depict a politician, typically, alone, with his lower garments on fire. Usually, the verbal content in the speech bubble triggers a topic that the politician is represented as being dishonest about. For example, a cartoon by Steve Bright for the *Sun* in 2012 depicts the Conservative Chief Whip Andrew Mitchell with flames blazing from his pants saying: 'who are you calling a ------- liar?' The use of a swear word trigger the context of Mitchell's denial of having used the phrase 'fucking plebs' to policemen in the so-called Plebgate affair. The meaning is reinforced by depicting him with an elongated nose as this refers to the character Pinocchio who, in the children's fairy story, was punished for lying by the lengthening of his nose. There is visual hyperbole in both the size of the fire and the duplication of references to lying that contrasts with the verbal euphemism of replacing a swear word with dashes. The visual exaggeration therefore makes the satirical comment on his behaviour towards the police that it was an over-reaction.

A number of cartoons representing politicians as lying appeared at the time of the Gulf War where it became a widespread view that politicians were creating a cause for war by lying about the nature of the weapons possessed by the former Iraqi leader Saddam Hussein, and the danger they posed to Britain, in order to justify the invasion of Iraq. Indeed, the politician who is most represented in this group is Tony Blair; a typical one by Steve Bell of the *Guardian* in 2003 is shown in Figure 10.6.

Here a large George W. Bush and a very small Tony Blair are both depicted with their pants on fire implying that they are both lying. The size activates a concept POWERFUL IS BIG and shows Bush as more powerful than Blair. It is significant that a visual stylistic feature of Steve Bell is that he always represents Tony Blair with sticking out ears; in this cartoon this attribute is also ascribed to George W. Bush; the sharing of this attribute is a visual metaphor that implies that they were equally complicit in the lie – here the lengthening ears take over the role of the lengthening Pinocchio nose as a symbol of lying. The visual grammar argues that they were lying about the extent of the evidence for weapons – referred to in the metonym 'no smoking guns', where a smoking gun stands for incriminating evidence of having fired the gun and, in this case, of Saddam having possessed weapons of mass destruction. The satirical comment relies on cultural knowledge that the punishment for lying is to have one's undergarments catch fire and it would be difficult to interpret this from visual grammar alone. In these cartoons the thing they are trying to conceal becomes revealed through their clothes catching fire, but it is significant that their 'pants' are

**Figure 10.6** Liar, liar pants on fire

located below the level of the desk – and hence out of sight. This implies a type of moral order where deception is punished by the forces of nature. The emergence of a hidden truth suggests the concept PURIFICATION IS FIRE. There is also a secondary visual metaphor associating George W. Bush with monkeys by his hand and its proximity to a banana implying GEORGE BUSH IS A MONKEY, however, on close examination both politicians are shown to have simian hands implying that their bodies are as similar as their policies and the morphing of their physical attributes implies a shared morality. As may be expected in a work by Steven Bell – a widely acclaimed cartoonist – there is a complex layering and interweaving of visual and verbal elements in multimodal metaphor.

## Keep the home fires burning

Eight cartoons include the phrase '*Keep the home fires burning*' in their captions. The expression 'Keep the home fires burning' originated in a patriotic First World War song composed in 1914 by Ivor Novello and was first published as '*Till the Boys Come Home*'; it became very popular during the war among troops and in the UK as it satisfied the nostalgia of the troops for a home that many of them would never be able to return to. It subsequently features in a number of very popular films including *Oh What a Lovely War* (1969) and *Chariots of Fire* (1981). Like the previous catchphrases illustrated in cartoons, it serves as a cultural meme to which reference is made across diverse genres, one of which is the political cartoon. It occurs mainly in the lower end of the press – such as the *Mirror*. However, it is significant that the most recent of these was in 1984 suggesting that the phrase has become eroded as a cultural reference point. The image of the home fires has a long cultural history – going back to the original domestic fire of the Roman households, which was later retained in the form of the hearth: the controlled fire that stands for emotional warmth, domesticity and reflection.

Perhaps nowadays the expression is associated with a less fashionable patriotic perspective; for example, the most recent use of the phrase is by Peter Brookes of the *Times* in May 1984 where it is in a 'singing' speech bubble for the Chancellor Geoffrey Howe who has his arm around Margaret Thatcher's shoulder. They are depicted as comrades in arms and there is a caption in large bold type that reads 'Britain needs a strong voice in Europe'. Although the sentiment is surprisingly contemporary at the time of writing, the very traditional style of a comic with a Second World War story represents these values as out of keeping with the climate of European cultural unity. The decline in use of fire-related expressions is an indicator of shifts in social attitudes. More generally, with the growth of visual literacy there is less reliance on the verbal element of cartoons, therefore making fixed phrases relatively less attractive to the cartoonist as an expressive resource.

## Bonfires & Guy Fawkes

A further group of fifteen cartoons contain a bonfire with some type of a man-made fire that has an association with Guy Fawkes in which either a person or an entity is being burnt. These cartoons tend to occur in the mid- and lower-market press. The people represented on the bonfire include Theresa May (2014); people without visas (2012); company directors (1966); Joseph Stalin (1961); entities that are burning include money, trading stamps and political policies that have been abandoned. There is evidence of the frame ANGER IS FIRE where the anger of a social group or individual leads them to burn someone or something that is usually indicated by words within the image. There is some reference to the cultural tradition of bonfire night when in Britain it has been traditional to burn the effigy of a man to commemorate the punishment of the Catholic activist Guy Fawkes who sought to blow up the House of Commons in 1605 (the name 'Guy Fawkes' features in twenty-two cartoons). However, the satire from these cartoons rejects the view that the bonfire is a justified act of social retribution for a wrongdoing. The fire is a controlled fire that has been deliberately started and makes the satirical comment that those who have started the fire are wasteful, for example, by burning money, or that they are making a disproportionate response to a social problem. For example, the image of a Guy Fawkes burning is accompanied by a speech bubble for one of the onlookers saying 'Apparently this is what they do to people without proper visas' (Sanders, *Independent*, 11 May 2012).

Figure 10.7 by Nicolas Garland for the Sunday Telegraph in 1992 depicts the members of the Conservative Party (Douglas Herd, John Major and Normal Lamont) as plotting the explosive issue of the Maastricht debate over Britain's entry into the

**Figure 10.7** Guy Fawkes

European Union and then pouring cold water on it. Although they intend to start a fire that would have been destructive, they are depicted as changing their position as they now sought continued membership of the European Union but wanted to opt out of the euro. This paradoxical position is emphasized visually by the strong contrast between light and dark and by the contrast between fire and water.

Interpretation of the cartoon relies on recognition of the individual politicians and on the potentially severe repercussion arising from the Maastricht debate; it also requires knowledge that the intentions of Guy Fawkes was to explode the House of Commons, rather than to abort his plan. But interpreting the multimodal metaphor is equally important in reading the cartoon.

## The Olympic torch

The Olympic torch offers cartoonists a fire symbol that readily activates a cultural frame of reference, and is a symbol based on the frame PURIFICATION IS FIRE, with origins going back to the Sacred or Eternal Fire that was always kept burning to remind people of their shared ideals. Given its familiar status as a symbol for purity, it is not surprising that it is frequently relied on by cartoonists and features in forty-six different cartoons; nor is it surprising that these feature predominantly during years when the Olympic games were held, for example, there were eleven 'Olympic torch' cartoons in 1968, but no further cartoons with this theme until 1972 (the Munich Olympics) when it occurs six times; there are thirteen cartoons that refer specifically to the London Olympics of 2012. The majority of occurrences are in mid-market papers such as the *Daily Mail* and the *Daily Express* that rely more on familiar tropes since they can be readily accessed by readers.

The Olympic torch serves as a visual metonym for the Olympic games and is a shorthand reference to an event that is salient for readers. The torch is a widely recognized symbol and offers itself readily to satire as it is commonly used to indicate a lapse from the ideals symbolized by the Olympic games; for example, in the year before the Olympics were held in London, there had been extensive rioting and looting of shops in events following the shooting of a criminal suspect. A cartoon by Morten Morland for the *Times* of 10 August 2012 (one year later) makes explicit reference to this by depicting a running hooded figure holding aloft a torch in a bottle containing an explosive while in the background a similar figure is shown igniting a shop window that features London's Olympic logo. In another cartoon, a profile of the Olympic torch with idealistic achievements written on the flames such as 'End of Apartheid' and 'One Man, One Vote' is shown in a large frame, the other frame depicts a hand holding aloft a new pair of trainers in a box with a flame in the background.

There is nothing new about strong satirical comment on societies that fail to live up to the ideals they espouse, and the Olympic torch offers the cartoonist an archetypical symbol of hypocrisy or a dramatic failure to live up to ideals. Figure 10.8 shows a cartoon by Michael Cummings for the Daily Express in 1972 from 6 September 1972 when the Israeli Olympic team were held hostage at the Munich Olympics; the cartoon depicts Adolph Hitler passing on a baton shaped as the Olympic torch to an Arab

**Figure 10.8** The Olympic torch

runner with the words 'Anti-Jewish' written on the torch. The baton-torch is itself a blended image for the enmity by different social groups towards the Jews and is reinforced by a horizontal vector formed by the smoke. This then fragments into a stream of bubbles, each of which contains a swastika.

The cartoon implies the complete inversion of the original Olympic ideal that all conflict should cease for the duration of the Games. A cartoon by Dan Brown of the *Independent* (11 August 2011) depicts Georgiou Papandreou, the leader of Greece, in flames clutching an Olympic torch that has set him alight; this is another example of a topic-triggered visual metaphor that offers satirical comment on the plight of Greece following the 2008 financial crisis. The cartoon makes the ironical comment that it is the nation where the Olympic games were first held that has suffered the most from the global financial crisis.

### The ashes

Another readily available cultural frame for British audiences is the cricket contest between England and Australia known as 'the Ashes'; the term refers to the periodic series of five fiercely competed cricket matches between the national teams. Twenty-four cartoons – mainly from mid-market papers – give some form of visual or verbal reference to the Ashes. The name originates from a satirical pseudo obituary written in the *Sporting Times* after Australia's first text victory in 1882 at the Oval. The satirical obituary referred to the death of English cricket and proposed that the body should be cremated and 'the ashes taken to Australia'. Subsequently, at some point a bail (a small wooden object that forms part of the target at which the bowler aims and which the batsman must protect) was burnt and its ashes placed in a small urn, a replica of which has subsequently been awarded to the victorious team.

Many of the earlier cartoons make some sort of cultural reference to the high level of competitiveness that characterizes the competition. For example, one by Paul Thomas of the *Daily Express* (25 November 2013) depicts the Australian transvestite comedian Barry Humphries wearing pads and holding a bat on stage with a guardsman saying: 'looks like she is very pleased about the Ashes' and in a framed box in the corner are the words 'Aussies win first test'. Another from the *Daily Mail* in 1971, when Britain was negotiating possible membership of the Common Market (European Union), depicts the former Prime Minister Edward Heath saying: 'and you can expect much stiffer terms now we've got the Ashes'. However, in around one third of this group of cartoons the phrase 'The Ashes' does not appear and is expected to be retrieved from context indicating the anticipated familiarity of this culturally based sports frame – in spite of the relative decline of cricket as a national sport. Effectively, 'the Ashes' symbolizes national sporting pride rooted in the desire to avoid experiencing again the humiliation associated with the original defeat. So, it has become a symbol for national humiliation as much as of national pride and hence is often treated this way in this satirical genre.

## The phoenix

The phoenix is another readily accessible cultural frame that is frequently drawn on by political cartoonists. There are forty-nine cartoons including some form of satirical representation of this bird; its origins are in Greek mythology where the phoenix – associated with the sun – rose from out of its own ashes and symbolized cyclical rebirth and regeneration. The majority of these cartoons are towards the higher end of the press market in newspapers such as the *Guardian* and the *Times* probably because of the classical reference. The phoenix emblem is used to comment on a politician or situation where good is believed to be coming out of bad. However, this potentially good outcome is more commonly represented satirically in cartoons by ugly phoenixes that look unlikely ever to fly. For example, Figure 10.9 depicts a cartoon by Scott Clissold of the *Sunday Express* showing a phoenix whose head is fused with that of David Cameron. This 'Cameron-phoenix' is depicted as rising out of ashes comprised of former leaders of the Conservative Party. There are speech bubbles for two observers, a couple, who make the contrasting comments: 'it's a phoenix' and 'You sure it's not another turkey?'

The cartoon satirizes Cameron for appearing to be more than he is, and implies that the hopes that he aspires to will meet the same fate as that of the previous Conservative Party leaders whose heads are depicted in a smouldering pile of ashes from which the Cameron-phoenix is rising. There are five cartoons where the head of a politician is morphed onto a phoenix body; these are intended to comment satirically on trusting in the hopes offered by these leaders. For example, a cartoon by Nicholas Garland of the *Daily Telegraph* in November 1978 shows an Indira Gandhi head on a phoenix body arising out of ashes with the labels 'corruption', 'scandal' and 'charges'. Sometimes

**Figure 10.9** 'The Cameron-Phoenix'

the false hope represents a situation, for example, in a cartoon by Chris Riddell for the *Observer* in April 2005 a fat golden phoenix ridden by a small, suited capitalist clutching a bag of gold is rising away from the ashes of the car manufacturer Rover. A speech bubble from the capitalist's mouth says 'Market forces, I love 'em!' Generally, as might be expected in a satirical genre, the cartoonist does not offer the phoenix as a symbol of regeneration, so much as one of misplaced hope.

**The dragon**

A large group of eighty-nine cartoons draw on the symbolism of the dragon to provide satirical comment on an affair of the day. The cartoonist David Low has as many as twenty cartoons that include the dragon as a subject. The politicians commonly represented as a dragon include Edward Heath (eight) and Mao Tse-tung (six). These fire-breathing and culturally diverse mythological creatures provide a potent, visually dramatic and culturally accessible symbol that captures the viewers' attention. They also offer plenty of scope for visual creativity in blending together features of different animals: lions, serpents, eagles and dinosaurs.

'Dragon' cartoons can have referential meaning in one of three ways: those depicting a social ill in a label – usually on the dragon's chest; a human head blended on to a dragon's body, and those that serve as a metonym for China – typically with 'China' in a label on the dragon's body. Social ills that are represented as dragons include unemployment, inflation, trade unions, tariffs and capitalism. Twenty-one cartoons (around 25 per cent of all dragon cartoons) refer to China; for example, one by Christian Adams for the *Daily Telegraph* in October 2014 shows a very large red dragon sitting on a pile of gold; it is being approached by a very small George Osborne (the British Chancellor of the Exchequer) St George who is holding a begging bowl in one hand and a Union Jack shield in the other. The cartoon comments satirically on Osborne's covert motives in making an official visit to China with the intention of gaining trade that could benefit the British economy.

The association of China with dragons is not recent in cartoons as there is one from the *Star* from September 1926 that shows westerners referred to in the image as 'Foreign Debbils' sitting on the back of a dragon that is feeding on red fire from a bowl with the label 'A dragon with indigestion'. The cartoon is making a comment on the Civil War in China when the Kuomintang under Chiang Kai-Shek had just captured the port of Hankou. One of the characteristics of the group of Chinese dragon cartoons is that none of them have a human face transposed onto the dragon, so they are always based on the metaphor CHINA IS A DRAGON rather than using metonyms in which the leader may stand for the nation.

There are also a number of different options as regards how evaluation is expressed: they can simply represent the entity depicted as a dragon as harmful and potentially threatening, or they can be ironic, for example, by an image of a small dragon lacking the prototypical attributes of power, flight, breathing fire and so on (rather like the phoenixes discussed in the previous section). Awful looking dragons are typically used to profile dangerous aspects of whatever is represented as a dragon-based frame such as ANGER IS A DANGEROUS ANIMAL – since the dragon combines the attributes of several different types of potentially dangerous animal. For example, a cartoon by Clive Collins for *The People* in December 1970 represents the Trade Union Congress as a multi-headed dragon with the heads of various Trade Union leaders with open mouths out of which smoke is spewing over a vulnerable St George. By contrast, a cartoon by Christian Adams for the *Daily Telegraph* in September 2014 depicts a red Welsh dragon with a pusillanimous body and Obama's head. The mouth is open emitting very small puffs of smoke, making a satirical comment on Obama's rhetorical power and implying that it has become ineffectual – especially for a passionate Welsh audience.

Another option is for the dragon's role to be put in the background and prominence placed on St George as the dragon slayer. The identity of the heroic St George role can either be that of a known-individual or a generic category such as a nation state, by showing St George holding a shield depicting a national flag. For example, a satirical cartoon in the *Daily Telegraph* depicts the radical-left wing politician Tony Benn as St George riding on a white horse and slaying the dragon of capitalism; he is leading a top-hatted capitalist with a rope around his neck and riding towards the 'bright future' of 'socialism' and away from 'war clouds'; a volcano is spewing out multi-national smoke. There is extensive use of motion lines for the clouds, the volcano and Tony Benn. The image appears to fuse the myth of St George with the story of Don Quixote as Tony Benn is represented as distracted, looking backwards while riding a horse; the motion lines suggest that he is likely to fall off at any moment – so not a steady rider.

However, it is more typical for the satirical representation to be expressed through the image of the dangerous fire-breathing dragon rather than the heroic St George. For example, a cartoon by Emmwood in October 1968 for the right wing *Daily Mail* from October 1968 depicts Enoch Powell as a fierce snake-like dragon wrapped around Trafalgar's column on which the Tory Party is precariously poised (see Figure 10.10). A bland faced St George is shown with a shield with the ironic label: 'make life better'. Powell had recently given his so-called Rivers of Blood speech in which he had highlighted the dangers of immigration and the image of the Powell dragon shows him with a long and fiery tongue. The implication seems to be that though he is dangerous because he threatens the unity of his party, Enoch Powell is also exciting, passionate and visionary; it is significant that Powell's eyes are wide-open while those of St George are closed, suggesting that the nation is blind as to its future.

It is not only British politicians that are depicted as dragons, a cartoon from August 2011 by Morten Morland of the *Times* shows a cartoon sequence of a dragon with Hosni Mubarak, the former president of Egypt who was associated with dictatorial leadership. The Mubarak dragon is show as a fierce dragon destroying very small opponents in the first three frames, but in the final frame he is shown as a frail dragon lying on the ground with two lawyers saying 'Our client is too frail to face justice.' So, here the role of the dragon has undergone a complete reversal from being a symbol of authoritarian power to an ailing creature that is in the vet's waiting room and barely warranting our pity.

**Figure 10.10** Enoch Powell as dragon

# Summary

In this chapter, I have argued that fire is attractive to cartoonists because – as well as being relatively easy to draw – it activates emotions arising partly from the metonymic role of fire that links it with danger and social disorder, and partly from its metaphoric association with anger. I have illustrated this by showing how the suppressed anger of politicians (and other public figures) can be conveyed by visually blending the politician with a volcano. Readers interpret political cartoons through an interactive process of psycholinguistic hypothesis formation and rejection that is assisted by discursive knowledge and visual literacy aided by a set of visual and verbal cues provided by the cartoonist. Discursive knowledge involves understanding the purpose of the genre, reading the cartoonist's intention and establishing correspondences between represented persona and events and the actions and behaviour of real politicians in the real world. Visual literacy involves the ability to interpret motion lines, labels and speech bubbles, elements of visual distortion involved in the caricature, vectors and other visual elements that contribute to understanding the narrative theme.

Along with discursive knowledge and visual literacy, readers also require cognitive skills when understanding visual and verbal metaphors. In the case of fire metaphors, I have illustrated this with reference to an ability to recognize a cognitive script for anger and its associations with increased bodily heat based on the frames EMOTION IS FIRE, EMOTION IS A FORCE and ANGER IS FIRE. Fire also serves as a metonym for civil and social disorder based on the frame FIRE FOR CRISIS. I have also illustrated these cognitive scripts by describing nine common narrative themes that occur in cartoons where fire is depicted. As a fundamental component of human experience, fire offers a readily available set of frames for political cartoonists and provides a source of humour and cognitive enrichment for their readers.

# Appendix 1 – British Sample

| POLITICIAN | SPEECHES | WORDS |
|---|---|---|
| Tony Blair | 26 | 101,533 |
| David Cameron | 30 | 83,361 |
| Margaret Thatcher | 11 | 73,421 |
| Enoch Powell | 26 | 50,904 |
| Boris Johnson | 6 | 14,079 |
| Winston Churchill | 25 | 32,217 |
| Gordon Brown | 8 | 31,560 |
| Hazel Blears | 6 | 17,297 |
| Peter Hain | 6 | 16,510 |
| Margaret Harman | 6 | 15,101 |
| Alan Johnson | 6 | 15,314 |
| Ken Livingstone | 2 | 9,245 |
| Ed Miliband | 3 | 19,424 |
| Nic Clegg | 2 | 8,616 |
| Michael Howard | 2 | 7,102 |
| William Hague | 2 | 12,702 |
| TOTAL | 167 | 505,324 |

# Appendix 2 – American Sample

| POLITICIAN | SPEECHES | WORDS |
|------------|----------|-------|
| Roosevelt | 10 | 32,545 |
| Truman | 8 | 41,131 |
| Kennedy | 4 | 18,670 |
| Martin L. King | 14 | 53,000 |
| Nixon | 7 | 25,598 |
| Johnson | 6 | 29,321 |
| Eisenhower | 2 | 4,200 |
| Carter | 2 | 4,670 |
| George W. Bush | 16 | 40,222 |
| Reagan | 13 | 78,419 |
| Condoleezza Rice | 23 | 48,593 |
| Clinton | 9 | 50,659 |
| Obama | 19 | 63,486 |

# Notes

## Chapter 1

1 http://www.stjoan-center.com/Trials/sec20.html (accessed 15 November 2015).
2 Bocanegra, *Auto de la Fee*: 160–61, in Cañeque (1996).
3 http://www.bbc.co.uk/news/world-middle-east-30083303 (accessed 15 November 2015).
4 Lawrence: 1917 *Look! We Have Come Through!*
5 http://www.biblegateway.com/quicksearch/?qs_version=NKJV&quicksearch=fire&begin=73&end=73 (accessed 15 November 2015).
6 http://corpus.quran.com/search.jsp?q=fire&s=1&page=3 (accessed 15 November 2015).

## Chapter 2

1 http://corpus.byu.edu/coca/ (accessed 15 November 2015).
2 Here and elsewhere in the book semantic fields and concepts are in upper case.
3 Firth (1957: 11).

## Chapter 4

1 https://www.jewishvirtuallibrary.org/jsource/judaica/ejud_0002_0016_0_15772.html (accessed 4 November 2015).
2 http://www.holyfire.org/eng/index.htm (accessed 15 November 2015).
3 Naphtha is a flammable oil containing various hydrocarbons. It is obtained by the dry distillation of organic substances such as coal, shale or petroleum (OED).
4 The Torah derives from the Hebrew word for 'root' and is the first five books of the Tanakh: Genesis; Exodus; Leviticus; Numbers and Deuteronomy.
5 Glossolalia is 'The phenomenon of (apparently) speaking in an unknown language, especially in religious worship. It is practised especially by Pentecostal and charismatic Christians'. Oxford Reference Online (accessed 23 September 2015).
6 2 Maccabees are part of the Catholic and Eastern Orthodox Canons, but not part of the Protestant Old Testament or the Jewish Bible.

## Chapter 5

1 Zoroaster is from the Greek form of the name Zarathushtra.
2 For a detailed summary of fire in Zoroastrianism, visit http://www.iranicaonline.org/articles/atas-fire.

3 Magi is from the Greek plural form *magoi* (singular *magos*), from the Old Persian *magush*. The Sasanians called their priests *mow, mowbed, herbad, dastur*, along with some more secular titles (such as 'judge').
4 Boyce 1987, see http://www.iranicaonline.org/articles/atas-fire (accessed December 2015).
5 http://www.iranicaonline.org/articles/atas-fire (accessed December 2015).
6 It is available online at http://www.avesta.org (accessed December 2015).
7 http://www.iranicaonline.org/articles/atas-fire (accessed December 2015).

## Chapter 6

1 Griffith (1896) available at http://www.sanskritweb.net/rigveda/griffith.pdf (accessed 15 November 2015).

## Chapter 7

1 Families made homeless by riots will be compensated. *The Guardian*, Thursday 11 August 2011.

## Chapter 8

1 The corpus was created as part of the SAMUELS project (Semantic Annotation and Mark-Up for Enhancing Lexical Searches), 2014–2016. The 7,545,101 texts (by nearly 40,000 individual speakers) were created as a corpus by the 2011 JISC Parliamentary project by Jean Anderson and Marc Alexander.

## Chapter 9

1 http://www.bartleby.com/124/ (accessed December 2015).

## Chapter 10

1 http://en.wikipedia.org/wiki/List_of_editorial_cartoonists (accessed 15 November 2015).
2 Most recently with the assassination of twelve staff (including five cartoonists) of the satirical magazine *Charlie Hebdo* by two Islamist gunmen in January 2015.
3 http://www.cartoons.ac.uk (accessed 15 November 2015).

# References

Allan, K. (2001), *Natural Language Semantics*. Oxford: Blackwell Publishers Ltd.

Aston, M. (1993), *Faith & Fire: Popular and Unpopular Religion, 1350–1600*. London and Rio Grande: Hambledon Press.

Bachelard, G. (1964), *The Psychoanalysis of Fire*. Boston: Beacon Press.

Betteridge, T. (1999), *Tudor Histories of the English Reformations, 1530–83*. Aldershot: Ashgate Press.

Boyce, M. (1968), 'On the Sacred Fires of the Zoroastrians'. *Bulletin of the School of Oriental and African Studies, University of London* 31 (1): 52–68.

Boyce, M. (1997), 'Zoroastrianism'. In J. R. Hinnells (ed.) *A New Handbook of Living Religions*. London, New York etc.: Penguin. pp. 236–260.

Brown, P. (1975), 'Society and the Supernatural: A Medieval Change'. *Daedalus* 104 (2): 135–138.

Burrow, J. (2008), *A History of Histories*. New York: Alfred A. Knopf.

Cañeque, A. (1996), 'Theater of Power: Writing and Representing the Auto de Fe in Colonial Mexico'. *The Americas* 52: 321–343.

Canetti, E. (1960), *Crowds and Power*. Harmondsworth: Penguin.

Charteris-Black, J. (2004), *Corpus Approaches to Critical Metaphor Analysis*. Basingstoke and New York: Palgrave-MacMillan.

Charteris-Black, J. (2011), *Politicians and Rhetoric: The Persuasive Power of Metaphor*. 2nd edn. Basingstoke and New York: Palgrave-MacMillan.

Charteris-Black, J. (2014a), *Analysing Political Speeches: Rhetoric, Discourse and Metaphor*. Basingstoke and New York: Palgrave-MacMillan.

Charteris-Black, J. (2014b), 'Political Style: A Study of David Cameron'. In P. Stockwell and S. Whiteley (eds) *The Handbook of Stylistics*. Cambridge: Cambridge University Press. pp. 536–557.

Croft, W. (1993), 'The role of domains in the interpretation of metaphors and metonymies'. *Cognitive Linguistics* (4–4): 335–370.

El Refaie, E. (2009a), 'Metaphor in Political Cartoons: Exploring Audience Responses'. In C. Forceville and E. Urio-Aparisis (eds) *Multimodal Metaphor*. The Hague: Mouton de Gruyter. pp. 173–196.

El Refaie, E. (2009b), 'Multiliteracies: how readers interpret political cartoons'. *Visual Communication* 8 (2): 181–205.

Fauconnier, G. and Turner, M. (2002), *The way we Think: Conceptual blending and the mind's hidden complexes*. New York: Basic Books.

Firth, J. R. (1957), *Papers in Linguistics (1934–1951)*. Oxford: Oxford University Press.

Forceville, C. (1996), *Pictorial Metaphor in Advertising*. London: Routledge.

Forceville, C. (2008), 'Metaphor in Pictures and Multimodal Representations'. In R. W. Gibbs (ed.) *The Cambridge Handbook of Metaphor and Thought*. Cambridge: Cambridge University Press. pp. 462–482.

Foucault, M. (1975), *Discipline and Punish: the Birth of the Prison*. New York: Random House.

Fraser, J. G. (1930), *Myths of the Origin of Fire*. London: MacMillan & Co.

Gibbs, R. W. (1990), 'Pyscholinguistic Studies on the Conceptual Basis of Idiomaticity'. *Cognitive Linguistics* 1: 417–451.

Gibbs, R. W. (1999), 'Researching Metaphor'. In G. Low and L. Cameron (eds) *Researching and Applying Metaphor*. Cambridge: Cambridge University Press.

Gibbs, R. W. and O'Brian, J. (1990), 'Idioms and Mental Imagery: The Metaphorical Motivation for Idiomatic Meaning'. *Cognition* 36: 35–68.

Goatly, A. (2007), *Washing the Brain: Metaphor & Hidden Ideology*. Amsterdam and Philadelphia: John Benjamins.

Goudsblom, J. (1994), *Fire and Civilization*. London: Penguin.

Grady, J. E. (1997), *Foundations of Meaning: Primary Metaphors and Primary Scenes* (Unpublished PhD dissertation, University of California, Berkeley).

Grady, J. E. and Johnson, C. (2002), 'Converging Evidence for the Notions of Subscene and Primary Scene'. In R. Dirven and R. Pörings (eds.) *Metaphor and Metonymy in Comparison and Contrast*. Berlin: Mouton de Gruyter. pp. 533–554.

Griffith, R. T. H. (trans.) (1896), *The Hymns of the Rigveda* 2nd edn. Kotagiri: Nilgiri.

Hodges, C. F. (2011), *His Sexy Bad Habit*. New York: Defina Books.

Hopkins, T. J. (1971), *The Hindu Religious Tradition*. Andover: Cengage Learning.

King, J. (2006), *Foxe's Book of Martyrs and Early Modern Print Culture*. Cambridge: Cambridge University Press.

Kövecses, Z. (2000), *Metaphor and Emotion: Language, Culture, and Body in Human Feeling*. Cambridge: Cambridge University Press.

Kövecses, Z. (2002), *Metaphor: A Practical Introduction*. Oxford: Oxford University Press.

Kövecses, Z. (2005), *Metaphor in Culture*. Cambridge: Cambridge University Press.

Kövecses, Z. (2008), 'On Metaphors for Emotion: A Reply to Ayako Omori'. *Metaphor and Symbol* 23 (3): 200–203.

Kövecses, Z. (2013), 'The Metaphor–Metonymy Relationship: Correlation Metaphors Are Based on Metonymy'. *Metaphor and Symbol* 28: 75–88.

Kress. G. and van Leeuwan, T. (2006), *Reading Images: The Grammar of Visual Design*. London: Routledge.

Lakoff, G. (1987), *Women, Fire and Dangerous Things: What Categories Reveal about the Mind*. Chicago: University of Chicago Press.

Lakoff, G. (1993), 'The Contemporary Theory of Metaphor'. In Ortony, Andrew (ed.) *Metaphor & Thought*. 2nd edn. Cambridge: Cambridge University Press. pp. 202–251.

Lakoff, G. and Johnson, M. (1980), *Metaphors We Live*. Chicago: University of Chicago Press.

Lakoff, G. and Johnson, M. (1999), *Philosophy in the Flesh: The Embodied Mind and Its Challenge to Western Thought*. New York: Basic Books.

Lakoff, G. and Kövecses, Z. (1987), 'The Cognitive Model of Anger Inherent in American English'. In Dorothy Holland and Naomi Quinn (eds.) *Models in Language and Thought*. Cambridge: Cambridge University Press. pp. 195–221.

Lakoff, G. and Turner, M. (1989), *More than Cool Reason: A Field Guide to Poetic Metaphor*. Chicago: University of Chicago Press.

Lawrence, D. H. (1917), *Look! We Have Come Through!* London: Chatto & Windus.

Lawrence, D. H. (1928), *Lady Chatterley's Lover*. Florence: privately published.

Le Bon, G. (1895), *Psychologie des foules*. Paris: Felix Alcan.

Mitchell, P. (2012), *Contagious Metaphor*. London and New York: Bloomsbury.

Morgan, K. O. (2009), *The Oxford Illustrated History of Britain*. Oxford: Oxford University Press.

Musolff, A. (2010), *Metaphor, Nation and the Holocaust*. New York and Oxford: Routledge.

Pyne, S. (1992), *Burning Bush: A Fire History of Australia*. London: Allen & Unwin.

Pyne, S. (2001), *Fire: A Brief History*. Washington: University of Washington Press.

Quinn, N. (1991), 'The Cultural Basis of Metaphor'. In J. W. Fernandez (ed.) *Beyond Metaphor: The Theory of Tropes in Anthropology*. Stanford, CA: Stanford University Press. pp. 57–93.

Rose, J. (2011), *Zoroastrianism: An Introduction*. London: IB Taurus.

Seip, T. (2003), 'Political Cartoons'. In *Encyclopedia of International Media and Communications*. New York: Columbia University. pp. 527–542.

Semino, E. (2008), *Metaphor in Discourse*. Cambridge: Cambridge University Press.

Sontag, S. (1991), *Illness as Metaphor and AIDS and Its Metaphors*. Harmondsworth: Penguin.

Staal, F. (2008), *Discovering the Vedas*. London: Penguin.

Thomas, K. (1971), *Religion and the Decline of Magic Studies in Popular Beliefs in Sixteenth and Seventeenth Century England*. London: Weidenfeld and Nicolson.

Warneken, F. and Rosati, G. A. (2015), 'Cognitive Capacities for Cooking in Chimpanzees'. *Proceedings of the Royal Society B* 282 (1809).

# Index

# Index of Conceptual Metaphors, Metonyms & Frames

Lightning Source UK Ltd.
Milton Keynes UK
UKHW02f0129210618
324570UK00003B/144/P